POLITICS, GOVERNANCE AND RELIGION

POLITICS, GOVERNANCE AND RELIGION

A *Study on the Administration of Hindu Shrines in Kerala*

Dr Rajagopal P.K.

KALPAZ

ISBN: 978-93-5324-941-0

First Published, 2022
Published by

Kalpaz Publications
C-30, Satyawati Nagar,
Delhi – 110052
Ph.: 011-47034999, 9811692060
www.kalpazpublications.com
E-mail: kalpaz@hotmail.com

Printed at: Gyan Press, Delhi.

Contents

Glossary

Avarnas	:	Lower caste Hindus.
Agamas	:	Traditional principles governing worship, means tradition.
Arat	:	Holy bath given to the festival images of the deities, when they are immersed in water on the final day of the annual festival.
Ayacut	:	The old settlements register in Travancore.
Brahmaswoms	:	Property belonging to Brahmins.
Chaturvarnya	:	Four-fold division of Hindu caste system.
Dasa	:	A servant.
Dalawa	:	Signify the office of the Chief Minister till the early19th century in Travancore.
Devaswoms	:	Religious endowments and property belonging to temples.
Dewan	:	Chief Minister of an erstwhile Indian state.
Illam	:	The house of the Nambuthiri Brahmins.
Jatha	:	Procession.
Kacham	:	Agreement.
Karalar	:	Tenants of temple lands
Karanavan	:	The eldest male member of a taravad.
Karakkar	:	The people of a Kara or a village.
Koviladhikarikal	:	The office in charge of the temples.
Melkoma	:	Over lordship.
Ooranma	:	Administration by the people of the village.

Ooranma Devaswom	:	Temples founded or managed by Ooranmakkar.
Ooranmakkar	:	Land lords who are in sole management of certain temples.
Pandaravaka	:	Belonging to the Government.
Pattom	:	A kind of lease.
Pooja	:	Daily ritual.
Satyagraha	:	Any kind of protest action.
Savarnas	:	High caste Hindus.
Sanketams	:	Were medieval temple corporations of Kerala which enjoyed semi-autonomous power in its areas.
Tindal	:	Caste pollution.
Tanthri	:	High Priest or a person authorised to perform rituals in temples.
Thrippadidanam	:	Dedication of the state to the deity.
Uraler	:	Owners or trustees of temples.
Viharas	:	Shrine.
Uttupura	:	A free feeding house for Brahmins.
Yogam	:	Council.
Yogakkar	:	Members of the yogam.

Abbreviations

ABASS	:	Akhila Bharata Ayyappa Seva Sangham
BJP	:	Bharatiya Janata Party
BDJS	:	Bharat Dharma Jana Sena
CDB	:	Cochin Devaswom Board
CLA	:	Cochin Legislative Assembly
CLC	:	Cochin Legislative Council
CITU	:	Centre of Indian Trade Unions
CPI	:	Communist Party of India
CPI (M)	:	Communist Party of India (Marxist)
CSDS	:	Centre for the Study of Developing Societies
DGB	:	Devaswom Governing Bodies
GDMC	:	Guruvayur Devaswom Managing Committee
GoK	:	Government of Kerala
HAV	:	Hindu Aikya Vedi
HRCE	:	Hindu Religious Charitable Endowment
INC	:	Indian National Congress
IUML	:	Indian Union Muslim League
KCHR	:	Kerala Council for Historical Research
KDMC	:	Koodalmanickam Devaswom Managing Committee
KHC	:	Kerala High Court
KLA	:	Kerala Legislative Assembly
KPSC	:	Kerala Public Service Commission
KPCC	:	Kerala Pradesh Congress Committee

KSAR	:	Kerala State Administration Report
KTPC	:	Kerala Temple Protection Council
LDF	:	Left Democratic Front
MDB	:	Malabar Devaswom Board
MHRCEA	:	Madras Hindu Religious Charitable Endowment Act
MLA	:	Member of Legislative Assembly
NDP	:	National Democratic Party
NSS	:	Nair Service Society
PIL	:	Public Interest Litigation
PSP	:	Praja Socialist Party
PWD	:	Public Works Department
RSP	:	Revolutionary Socialist Party
RSS	:	Rashtriya Swayamsevak Sangh
SKS	:	Sabarimala Karma Samithi
SNDPY	:	Sree Narayana Dharma Paripalana Yogam
SNM	:	Sree Narayana Movements
STNCA	:	South Travancore Native Christian Association
TAC	:	Temple Advisory Committee
TAR	:	Travancore Administration Report
TCHRIA	:	Travancore Cochin Hindu Religious Institutions Act
TDB	:	Travancore Devaswom Board
UDF	:	United Democratic Front
UTUC	:	United Trade Union Congress
VHP	:	Visva Hindu Parishath

P S Sreedharan Pillai
Governor of Goa

Raj Bhavan
Goa-403004

Foreword

"Those who believe that politics and religion do not mix understand neither" said Albert Einstein. On the same lines Mahatma Gandhi had said that "those who say religion has nothing to do with politics do not know what religion is". He had said this in the context of moral values that form the basis of all religions and he believed that politics must be guided by ethics drawn from religions. The thoughts of these great man show that religion has been an ennobling and uplifting presence in the body politics. In all the conflict and disorder that often characterises human life religion has been endowed with the power to demonstrate that the bonds of humanity do exist.

Since centuries the topic of politics and religion has perpetually provoked passionate debates across a wide spectrum of society. The connections between religion and political life are profound, significant and worthy of serious examination. Therefore, I am happy that Dr. Rajgopal P.K. is publishing a book on "Politics, Governance and Religion" which is a study on the administration of Hindu temples in Kerala by the state regulated Devaswoms governing bodies, their politics organisational structure, temple regulated legislations and amendments, response of political parties, civil society and organisations over such concerns related to temples. The study also contains special analysis of the recent women entry issue in Sabramala. The study illumines connections between two explosive subjects and deepens our understanding of the issues and problems involved.

Having read this book, I am of the view that the right question should not be whether religion and politics should be separate but what should be the exact re!ationship between these two so that harmony prevails in society. In this regard, this book has number of recommendations such as the codification of Devaswom laws, radical administrative reforms and restructuring which I believe are all the need of the hour. Though the focus of the study is Kerala where temples are closely associated with the life of people I strongly believe that similar situation prevails in the rest of the country. The recommendations of the author are relevant to other states and regions also. This book by Dr. Rajgopal.P.K is an interesting and fresh look at this very sensitive topic. The author however, on the issue of women's entry in Sabarimala could have shed more light on the analysis content rather than an exhaustive sequence of facts and events. I would like to express my opinion that Kerala Temples should be free from the clutches of political set up. Further without any hesitation, I can tell that in Sabarimala, old traditions should be continued regarding women entry.

In conclusion, this book is a welcome addition to the public discourse on a topic that is very important and relevant to our times. I am sure the book will be very useful for devotees, temple administrators, politicians and help them to ruminate about the issues and problems highlighted by the author. Therefore I would like to encourage all book lovers to read this book so as to enlighten and broaden their horizons of knowledge and understanding.

P.S. Sreedharan Pillai
Governor of Goa

Preface

Politics, Governance and Religion: A *Study on the Administration of Hindu Shrines in Kerala* is a revised version of my thesis submitted to the University of Kerala for the award of PhD degree. The study explores the state-temple relations in a secular polity, concerns of devotees regarding the issues prevailing in the administration of Devaswoms at the auspices of the state, possibilities of a unified Devaswom administration for the betterment of both the temples and the employees and also enquires better alternative administrative systems for the temples in the state. In Kerala, majority of Hindu shrines are managed by the state regulated Devaswom governing bodies. Private temples and their administration are excluded from the ambit of the study as they are managed by diverse agencies like family trusts, caste and religious organisations and most of them are not coming under the purview of public institutions. As such they lack centralised authority for governance, state interference and lack of uniformity in their administration.

Temples, popularly known as *Devaswoms* cater the spiritual and cultural aspirations of Hindus and occupy a predominant place in the socio-political, economic and cultural scenario of the state. The historic Temple Entry Proclamation had broken the caste fetters and ensured social justice to the marginalised. Owing to the power, influence and wealth of the temples, the Government took over their administration in disguise of corruption in 1811. When monarchy gave way to democracy the temples were also entrusted with the popular Government. Due to the progressive land legislations of the State Government large tracts of landed properties belonged to the temples were lost that affected the revenue of the temples considerably.

The state of Kerala was formed on 1st November, 1956, comprising of the erstwhile Travancore, Cochin and Malabar regions. The temples in these three regions followed their own laws for governance in the pre-state formation era and no specific steps were taken by the State Government for the unification of Devaswom laws even after sixty years of the state formation. The Travancore and Cochin Devaswom Boards were constituted in 1949 for the administration of temples as per the tripartite agreement instituted by the rulers of the respective states with the Union Government and a Covenant at the time of the integration of Travancore and Cochin States. Today the Travancore Devaswom Board (TDB) and Cochin Devaswom Board (CDB) manage temples as per the provisions of Travancore Cochin Hindu Religious Institutions Act, 1950. The Temples in Malabar region were brought under the supervision of the Malabar Devaswom Board constituted as per the Madras Hindu Religious Endowment (Amendment) Act 2008.The administration of Guruvayur and Koodalmanickam temples were taken over by the Government in 1971 and their administration were made viable under the respective Devaswom Acts.

As a secular state, the Government is not expected to interfere in the internal administration of religious institutions, but in Kerala the administration of temples is carried out by Devaswom governing bodies and the Government control over them gradually paved the way for the politicisation of its administration. A secular state's intervention may be viewed as paradoxical as the religious institutions of other communities are largely left free for deciding their own religious affairs. Politicisation of administration is one of the grave issues faced by the temples in the state; the study delves deep into this aspect. Politicisation and the nomination of non-believers in the Devaswom governing bodies posed a challenge to the beliefs and traditions of temples. Other grave administrative issues such as trade unionism, lacks of unified Devaswom law, corruption, mismanagement, land encroachment etc., are also given due consideration in the study. Issues like women entry in Sabarimala, appointment of non-Brahmin priests, temple entry for non-Hindus, economic reservation to forward castes in Devaswom services etc., are also reverberated in the state polity. All these issues are incorporated in the study.

The study also discussed in detail the organisational structure, income and expenditure and a comparative analysis of five Devaswom governing bodies. It also gives suggestions to improve temple administration in an effective and fool proof manner. The work mainly focused on the period after the formation of the state of Kerala on democratic basis. The information regarding the administration of Devaswom governing bodies have been obtained through direct interview with the higher officials including administrative personnel, members and former Presidents of Devaswom committees. Interactions were also held with leaders of major political parties, religious organisations and community organisations. A few major temples under various Devaswom governing bodies are visited and collected information from the Devaswom offices, devotees and temple employees. A data sheet is prepared for conducting field study and collecting information from Devaswom Boards and temples. Various Commission Reports, Administration Reports, various Verdicts of the High Court and Supreme Court, Devaswom Manuals and Legislative Proceedings are extensively referred for the study. Secondary sources of the study include books, journal articles, periodicals and newspapers, doctoral theses, online journals and internet sources.

In preparing this work, I am indebted to a large number of individuals for their relentless support and encouragement. First of all I have to express my sincere gratitude to my Research Supervisor, Dr Jitha. S. R, Principal, Sree Narayana Guru

College for Advanced Studies, Chempazhanthy for her help and support. Her encouragement and inspiration have instilled confidence to realise my work. I express my indebtedness to Dr S. Sujatha, Principal, NSS Hindu College, Changanacherry, Dr T.V. Muralivallabhan and Dr Vineetha. N R for their sincere cooperation and support for publishing the work. I would like to thank my colleagues in the Post Graduate and Research Department of Political Science, NSS Hindu College, Changanacherry and the staff of the offices of various Devaswom governing bodies for providing necessary help and guidance. I am grateful to the University Grants Commission (UGC) for the award of the two-year teacher fellowship (FDP) for completing my Ph.D research work. I gratefully acknowlldge the kindness of Adv. P.S. Sreedharan Pillai, the Hon'ble Governor of Goa who readily agreed to write a foreword to this book. An eminent writer as well as a scholar, he is the right person for the purpose. Thanks are extended to Sri. K.S. Vijayan, State Vice President of Kshetra Samrakshana Samithi for his relentless support and help.

Thanks are due to my beloved parents for their affectionate blessings. My sincere thanks are extended to my wife Sreekala. K, Assistant Professor of History, Government College, Nedumangad, Thiruvananthapuram for the constant support she provided in the publication of this work. Thanks to my children Nandagopal and Naveengopal for their loving support and encouragement. I am greatly indebted to the God Almighty Lord Guruvayoorappan for the blessings showered on me for the successful completion of the work. Last but not least I am obliged to Kalpaz Publications, New Delhi for undertaking the responsibility of publishing the book.

Dr Rajagopal P.K.

Introduction

Kerala is renowned for communal harmony and religious toleration for centuries. Religious institutions of various communities like temples, mosques, churches etc., stand as icons of Kerala's secular fabric. Our secular culture is embedded with religions and not a departure from them. Hinduism is not only a religion, more than that, a way of life. Temples and idol worship become integral parts of Hinduism. The routine life of a Hindu is, in one way or the other, closely associated with temples. Though the temples were once citadels of conservatism, later they became the centres of socio-cultural renaissance. The role played by Hindu reformers like Sree Narayana Guru, Chattambi Swamikal, Ayyankali, Mannathu Padmanabhan, V.T. Bhattathirippad and Pandit Karuppan in demolishing caste-based ostracism and providing social justice to the depressed sections is great. Aruvippuram temple consecration inaugurated a social revolution and became the vanguard of temple entry movements in Kerala.

Temples in Kerala popularly called as *Devaswoms* were managed by *uralers* (temple trustees) or *karakkars* and the King wielded *melkoima* rights over their administration. The widespread corruption by the *uralers* necessitated the intervention of the state in temple administration. Dewan Col. Munro in 1811 took over the administration of temples along with their properties which declined considerably the power and influence of temples and their trustees in society. He amalgamated temple revenue and properties with the state revenue and entrusted temple administration with the Revenue Department, one of the overloaded departments in the state.

This resulted in the lack of giving proper attention to temple affairs. A separate Department for Devaswoms was created in the state of Travancore solely for the administration of temples in 1922. Later in 1949, as part of the integration of Travancore and Cochin princely states, Devaswom Boards were created for the administration of temples in the respective states. As per the then existing rules, they should be free from governmental involvement, but in practice, they are functioning under the directions of the Devaswom Department of the Government. This governmental intervention is justified on the ground that it is necessary to eliminate corruption from their administration. But the fact is far from reality as the governmentally nominated members are indulging in corrupt practices and none of them are being punished, but escaped due to their political influence. Thus, the temples in Kerala have often become the playground for politics with successive governments in power. Temple assets are mismanaged and temples become the hotbed of maladministration. In the past, that is, before the formation of Kerala state, temples were under the direct control of the state. The continuation of state control over temples even after the process of democratisation of the state led to the politicisation of its administration. The 26th amendment of the Indian Constitution of 1971 abolished the Privy Purse and thus even the nominal right enjoyed by the King over temple administration came to an end and his powers were transferred to the Hindu Ministers.

Interference of a secular state over the administration of religious institutions of a particular community is ironical. In Kerala, Hindu temples are governed by state-controlled Devaswom Boards constituted through nomination and election processes in which Hindu Ministers and MLAs only can participate. The so-called secular state's intervention over temples has created controversies in state politics. Secularism implies the state to maintain an equi-distance policy between itself and religious institutions, but in Kerala there exist a state-temple nexus for over a long period. This relationship is not only a phenomenon limited to Kerala state, but various other state governments in India who have approved administrative control of the state over temples. In the *Chidambaram Temple Case* of 2014 the Supreme Court observed that temples may be taken over for short periods to sort out problems, but it must be handed over to the Trustees after evils are remedied. The verdict of the Supreme Court is a warning to the state interference over temple administration.

The study focuses on the issues that are prevailing in the administration of temples in Kerala by the state-regulated Devaswom governing bodies, their politics, organisational structure, temple related legislations and amendments, response of political parties, civil society and Hindu organisations over such concerns related to temples. A special analysis of the recent women entry issue in Sabarimala is also incorporated in the study. The study centres on the administration of temples under Devaswom governing bodies only. Though a comprehensive view on the politics of temple governance in the state is aimed at, emphasis has been given to Travancore Devaswom Board being the leading Devaswom Board in the state managing 1248 temples including the highly reputed Sabarimala temple. The study is focused on the period after the state formation on democratic basis. The important issues identified for analysis in this study are:

(1) Influence of Hindu temples on Kerala society and the evolution of the state-temple relations.

(2) The nature of intervention of the Government of a secular state over the administration of a particular religious institution in the context of the rights of devotees.

(3) Lack of uniformity in the composition of various Devaswom governing bodies and the need for a uniform Devaswom law in the state.

(4) The issues prevailing in the administration of temples and the attitude of political parties, Hindu organisation and civil society towards them.

The administration of temples in Kerala is seen immerse with issues and controversies. Politically appointed Devaswom Boards are handling the administration of temples and naturally temples become a fertile land for politicians to enhance their influence among the Hindu population. It has been often discussed on the issue of selection of Devaswom Board members by Hindu MLAs and Ministers; here a question arises whether the Hindu Minister or MLA needed to be a believer in God and temple worship. The Hon'ble High Court of Kerala has pronounced that faith in God and temple worship alone makes a Hindu MLA competent to take part in the election of members to Devaswom Boards. However, non-believers are also participating in the election and often being nominated to Devaswom Boards. But in a sense the concept of Hindu MLAs and Ministers is itself contradictory to the spirit of secularism envisaged in the Constitution. Political activism can be seen even in the Temple Advisory Committees that are representing the interests of devotees. The Constitution of India envisages a secular domain with a separation of religion and the state; accordingly, the state can regulate religious institutions, but should not interfere in their internal administration. But in the South Indian states, especially in Kerala, the Hindu temples, by and large, are controlled by the Government. The Government justifies the state control over temple administration on the ground that temples are public institutions, once managed by the King.

Temples in Kerala are facing serious concerns most of them are of political and economic nature rather than spiritual. Temple assets are mismanaged, temple properties are alienated and temples become the hotbeds of maladministration and corruption. Corruption, misappropriation of funds, theft and mismanagement are associated with their administration. These facts are cited as the motive for the intervention of the state in the internal affairs of temples. Unfortunately, the system came into force for preventing maladministration has become more corrupted due to its excessive politicisation process. In order to enquire into the various problems exist in temple administration, the Government and the High Court of Kerala appointed Enquiry Commissions intermittently; these Commissions suggested radical reforms, but no serious efforts are being taken by the various Governments for implementing them. Kuttikrishna Menon Commission (1964) and K.P. Sankaran Nair Commission (1984) Reports provided valuable suggestions for improving the administration of temples. Politically affiliated trade unions are active among temple employees and their direct action methods like strike, demonstration etc., often affect the serene atmosphere of temples.

While considering the economy of the state of Kerala, heavy influx of pilgrims even from other states to major temples like Sabarimala and Guruvayur add a huge source of revenue to the government treasury. The state provides annual contributions to temples in the form of annuity and renovation grant to various Devaswoms in the state, but this amount is meagre compared to the properties of temples taken over by the government in the past. Vast tracts of landed properties of temples have been lost due to the progressive land legislations of the State Government and because of this a number of temples are now fighting for their existence.

Currently, the Devaswom administration faces many serious pitfalls. Very few temples under the Devaswom governing bodies are self-supportive and a common pool fund system exists for their financial management, except in Malabar Devaswom. Malabar temples are functioning independently under respective trustees and Malabar Devaswom Board has only supervisory powers. The Law Reform Commission in 2017 recommended taking over of all temples and put them directly under the control of the MDB. Another interesting fact is that while the administration of thousands of temples under the TDB is vested with a three-member Board, at the same time that of Guruvayur and Koodalmanickam Devaswoms consists of seven-member Boards. This results in the wastage of Devaswom fund which can be used for the well-being of temples. The SC in 2019 issued directions to the State Government to consider a separate administrative set up for the Sabarimala Temple that created concern to the existence of Travancore temples. Also issues like a separate administrative set up for Sree Padmanabhaswamy Temple, plea for dismantling of Devaswom Boards in the state are under the consideration of the Apex Court.

Besides the numerous issues prevailing, the question of women entry in Sabarimala created heated debates from various corners. The State Government's attitude towards the Supreme Court verdict on women entry has created resentment among Hindu organisations. The grave administrative issues faced by the temples such as political interference, nomination of non-believers to Devaswom managing committees, trade unionism among temple employees, corruption, mismanagement, favouritism, misappropriation of funds, pathetic conditions of temples, land encroachment issue, shortage of finance, theft etc., are analysed through the study. The appointment of non-Brahmin priests, entry of non-Hindus in certain temples, economic reservation to forward castes in Devaswom recruitment etc., are the other issues debated. Environmental impact of pilgrimage in the hill shrine, Sabarimala needs to be solved amicably. It is an interesting fact that a section of Hindus is not aware of even the administrative machinery prevailing for temple governance and believes that the income of temples is directly credited to the government exchequer. A secular state's intervention in the religious affairs of a particular community is resented by a large section of people. Such a control may be seemed as paradoxical as the religious institutions of other communities are largely left free for deciding their own religious affairs. The study has become more significant in the contemporary socio-political scenario of the state after the SC verdict on women entry in Sabarimala and its imprints in state politics.

The major objectives of the study are to analyse the nature of the state-temple relations and the issues faced in the administration of temples in the state. Successive Governments in power interfere in the administration of temples by amending Devaswom Acts, issuing Ordinances, nominating their own members to the Devaswom Committees etc. Politics of temple administration in Kerala and other manifold administrative problems are analysed in this study.

1

State and Temples

Kerala, the 'God's own country' and the land of magnificent shrines, is famous for social reform movements and other political movements associated with temples. It is the first state in India where the historic Temple Entry Proclamation facilitated all the believers to worship in temples without any distinction. The presence of amazing great temples makes the land a spiritual tourist destination of South India. Temples in Kerala are renowned for their sanctity and serenity, art, architecture, festivals and mode of worship. Temples definitely occupy a significant place in the lives of the Hindu populace. The temple is an institution of antiquity which has played a notable role in the spiritual life of the people and their socio-cultural, economic and political dealings.

When and where the practice of idol worship started remains in obscurity. The temples and idol worship in the system of Hindu religion has been explained in ancient scriptures. *Vishnu Samhita* says that it is not possible for anyone to contemplate any god without his image (Pillai, Vol. IV, 1996: 553). But according to Max Muller, the Vedas not refers to any idol worship and it may be a later degradation of the more primitive worship of ideal gods (1867: 38). However, it can be surmised that the worship of images in the land is a post-Buddhist development. The Buddha *viharas* became the centres of Buddha worship in image form and later several of them were transformed into Hindu temples after Buddhism was on the wane. Though Buddhism was disappeared from the land, it had left its imprints upon Hinduism in the form of temples, idol worship, festivals and processions. The artistic and architectural styles of Kerala temples also bear evidence of Buddhistic influence (Menon, 2010: 15). The deity of *Sastha* in Sabarimala temple is widely recognised as the Hinduistic version of Buddha· though scholars like M. G. S. Narayanan disagree with it. Snake worship in Kerala is also associated with the Buddha tradition.

Temples and Society

Temples become the symbols of spirituality and Hindu culture. Hinduism, one of the world's oldest religions is a way of life rather than a form of worship. Spirituality is the hallmark of Hindu culture. Temples have exerted enormous influence on society as they accommodated the interest of different sections of the Hindu society. Life of the vast majority of the Hindu population is even now closely associated with the temple and temple related activities. Their influence on the socio-cultural, economic and political lives of an ordinary man is very significant.

While examining the history of the land, it can be seen that Kerala society became a temple centred one since her medieval times when the 2nd Chera Emperors or the *Kulasekharas* was on the suzerainty here. The Kulasekhara period, in the 9th century was a major landmark in the history of temples in Kerala. Renowned as the *golden age* in the history of temples, the period witnessed the emergence of the first Bhakti Movement and the resurgence of Hinduism led by Sri Sankara (Jayashanker, 1997:12) The Bhakti movement became instrumental in establishing a number of Saiva and Vaishnava shrines under the aegis of *Nayanars* and *Alwars*. Structural temples were extensively built during this period. The greatest development of the medieval period in Kerala was the rise of temples to prominence in the society. The temples which began as a centre of worship and as the nucleus of the Brahmin colony began to increase in space and engage in political activities (Kunjan Pillai, 1970: 253).

Another development in the history of temples in Kerala is the close link that they had established with the ruling dynasties. Several temples in the state were founded and patronised by the Royal families. Marthanda Varma, the maker of modern Travancore, dedicated the state to his family deity, *Sree Padmanabha* which became a major event in the religious and political history of the kingdom. Sree Padmanabhaswamy temple is the tutelary deity of the Travancore dynasty and like that Sree Poornathrayesa temple, Thrippunithura was originally belonged to the Cochin royal family. Even today, these temples enshrine as the icons of the royal power. The rulers of the erstwhile princely state of Travancore introduced two important social reforms centred on temples deriving authority from the laws legitimising state intervention introduced by the British. The first reform was introduced in 1925 when Rani Sethu Lakshmi Bai was the Regent of the State of Travancore, as Sri Chithira Thirunal Bala Rama Varma was a minor, abolished *Devadasi system* and animal sacrifices in temples under the Travancore Devaswom (Madhusoodhanan, 2010: 152). The *Temple Entry Proclamation* on 12th November, 1936 enshrines as a turning point that ensures social justice to the downtrodden classes.

Temples in Kerala are the symbols of great cultural legacy and they become agents of developing, consolidating, transmitting and conserving the heritage of high culture (Veluthat, 2009: 6). They imparted knowledge on temple arts, mural paintings, temple instruments, Vedas and Upanishads and religious discourses. Several art forms like *Kudiyattam, Chakyar Koothu, Mohiniyattam, Kathakali, Ottanthullal, Theyyam, Padayani* etc. were born, flourished and enriched the temple premises. It can be seen that in the field of cultural activities, the temples contributed much more than any other institution in the state. Temples in Kerala are reputed for their architectural splendour and marvelous festivals.

Social Composition of Travancore Hindu Society

As a social institution, temples embody the social structure of a bygone period. An analysis of the social structure existed in state of Travancore is relevant here. It was essentially a Hindu dominant state where the Hindu people remained hierarchically ordained castes, based on ritual status, concepts of purity and pollution and property ownership (Census, 1894: 647-48). A *chaturvarnya* model of relationship attached to temple functions as existed in the traditional Hindu society of Travancore. The *savarnas* like Brahmins and Nairs constitute the upper strata monopolised all the spheres of state administration, particularly, temple administration. The so-called *avarnas* including Ezhava, Pulaya, Paraya communities were the socially inferior groups in the caste hierarchy. Certain *social distances* were observed between them and caste Hindus enforced *social apartheid* on the *avarnas* by triple weapons of untouchability unapproachability and unseeability. Communities and sub-castes were formed in a temple centred society on the basis of hereditary occupation; each group had its allotted place (Narayanan, 1972: 3). Unable to bear the social exclusion, the agitated sections resolved to disown Hinduism and Hindu Gods (Desai, 1937: 24). This led to a mass conversion of the untouchables. The Travancore Census of 1931 pointed out that about five lakhs *avarnas* left Hinduism in the last fifty years (Pillai, 1932: 389).

In the 19th century, temples witnessed a series of movements for achieving equality against caste-based discriminations. The movement for eradication of untouchability and temple access by the lower caste people drew inspiration from social reformers like Vaikunda Swamikal, Chattambi Swamikal, Sree Narayana Guru, V. T. Bhattathirippad, Ayyankali, Mannathu Padmanabhan, Kumaran Asan and T. K. Madhavan and caste-based organisations like SNDP Yogam, Yogakshema Sabha and NSS. The Indian National Congress under the aegis of Mahatma Gandhi also urged the movement for freedom of worship. Moved by the spirit of Sree Narayana Guru's message *to get strengthened through organisation,* Sadhu Jana Paripalana Sanghom was formed by Ayyankali in 1907 which became the predecessor of modern Dalit consolidation movements in Kerala.

Temples and Social Reform Movements

Temples act as an integrating force among different strata and substrata of the Hindu community. Earlier, they acted as a disintegrating factor by segmentalising Hindu community on caste lines. The lower strata in the caste hierarchy were kept aloof from the vicinity of God. Their status was at low ebb that they were subjected to all kinds of disabilities. They were not only allowed to enter into temples but not to walk through even the streets of the temples and the higher castes. In course of time, the Temple centred socio-religious movements could secure social equality and social justice to all the Hindus. Thus, Kerala became the first state in India where the right to worship is guaranteed to all sections of Hindus irrespective of their birth status. This could be achieved as a result of the reforms by progressive leaders like Sree Narayana Guru, Chattambi Swamikal, Ayyankali etc., who questioned the Brahmanic monopoly in temple affairs.

Agitations for Civic Rights

20th century Travancore witnessed an eventful agitation for securing social justice and equal opportunities to all classes. The Revenue Department, one of the major departments of the State Government was fully dominated by *savarna* communities due to the fact that Devaswom management was vested with it. The non-caste Hindus and non-Hindus denied employment opportunities in the department. The aggrieved communities demanded that they should be given complete freedom of access to all those institutions set up out of public funds (Shaji, 2017: 123). They raised voice for the immediate separation of the temple administration from the Land Revenue administration. The distribution of Government jobs in 1922 show that the *avarnas* were discriminated (see Table).

Table 1.1: Distribution of Government Jobs between Savarnas and Avarnas (as of 1922)

Caste	Salary up to 20 pm	Percent	Salary between Rs. 20-50 pm	Percent	Salary above Rs 50 pm	Percent	Total	Percent
Caste Hindus (Savarnas)	3,325	97.1	388	91.25	104	90.43	3,817	96.30
Non- caste Hindus (Avarnas)	99	2.90	37	8.75	11	9.57	147	3.70
Total	3424	100	425	100	115	100	3,964	100

Source: George Mathew, Communal Roads to A Secular Kerala, 1989, p. 71.

The table indicates the upper castes domination in government sectors as 96.3 % of the posts were occupied by them. The savarna castes constituted only a microscopic minority of the total population and the vast majority remained excluded from government jobs. One of the reasons for this inadequacy was the ban on appointments of avarnas and non-Hindus in the Revenue Department. At the beginning of the 20th century, fiery debates were held in the Sree Moolam Popular Assembly on the issue of Devaswom separation from the Revenue Department. Representatives of Christian groups such as South Travancore Native Christian Association (STNCA), Nagercoil and Travancore and Cochin Christian Association (TCCA), Kottayam had urged Devaswom separation to facilitate their entry in the revenue services. Both the Hindus and non-Hindus untiringly demanded separation of Devaswom by any means. Non-Hindu communities complained about the spending of lakhs of rupees from the state treasury to temples and in turn, demanded merging of temple fund to the common fund that irritated the Hindus. In this context, the only solution before the government was nothing other than separation of Devaswom from Revenue.

To pressurise their demand effectively, the Christian, Ezhava and Muslim communities jointly formed a Civic Rights League in 1919. In the same year, the government appointed Krishna Iyengar, a Forest Settlement Officer to study the issue of separation of Devaswom from Revenue Department and to submit a report. The Report submitted by him favoured the separation of all government-owned Devaswoms from the Land Revenue Department and the formation of a separate Devaswom Department in direct correspondence with the government (Kumar, 1994:108). The Civic Rights League submitted a memorandum to M. Krishnan Nayar, the Dewan of Travancore in February 1920 consisted of five important demands including separation of Devaswom from the Land Revenue Department. T. K. Madhavan was one among the signatories of the memorandum.

Dewan Krishnan Nayar assured that appointments would be done purely on merit and not with reference to caste, creed and colour and that no particular class would be excluded (Menon, 1972: 284). On the basis of this and the recommendations of Krishna Iyengar's committee report, the government appointed a Mixed Committee of Hindu and Non-Hindu members on April 1920 to investigate the question of separating the administration of Devaswoms from the Land Revenue Department and the financial implications of such a change. The committee submitted its report recommending separation of Devaswoms from the Land Revenue Department for their efficient administration. There was a dissenting note of P. K. Narayana Pillai, a member of the Committee to the effect that the assumption was only of management; the role of the state was to be limited to that of a trustee. The government considered it necessary to take a legal opinion before finally deciding what action they should take. Accordingly, a reference was made to the Advocate General of Madras, Dr C. P. Ramaswamy Iyer; the Advocate General agreed to the minority view. Taking into account of the recommendations of the Devaswom Separation Committee and the report of Krishna Iyengar, Raghaviah, the Dewan decided to advise Maharajah Sri Mulam Tirunal, to issue a proclamation separating the Devaswoms from the Department of Revenue. Accordingly, the Maharajah issued a Proclamation on 12th April, 1922 separating the Devaswom from the Revenue Department. Creation of the Devaswom Department was a milestone in the history of temple administration in Kerala.

Temple Entry Movement

For assuring social justice and securing freedom of movement along the temple roads, a chain of historical movements were conducted. The *avrna* classes were prohibited to enter the premises of temples on the belief that the pollution due to their entry would affect the deity inside the *sanctum sanctorum*. Temples are built in such a design that the four walls surrounded the temple should be a barrier against contamination or pollution. Even their entry in the temple roads was prohibited by exhibiting prohibition boards (*Theendal palakas*) in front of the approach roads adjacent to major temples. Such prohibition existed in temples of the central and southern part of Travancore like Vaikom, Thirunakkara, Haripad, Ambalappuzha and Sucindram. When the low caste people got educated, they resented this practice and their resentment found expression in the creation of their own temples where they freely worshipped without any distinction (Thampi, 1942: 129). It is curious to see that in some temples under the control of Ezhavas, the Harijans were denied entry. In the Jagannatha temple, Thalasserry consecrated by Sree Narayana Guru, Harijans were not admitted, but later they got temple entry with the intervention of Guru (Vasanthan, 2006: 113).The social reformers gave priority to break Brahmin monopoly in all walks of life especially in the affairs of temples. Sree Narayana Guru revolutionised the movement consecrating *Siva* deity at Aruvippuram near Neyyattinkara in 1888 that broken the Brahmin hegemony in temple affairs that sowed the seed of a series of agitations for achieving religious freedom and freedom of worship. This event is enshrined as a milestone in the history of temple administration in Kerala.

The issue of denial of freedom of movement around temples was raised in the Sree Moolam Assembly many a time by Ezhava leaders T. K. Madhavan and Kumaran Asan. Kumaran Asan demanded the removal of signboards in front of the temples of Vaikom, Sucindram and Thirunakkara. It is worth to mention here that *savarna* leaders and organisations also took up the issue seriously. In 1917, C Raman Thampy, a judge of the Travancore High Court suggested that the temples should be thrown open to all became the first *savarna* voice in Travancore exhorting the Ezhava community to work for temple entry in a public meeting at Kollam (Shaji, 2017: 156). SNDP Yogam, NSS and Nambudiri Yogakshema Sabha in their annual meetings passed series of resolutions demanding temple access to the depressed castes.

Meanwhile, during the Civic Rights Movement, some Ezhava leaders demanded to include the issue of temple entry in their programme. But the Christian groups stoutly refused to include it because it was a religious question that should be settled between caste Hindus and non-caste Hindus (TLC, 1925, February 6). According to Robin Jaffrey, Civic Right League had been quick to forget the anti-untouchability aspects of its original programme when the major grievance of educated Syrian Christians was met. This made T. K. Madhavan, the chief architect of the temple entry movement in Travancore to rethink the Christian alliance and give importance to make alliance with the educated and progressive *savarna* leaders (1978:148-49).

Ezhavas who constituted a sizable portion of the Travancore population made rapid progress in the educational sphere and felt that the caste-based discrimination and distance pollution were detrimental to their moral development. They constituted the upper strata among the lower caste population. On 12th December 1919, a meeting of nearly 5,000 Ezhavas was held at Kanichukulangara in Alappuzha district under the presidentship of C. V. Kunjiraman had called for securing admission in the state-managed temples (Menon, 1972: 116). Ezhava members in the Sree Moolam Assembly demanded for the Ezhavas the right to enter temples and worship the deity as freely as caste Hindus. In 1920, Kumaran Asan presided over a religious meeting at Varkala and called upon the Ezhavas to boycott the caste Hindu temples (Sadasivan, 2000: 524). He raised the issue in the 17th session of the Assembly in 1921. S. Padmanabha Panicker, a nominated member, brought the attention of the house to the display of signboards at Tirunakkara temple in Kottayam (TSMPA, 1921, March 11). The issue existed in Manakkad Sastha temple, Trivandrum by displaying bamboo boards prohibited the use of footpaths attached to the temple by the non-caste Hindus was raised in the TLC by Kumaran Asan (TLC, 1921, June 2). Forty-six Hindu members of the Assembly signed a memorial in 1922 and submitted to the Government demanding temple entry.

Vaikom Satyagraha

Vaikom Mahadeva temple is an ancient Hindu temple in the Central Travancore. It was a very old *ooranma* institution and the temple and its property were taken over by the government during the time of Col. Munro (TLC, 1925, February 6: 675). The temple was placed under the Devaswom department after its formation in 1922 and later transferred to the TDB. The temple witnessed the historic movement for attaining freedom of worship for the so-called untouchable sections. Roads adjacent to Vaikom temple were inaccessible to the non-caste Hindus and prohibitory boards were displayed on all sides of the temple. At the same time non-Hindu communities used these roads without any restriction. There was an order of the Magistrate prohibiting the use of the road by the non- caste Hindus. Vaikom Satyagraha was really a movement for freedom to travel adjacent to temple roads and considered as a pioneer movement for temple entry.

Meanwhile, Vaikom Satyagraha was designed as a movement for eradicating untouchability by Indian National Congress as part of the freedom struggle after T.K. Madhavan's proposal to make the anti-untouchability movement as a constructive programme. In its Kakinada session (1923), Congress adopted the programme and decided to form anti-untouchability committees in each and every village. An anti-untouchability committee was thus constituted under the auspices of Kerala Pradesh Congress Committee with T.K. Madhavan, K. Kelappan, Kuroor Neelakandan Nambuthiri and others as its members. In January 1924, the Congress in its Ernakulam session passed a resolution which demanded the right to entry of the lower caste Hindus into temples (Fic, 1970:11). But it is interesting to note that the plea for temple entry of the inferior castes were not included in the charter of demands for the Vaikom Satyagraha.

On March 12, 1924, Gandhi visited the *Maharani* (Queen) and Sree Narayana Guru to discuss the issue of denial of freedom of movement and the right to worship of the non-caste Hindus (Somarajan, 1986: 57). It was decided on March 29, 1924 that a *Satyagraha* would commence on the next day morning. On 30th March 1924, two untouchables- a Pulaya and an Ezhava along with an upper caste proceeded to the road around Vaikom temple and courted arrest and sentenced to six months imprisonment (Panicker, 2016: 214). The government favoured to preserve *status quo* and issued an order prohibiting the entry of untouchables beyond *theendal palaka (prohibition board).* Devaswom authorities and the government were bent upon suppressing the agitation. A positive development happened was the unconditional support rendered by the *savanna* castes to the noble cause. Gandhiji's appeal was a crucial factor in mobilising enlightened upper caste Hindu opinion in favour of temple entry. Almost every *savarna* reform association joined the historic movement. The Kerala Hindu Sabha, NSS, Yogakshema Sabha and Kshatriya Sabha endorsed the temple entry demand and some of them campaigned for it (Panicker, 2016: 219).

SNDP yogam also backed the movement with money, material and manpower. A combined conference of Nairs and Ezhavas was also held at Vaikom supporting the Satyagraha. *Savarna Jatha* was organised as per the suggestions of Mahatma Gandhi and led by Mannathu Padmanabhan from Vaikom to Thiruvananthapuram in order to express their solidarity with the demand for freedom of travel to the *avarnas*. Another *jatha* from the south led by M. E. Naidu arrived at Thiruvananthapuram on November 11, 1924. A memorial was submitted to the *Maharani*, but received only a disappointing reply that a decision on this important subject could be taken in the state legislature demanding the opening of temple roads to the *avarna* Hindus (Desai, 1937: 15).

On 2nd October 1924, a resolution was moved in the 6th session of Travancore Legislative Council by N. Kumaran, an Ezhava member urging the government that all roads around temples in Travancore be thrown open to all classes without distinction. In 1925, when the resolution came for discussion, the then Dewan T. Raghaviah stated in the Sree Moolam Popular Assembly that the approach of outcaste Hindus, unfortunately, would create pollution to the caste Hindus and temple deities, such custom had recognised by the Travancore High Court. The government is bound to carry out the law as it was interpreted by its court of Justice. Unfortunately, the resolution was rejected by one vote due to an unexpected move from an Ezhava member, Manager Parameswaran, brother of Dr Palpu. This incident produced a setback to the temple entry movement in Travancore. Finally, in 1925, a compromise formula was evolved at the meeting of Mahatma Gandhi with Maharani Sethu Lakshmi Bayi and accordingly temple roads were formally opened to all Hindus. It was an act of great magnitude with far-flung echoes, apart from being the first enactment of its kind in India (Gouri Lakshmi Bayi, 1998: 382). The Vaikom Satyagraha is rightly regarded as a turning point in the emancipation of Harijans as it was recognised as a preliminary step towards the major objective of opening the temples to untouchables (Ouwerkerk, 2004: 58). But this concession was not extended to other temples in Travancore.

Ambalappuzha Avarna Procession

Even after the Vaikom settlement, the roads around Ambalappuzha temple were not open to the untouchables. On August 18, 1925, when a few avarna people passed through the temple roads during pooja hours, savarnas questioned it. T. K. Madhavan arrived at the spot and discussed the matter with the temple authorities and finally, they conceded them permission for using the temple roads. The Ambalapuzha agitation was a natural or spontaneous move to fulfil a historic need, drawing inspiration and guidance from Vaikom Satyagraha (Bhai, 1986: 138).

Sucindram Satyagraha

A similar agitation took place at the Suchindram temple in South Travancore for obtaining passage of lower caste Hindu along certain roads reserved for upper caste people only (Kumar, 1994: 121). This issue was raised in the 12th session of Sree Moolam Popular Assembly in 1916 by Kumaran Asan who demanded the removal of the prohibition boards placed near the temple (TSMPA, 1916, March 1). As a result of the Satyagraha the authorities had agreed to open the road to all, but as the result of the protest from upper caste people, the roads continued to remain closed. Though these satyagrahas had failed to achieve their immediate goal, Vaikom and Suchindram Satyagrahas served as a preliminary step to achieve the right of temple entry later on (Perumal, 1937: 60). In 1928, all temple roads in Travancore were declared open for all Hindus without caste distinctions (Balakrishnan & Leeladevi, 1982: 64).

Guruvayur Satyagraha

Guruvayur temple is a very famous Sree Krishna temple in the erstwhile Malabar region where also the people of lower castes were denied freedom of worship. Guruvayur Satyagraha was really the first temple entry agitation in the state. At the Vadakara Session of the Congress in May 1931, a resolution was introduced by K. Kelappan which demanded temple entry for the *avarnas*. Guruvayur Satyagraha was launched by the KPCC in 1931 with the blessings of Mahatma Gandhi. Mannathu Padmanabhan was the president of Guruvayur Satyagraha Committee, constituted by the KPCC. On 21st October, 1931, a team of sixteen volunteers started route march to Guruvayur from a place near the Congress camp at Kannur under the leadership of T. Subramanian Tirumumbu (Sivathambika, 1991: 138). On 1st November, 1931 large number of volunteers assembled at Guruvayur and the Devaswom authorities resisted the volunteers with oppressive measures. P. Krishna Pillai was manhandled for having dared to ring the sacred bell in front of the *sanctum santorum*, a right exclusively reserved for the Brahmins by age-old tradition. The supporters of temple entry were enraged and forcibly removed the barricades around the temple. The temple authorities suspended the *pujas* and closed down the temple for a month (Nair, 2006: 17-18). The temple was re-opened only on 20th January, 1932. Zamorin argued that without temple entry being permitted in the neighbouring Cochin and Travancore, he could not allow it in respect of the Guruvayur Temple (Padmanabhan, 1998: 123).

On January 8, Guruvayur day was celebrated all over Kerala and the people involved in the movement extended support to a Bill on temple entry moved in the Madras Legislative Council by Dr P. Subaramanyan (Nair, 2006: 19). Gandhi suggested that a referendum on the issue be held among the *savarnas* in Guruvayur and its neighbourhood. Kasturba Gandhi, Urmila Devi and C. Rajgopalachari arrived on the scene to persuade the *savarnas* to agree to the demand for temple entry (Padmanabhan, 1998: 122). A referendum was conducted under the auspices of KPCC in Ponnani Taluk to ascertain the Hindu public response on the question of temple entry. Over seventy percent of the respondents favoured universal temple entry. Though the Guruvayur Satyagraha did not immediately result in the opening of either Guruvayur temple or other temples in Kerala to all Hindus, the movement helped to create a strong public opinion in the country in favour of temple entry and abolition of untouchability. It may be mentioned here that Guruvayur temple was thrown open to Harijans only in 1946 (Menon, 1962: 186). In fact, the real purpose of the *Satyagraha* was to regain the prestigious status of Hinduism through the weapon of temple entry Satyagraha by uniting the Hindus after removing the practice of pollution (Sivathambika, 1991: 141). In 1947, the Guruvayur temple was also opened for the entry of all Hindus.

Towards Temple Entry

The Temple Entry Proclamation was the first of its kind in the Indian subcontinent itself. The Proclamation guaranteed the right to freedom of worship to all people irrespective of caste and creed. On behalf of Mahatma Gandhi, a group of progressive men met the Diwan and discussed the question of temple entry for all Hindus. He constituted a Temple Entry Enquiry

Committee on 8th November 1932, to study the matter in detail. The Committee submitted its report in 1934. Majority members were of the view that temple entry should be allowed. Individual reports were sent by members, Changanacherry Parameswaran Pillai and M. Govindan wrote that all Hindus should be permitted to receive *darshan* of the deity standing in front of the *sanctum sanctorum*. Some others like Neelakanta Sharma opposed the view saying that the *avarnas* should be kept out of the temple compound (Padmanabhan, 1998: 123-24). On 3rd November, 1936 a memorial signed by 50522 *savarnas* of Travancore demanding temple entry to non-caste Hindu society submitted to the Dewan C. P. Ramaswami Iyer. Finally, the government resolved to throw open all public roads, public tanks, public wells etc maintained out of the general public funds to all classes of people irrespective of caste to which they belong.

On 12th November, 1936 Travancore Maharaja Sree Chithira Thirunal under the initiation of the Dewan C. P. Ramaswamy Iyer, temples in Travancore were thrown open to all people who are Hindus by birth or faith. Following the Proclamation, several private temples in the state were also thrown open to all Hindus for worship (GoK, 1938: 7). Temple Entry Proclamation is hailed as the *Magna Carta* of the marginalised sections in the Hindu community. Mahatma Gandhi paid a handsome tribute to the Maharaja for this great act of moral courage. Through this brave act, the king of Travancore would be remembered by future generations with gratitude (GoK, 1964: 21). Temple Entry Proclamation has been hailed by the world as the high watermark of religious and social reform ever inaugurated by a sovereign towards the emancipation of the backward sections of his subjects (GoK, 1937: 7). The King of Travancore met stiff opposition from some Orthodox quarters against the entry of *avarna* people in temples. Raja Raja Varma, the Devaswom Commissioner of Travancore state resigned forthwith. Many priests refused to perform *poojas* in the temples. Many of the orthodox Brahmins stayed away from the state temples which they considered polluted by the presence of *avarnas.* The Maharaja of Cochin refused to allow Namboodiri priests who had entered the polluted temples of Travancore to officiate in the temples of Cochin causing quarrel which went on for five years (Ouwerkerk, 2004: 99).

Temple Entry Movements in Cochin and Malabar

The Temple Entry Proclamation in Travancore created repercussions in the neighbouring state of Cochin. Temple authorities in Cochin were more conservative than the Travancore region. Like Travancore some of the major temples in Cochin, polluting castes were not allowed to worship. *Para* and *arattu* processions in connection with the festivals in Tripunithura, Chottanikkara temples were cancelled because they had to pass through the territory of Travancore area. Similarly, purification ceremonies were conducted in the Koodalmanickam temple, Irrinjalakkuda due to the entry of Travancore persons in the temple.

The Travancore Temple Entry Proclamation could not make any serious effects on the Malabar region too. In Malabar, the Zamorin was not in favour of the entry of *avarnas* in Guruvayur temple. Finally, Malabar Temple Entry Bill was introduced in the Assembly on 1st December 1938 by the Prime Minister Rajagopalachari. Later, the Madras Temple Entry Authorisation Act, 1947 made the temple entry a reality in the Malabar area also (Sivathambika, 1991: 241).

Kuttamkulam Agitation

The caste system in Cochin State was much more oppressive than that prevailed in other parts of Kerala. Kuttamkulam agitation was a protest movement of the lower caste people for securing freedom of movement around the roads of Koodalmanickyam temple in the erstwhile Cochin state. A prohibition board demarcating the boundary which avarnas could not cross, was placed near to the Koodalmanikyam temple, Irinjalakkuda and the untouchables were prohibited to walk from Kuttamkulam road to the west. While the Christians and Muslims had permission to walk through these roads, the *Pulayas* and other lower caste Hindus were prohibited to use these public roads. Several unfortunate incidents were happened when the upper caste Hindus objected the entry of lower-caste women in the temple passage. Organisations like SNDP, Samastha Cochin Pulaya Mahasabha and political parties like Prajamandalam, Labour Organisations like Beedi workers' organisation etc., protested against this injustice under the leadership of P. K. Kumaran Master, Saratha Kumaran, K.V. Unni, P.K. Chathan Master. Police resorted to oppressive measures against the agitators and finally, the roads near Kuttamkulam were opened to the untouchable classes (Remani, 2015). Thus, the untouchable classes got the right to freedom of movement along the Kuttamkulam road.

Travancore Cochin Temple Entry (Removal of Disabilities) Act 1950

Even after the Temple Entry Proclamation of 1936, freedom of worship was denied to non-caste Hindus in certain temples in the state. After the integration of Travancore and Cochin in 1949, a bill, the United States of Travancore and Cochin Removal of Social Disabilities Bill was presented in the Assembly by Chief Minister T. K. Narayana Pillai which ensured the protection of the downtrodden classes from all sorts of social disabilities. It is astonishing that even R. Sankar, one of the members of the Travancore Devaswom Board could not even go to Board temples because of caste disabilities (TCLA, 1949, November 29). In Travancore, the entry of all Hindus in the private temples was ensured as per the Travancore Temple Entry (Extension of Application) Ordinance of 1950. The Cochin Temple Entry Authorisation Proclamation in Cochin assured freedom of worship to all sections of Hindus in all Hindu temples, whether they were under government or private management. In November 1950, the Travancore- Cochin State Assembly passed the Travancore-Cochin Temple Entry (Removal of Disabilities) Act, accordingly, all the Hindus irrespective of their caste were entitled to enter any temple including private temples and offer worship (TCLA, 1950, November 2). The Travancore- Cochin Temple Entry (Removal of Disabilities) Act was a revolutionary measure in the true sense. It was a stride towards the attainment of social equality and a landmark in the history of the Travancore-Cochin State (Kumar, 2002: 101).

Historical Background of Temple Administration in Kerala: An Overview

The state of Kerala was formed on 1st November 1956 comprising of the territories of the erstwhile states of Travancore-Cochin and Malabar district. Since then, the state government made efforts to codify laws binding the temples of these three regions. It is interesting that though Travancore, Cochin and Malabar have merged to form the state of Kerala, the Devaswom Boards in the state are still known under these names. It was a great task before the State Government to make a uniform pattern of administration for its thousands of temples. The temples under the control of the rulers of erstwhile Travancore and Cochin became a part of Travancore and Cochin Devaswom Boards, except Sree Padmanabhaswamy Temple and Koodalmanickam Temple, Irrinjalakkuda. The year 1971 was an important year concerning temple administration in the State owing to the fact that the state government made special legislation for two leading temples with hereditary rights, Guruvayur and Koodalmanickam. In 2008, as per the directions of the High Court of Kerala, Malabar Devaswom Board was constituted for the administration of temples in Malabar area which were hitherto under the control of HRCE Department. There are several private temples in the state functioning beyond the purview of state regulation. The acts and regulations which were once in force regarding the administration of temples in Travancore, Cochin and Malabar regions were continued to be taken in the newly constituted state with specified changes.

Temple Administration in Travancore

Temple administration in Kerala has a long tradition associated with Kerala history, society and culture. Brahminical monopoly prevailed in the administration of temples then. *Koyiladhikaarikal* was the managers of various Devaswoms during the Perumal or Second Chera rule. This *adhikarikal* rose in power and in course of time established themselves as petty chiefs. Devaswom managers and trustees enacted rules and laws for the management of temple property and began to enforce these laws, independent of the king within the limits of their landed property (Menon, 1878: 79). Internal rifts and conflicts prevailed among temple trustees that affected the temple administration.

In the medieval period, temples emerged as a power centre in the agrarian society and economy, so naturally they had to perform a decisive role in the power structure relations of the period. Two types of property rights prevailed then, known as *Brahmaswom*, being the property belonged to the Brahmins and *Devaswom*, to the deity or temple. *Uralers* who were the Brahmin trustees of temples managed the temple lands (*Devaswom*) leased them to the *karalers*, the temple tenants. Thus, there developed a socio-economic system that had existed in Kerala for a long period of time. Land rights were conferred on the basis of the prevailing customs and traditions. *Poduvals* who managed both internal and external administration of temples (*purapoduval* and *akapoduval*) were also entitled to ownership of certain land. These changes effected favourable conditions for the emergence of a temple based Brahminical landlordism in the state. It is notable that during the period of the Perumals of Mahodayapuram in the medieval Kerala, certain administrative regulations known as *kacchams* were formulated to effect control over the administration of revenue and temple affairs.

In Travancore, mismanagement and misappropriation of temple funds by the uralers necessitated certain stringent action by the government. The King had been interfering in the administration of temples through their melkoima rights. The uralars, who collected the income from the properties of the temples, were only under the nominal or melkoima or supervision of the King (Raja, 1953: 52). In some cases, a synod of priests managed the temples. Temple Administration is carried out by these powerful priestly classes posed a serious threat to the tranquillity of the state. They were afforded a safe haven to malcontents and lawbreakers (Aiyer, 1931: 54). Thus, temple administration in Travancore ran parallel to the state administration and there often occured tussles between the two. These temple managers were so powerful that they could even control the sovereign and no ruler ruled the state without their consent and goodwill. Temples exercised their unlimited supreme power through the sankethams which played a dominant role in the social structure. The synods exercised judicial as well as executive power over sanketham lands owned by them, setting at naught the authority of the sovereigns. The existence of sacrosanct and superstitious forces in the country was a Damocles sword over the throne (Aiyer, 1931: 54).

Travancore was splitted up into a number of petty principalities and when Marthanda Varma came to the thrown in the first half of the eighteenth century, consolidated these principalities into a single state. In January 1750, he formally and solemnly dedicated the State to Sri Padmanabha, the tutelary deity of his family (Menon, 1955: 188). The regime of Marthanda Varma, the maker of modern Travancore, marks an epoch in the history of temple administration, as he was the first ruler to introduce a centralised administrative system for temples. In 1801, when Velu Thampi was appointed as Dalawa, he noticed the unlimited influence of temple trustees over the people by misusing their authority deliberately and misappropriating wealth. He proposed bringing Devaswoms under the control of the government that would neutralise the influence of Devaswom authorities over the people (Menon, 1878: 368). But he could not complete the mission as he lost his life and after his death, the temple trustees continued their corruption and maladministration unchecked by any state authority. Travancore state had a subsidiary alliance with the British government to whom it paid an annual tribute of Rs 8 lakhs (Aiyyer, 1903: 5).

The relationship between the state and temples had strained considerably during the period of Col. Munro as he tightened the bureaucratic set up over temple administration. During his time, the state of Travancore faced serious financial strain as the state debt amounted to nearly the annual revenue of the State, the most part of which was due to the East India Company as arrears of subsidy (Menon, 1878: 367). In order to bridge the fiscal crisis, Munro made several administrative reforms; the most important being the accumulation of a large amount of the wealth of temples to the state revenue. Temples in the state possessed large-scale landed properties and other valuable ornaments and as a step to rectify the abuses and corruption prevalent in temple administration, Munro took action to transfer them to the direct management of the government (Yesudas, 1977: 37).

Accordingly, he took over the administration of 348 major temples and 1128 minor temples with their properties and amalgamated it with state revenue through an executive order. These temples were known as Incorporated or Scheduled Devaswoms. Ward and Conner observed that the takeover of Devaswoms appeared to have been a judicious measure for the temple authorities in a way were functioning as a parallel source of power (1893: 108). Through the temple taken over process, Col. Munro got a chance to repay the long-standing and heavy arrears of subsidy payable to the British Government. Thus, Munro saved the state when it was in serious peril (Aiya, 1999: 380-81).

By the assumption of the Devaswoms, the state took over 62,000 acres of gardens and 5,48,000 paras of rice lands. The gardens yielded a rental of about Rs 50,000 annually, while the wetlands Rs 3,50,000, thus aggregating four lakhs of rupees and the expenditure was only Rs 2,50,000 and the surplus was Rs 1,50,00015. Besides these, there were other sources of income of a fluctuating character which flowed into the government treasury like daily offerings received in money and things, money thrown to hundis, earnings from the sale of boiled rice etc. (Pillai, 1996, Vol. II: 520). The annual income from these sources varied from 40,000 to 80,000 rupees (GoK, 1916: 206). According to Nagam Aiya, through this assumption of temples, the state gained an addition to its revenue (1999: 381).

Col. Munro entrusted revenue officers to supervise temple administration; rents collected were remitted in the state treasury and distributed an amount for the daily rituals of temples. The critics alleged that the bad stage of temples (shanidasha) began through this reform. It is assumed that the greater part of the enormous and unassessed wealth of temples had been transferred to the Christian missionaries for proselytizing activities (Sadasivan, 1977: 205). Entrusting temples with the direct supervision of the Revenue administration is a major landmark in the socio-political history of the state. As the Land Revenue Department had to perform overloaded works, they could not have time to spend for the effective supervision of temple administration. The accounts of temples were not regularly audited. The inefficient administration by the Revenue Department has been discussed in the legislative council since 1888.

As K. K. Pillay observed,

"resuming the history of temple administration, we find that change of control from uralers or yogakkar to the revenue

authorities did not prove an unmixed blessing. At any rate over the period from 1812-1922 contain defects in the administration persisted. True the tenants of the lands were treated better and were freed from minor extractions or oppression, the temple staff, too received a better treatment in the hands of the government officials. But with all that, it is doubtful whether the efficiency of the temple administration had improved" (2002: 169).

Again in 1903-04, Travancore Hindu Religious Endowments Bill was passed in the Travancore Legislative Council (TLC, 1903, December 5) which authorised the government to take over the direct management of private temples whenever necessary. Thus, the government had taken over the administration of 116 private temples. Their income came to be credited with the personal deposit and their expenditure was also separately charged. These temples were named as Unincorporated Devaswoms or Personal Deposit Devaswoms. Revenue from the temple was the main consideration for assuming the management of temples by the state (Madhusoodhanan, 2010: 53). PD Devaswoms are financially autonomous and wealthiest institutions with high income. With a view to secure better efficiency in the management and control of the Devaswoms, Chempaka Raman Pillai and Rajaram Rao were deputed in 1905 to investigate the question of regulating their expenditure both as regards *pathivus* and as regards their purification ceremonies. The administration of the Devaswoms by the state in course of time proved detrimental to the interests of the temples as far as their assets were concerned. The income from Devaswom lands became mixed up with the general revenue of the state and the Devaswom lands themselves became indistinguishable from government lands (TDB, 1968: 2-3).

In 1907, the Travancore Government deputed M. K. Ramachandra Rao, a judge of the Travancore High Court to enquire and report on the conditions of the Devaswoms in the state. His report indicated that the treatment of Devaswom land on the same footing as government land should be wrong. There was a general impression among the people that the Devaswoms are maintained out of the general revenue of the state. This created bitterness among sizable sections of Hindu community; they demanded a separate department for Devaswoms in the state for the effective management of temple administration. Thrivikramar Vasudevar, a member in the TSMPA in 1920 stated that it was highly desirable that the management of temples should be separated from the Land Revenue Department. But the separation should be done only after making out of an accurate list of the properties which originally belonged to the Devaswoms (TSMPA, 1920, March 3: 98). He also demanded to separate their supervision from the Land Revenue Department and to entrust their management to local committees consisting of the descendants of the donors of Devaswom lands, under the Superintendence of Government (TSMPA, 1921, March 10: 127). G. Idichandy a member from Mavelikkara constituency observed that the combination of Revenue and Devaswom duties for the same officer was indefensible in principles and injurious in operation and prayed for the early separation and the appointment of a commissioner in sole charge of Devaswom (TSMPA, 1907, January 9: 118).

Formation of the Devaswom Department

From the year 1873, it was the concern of the government to have an effort over the separation of Devaswom land from the government land. But the properties were incapable of identification and separation. Dewan Sheshiah Sastri pointed out that it had become difficult to separate Devaswom lands from those of the government (Pillai, 1996, Vol. I: 564). Ramachandra Rao Commission in its report on Devaswoms and Charitable Institutions in 1908 recommended the formation of a separate department for Devaswom administration in the state. He estimated Rs 47,000 as the annual expenditure on account of the creation of a new department for Devaswom

(Nair, 1999: 39-40). Considering the huge expenditure to be incurred on the creation of a department, the government decided to implement a few reforms in the prevailing system. The Travancore government, as an initial step towards addressing the grievances of non-Hindus regarding the denial of job opportunities in the Revenue Department, appointed Krishna Aiyangar, to study the issue of separation of Devaswom from Revenue Department and to submit a report. He favoured separation of the Devaswom Department from the Land Revenue Department in direct correspondence with the Government (Kumar, 1994: 108).

On April 1920, the government appointed a mixed committee of Hindu and non-Hindus to investigate the question of Devaswom separation and its financial implications. The Committee was required to report on the exact character of the assumption of the Devaswoms, the feasibility of separating their administration from the Land Revenue Department and the nature and cost of the additional staff that might be necessary if the organisation of a separate department be deemed desirable. The Committee submitted its report in 1922. On the basis of the Devaswom Separation Committee Report, Maharaja Sri Moolam Tirunal issued a Devaswom Proclamation according to which separate Devaswom Department was created. This was an epoch-making event in the history of temple administration in the state.

The expenditure in connection with the new Devaswom Department should be met from the general revenue of the state as per Section 7 of the Proclamation. A separate Devaswom fund composed mainly of a sum of Rupees 16 lakhs representing 40 percent of the recurring land revenue of the state and miscellaneous items of receipts such as offerings etc. The pay of the officers and establishment of the Devaswom Department was met from the general revenue of the state. Pay of the contingent employees in the department was met from the Devaswom fund sanctioned by the government (GoK, 1946:

168). Devaswom Commissioner was the head of the Devaswom Department. M. Raja Raja Varma, Efficiency Audit Officer was appointed as Devaswom Commissioner who prepared a scheme of proposals for the effective management of Devaswom Department which was sanctioned by the Government (GoK, 1923: 105). The Devaswom Proclamation of 1922 was historically significant as it redressed year long grievances of diverse sections of the society. The Proclamation enabled the government to appoint even those who did not have the right to enter temples to the Land Revenue Department (Nair, 1994: 5). While the management of the Government Devaswoms in the state was entrusted to the Devaswom Department, management of Sree Padmanabhaswamy Temple and PD Devaswoms and their properties were not under its control. The state Devaswoms were categorised into major, minor and petty according to the scale of expenditure.

In 1924, for the first time, Watts, a non-Hindu Dewan was appointed after Col. Munro. It was a turning point in the administrative history of temples in Travancore. Towards the close of 1925, the Dewan was relieved of his duties and responsibilities related to the administration of Devaswoms which was directly entrusted to the Commissioner under the sovereign, except in certain important matters for which the previous approval of the Dewan had to be obtained (TSMPA, 1932, March 10: 17). This arrangement was cancelled in 1930 and henceforth the Devaswom Department was placed under the control of Dewan with Devaswom Commissioner under him as the Head of the Department.

During the period of regent Maharani, many progressive reforms had been made like the abolition of animal sacrifice and devadasi system in temples and the opening of approach roads of Vaikom and some other important temples in Travancore for all. These reforms have given to Sethu Lakshmi Bai, an honoured place among the social reformers of modern Kerala (Menon, 1987: 209). In spite of these reforms, the majority of Hindus were not permitted to enter and worship in the temple. Temple entry movements such as Vaikom, Suchindram and Guruvayur Satyagrahas paved the way for a proclamation for temple entry by Sree Chithira Tirunal Bala Rama Varma. The Temple Entry Proclamation was a revolutionary step of the highest significance in the evolution of Indian social life.

There was a criticism that the State Government was spending less for the maintenance of the temples and religious matters than the amount of revenue accrued from the Devaswom properties and appropriating the balance of the income to the government. In the end, the legal position was taken whereby the government of the State accepted the obligation of maintaining the temples in an efficient condition and all law suits against them were barred (Menon, 1955: 197).

Integration of Travancore and Cochin and Formation of Travancore Devaswom Board

After the integration of Travancore and Cochin in 1949, the great concern before the respective governments was the Devaswom Administration. To examine all issues of integration, the Government of India appointed a Committee in 1949 under the Chairmanship of N. M. Buch. Even though full powers have been vested with the Ministers responsible to the legislature, some subjects like Devaswom and Religious Endowments made reserved by the respective rulers (GoK, 1949: 4). Article 8 of the Covenant provided for the formation of Travancore Devaswom Board for the administration of Devaswoms in Travancore and Cochin Devaswom Board for the administration of Devaswoms and Hindu Religious institutions in Cochin (See Appendix III 1). On August 1st, 1949, Travancore Cochin Hindu Religious Institutions Ordinance was promulgated by the Maharaja of Travancore as per Article 11 of the Covenant. Accordingly, TDB was constituted as per Section 3 of the Ordinance. The temples under the management of the Devaswom Department (constituted in 1922) were transferred to the effective control of the TDB. During the time of integration, TDB had 175 major Devaswoms, 371 minor Devaswoms, 882 petty Devaswoms and 125 PD Devaswoms (GoK, 1950: 6). The Ordinance was replaced by the Travancore-Cochin Hindu Religious Institutions Act 195.

With the State Reorganisation of 1956, Devaswoms in Travancore were also reorganised. Four Tamil speaking Taluks of South Travancore, Thovalai, Kalkulam, Agasthiswaram and Vilavancode were transferred to the Madras state forming Kanyakumari District. 490 temples of these areas were also separated and entrusted to the newly formed Kanyakumari Devaswom Board constituted under Madras Government Act 30 of 1959 and it started functioning from 1st April 1960. Consequently, the annuity was re-fixed at 46.5 lakhs including six lakhs of rupees towards expenditure in the Sree Padmanabhaswamy temple. Devaswom surplus fund was also to be divided into two parts in the ratio of 37.5 and 13.5, the smaller amount being payable to the Madras state. Accordingly, a sum of thirteen lakhs and fifty thousand rupees shall be charged on and paid out of the Consolidated Fund of the State of Tamil Nadu every year to the Devaswom Fund. The necessary amendments were made in the TCHRI Act, 1950 (GoK, 1964: 23). The provision was incorporated accordingly in Section 112 (1) (2) of the States Reorganisation Act, 1956 (Central Act 37 of 1956).

Constitutional Guarantee of Annual Grant (Article 290A)

Devawoms in Travancore got a statutory contribution from the government in lieu of compensation of the temple properties taken over by Col. Munro in 1811 AD. The Integration Committee Report specified that as the state had in the past taken over all properties of the temples, there was no escape from the obligation to maintain Devaswoms in a proper condition. According to V.P. Menon, the State would have no option but to return the properties to the temple. The State could not have it both ways, by refusing to return the properties while at the same time refusing to maintain the Devaswoms (1955: 197). The Report also stressed the need for adequate representation of the backward Hindus in the Board and the Devaswom fund to be utilised for benefitting a large section of people by avoiding unnecessary expenditure of feeding small sections and non-essential religious ceremonies (GoK, 1949: 35).

The annual government contribution to Devaswom upto 1931, as ensured in the Devaswom Proclamation of 1922, was a minimum of 16 lakhs. In 1932, this arrangement was altered and the contribution was fixed at 40 percent of the Ayacut and Sanchayam land revenue of the state (GoK, 1936: 235). The contribution for the subsequent years was therefore less than 16 lakhs. The whole contribution of 16 lakhs was however directed to be given only from 1937. As per the Land Tax Proclamation promulgated in 1946, a decade after the Temple Entry Proclamation; the government enhanced the annuity to the Devaswom from Rs 16 lakhs fixed in 1922 to Rs 25 lakhs. Again in 1948, immediately before the inception of responsible government, this contribution had been enhanced through a proclamation to 50 lakhs and an amount of one lakh was allotted to Sree Padmanabhaswamy Temple. The Hindu opinion persistently demanded not only the continued payment of the existing allotment, but also adequate compensation in respect of the properties taken over by the government and the profits derived from them (Menon, 1955: 197). Obviously, this plea could not be accepted; at the same time, it was impossible to decline the obligation of maintaining these temples as the state had taken over all their properties. The demand for incorporating specific guarantee for the regular allocation of funds for the proper administration of Devaswoms in Travancore and Cochin in the Constitution of India was raised by the Devaswom Central Committee and Ayyappa Seva Sangham in 1949 (Sadasivan, 2005: 89). Accordingly, the provision was made in the Constitution for the annual payment of Rs 51 lakhs by the Travancore- Cochin state to the Devaswom fund (Article 290 A of the Indian Constitution). Thus, the constitutional guarantee of annuity for Devaswom was secured. The annuity has been enhanced in 2004 to one crore by the government under the constant pressure from the stakeholders.

Temple Administration in Cochin

The state of Cochin was originally known as *Perumpadappu Nadu* and the ruling family is known as *Perumbadappu Swaroopam*. The word *Cochin* is popularly supposed to be a collection of two Sanskrit words *go-sri* means *prosperous with cows* (Menon, 1995: 2). Temples in Cochin were administered by *uralers* and the executive authority was vested with the chief elected by the Vedic Nambuthiris called *Yogam* (Menon, 1995: 323). The King exercised only a nominal rule over the affairs of major Devaswoms, but seldom interfered in the administration of minor Devaswoms.The state control over temple administration in Cochin began in the middle of the 18th century as a result of the confiscation of properties of the renegade chiefs who assisted the Zamorin while his invasion in the state. Subsequently, many of the *uralers* surrendered their temples to the government voluntarily (GoK 1984: 23; KHC,1990: 42). Besides, the Government had taken over several minor temples on the ground of mismanagement. The temple trustees called *yogathris* were powerful and posed a challenge to the royal authority and it was Sakthan Tampuran (1790-1805) who crushed their powers and their temples were brought under the government control. Thus, at the time of the state came under British supremacy, it had a large number of temples under its management (Menon, 1995: 325).

In 1812, Dewan Col. Munro took up the question of putting temple administration on a satisfactory footing. Taking advantage of the laxity in temple administration, the officers had grossly mismanaged the Devaswom and unlawfully enriched themselves at the temple income. Munro appointed a committee to prepare accurate registers of Devaswom properties and fixed scale of expenditure of temple rituals on daily, monthly and yearly basis. Accordingly, 179 Devaswoms were taken up as government temples and new *pathivus* were prescribed for them. Known as *Incorporated Devaswoms*, their properties were treated as government properties and the revenue from Devaswom merged with the revenue of the state and all Devaswom expenses were met from the public treasury (Menon, 1995: 325).

Later more number of temples came under government management but their funds were kept in separate accounts and they were called as *Unincorporated Devaswoms*. In 1897, a separate Devaswom Department was formed under a Superintendent and all incorporated and unincorporated Devaswoms were brought under it. Meanwhile, as per Cochin Hindu Religious Institutions Act of 1906, the Government took over some of the mismanaged private temples and such temples were called as *Assumed Devaswoms* (Jayashanker, 1997: 17). Conditions of the majority of incorporated Devaswoms were pathetic as they had no property and depended upon the state treasury for their existence. On the other hand, unincorporated Devaswoms were self-reliant and they earned high income exceeding their expenses. Thus, there was a great disparity in the financial position of two classes of Devaswoms (Menon, 1995: 327).

A Special Officer was deputed in 1907 to make an exhaustive investigation of Devaswom administration of the state and on the basis of his report; it was decided to be re-arranged. As per the Proclamation of 1910, all incorporated and unincorporated Devaswoms were brought under a single Devaswom Department. The separate *trust fund* was constituted and steps were taken to separate the receipts and expenditure of Devaswoms from the general revenue of the state (GoK, 1911: 12). All these Devaswoms under government were made as

Group Devaswoms. At the time of the assumption of temples by the government in 1812, the income from Devaswom lands was merged with state accounts. The progressive land legislation alienated large tracts of Devaswom land. Around 60,000 acres of land belonged to Devaswom Board temples were lost due to land reform legislation of the government. The Government allotted Rs 4.5 lakhs as annuity to the Board in lieu of this (GoK, 1984: 25); the amount is obviously inadequate. Thus, temples virtually lost their properties and income and they have to depend on the mercy of the government and devotees to meet their day-to-day expenses.

When the responsible government came into existence on 26th August 1947, the Government of Cochin (Amendment) Act, 1948 was promulgated; accordingly all reserved subjects were transferred to the control of the Council of Ministers, except palace, Devaswoms etc. (Chander, 1981: 4). Devaswoms were retained by the Maharaja. As per 50 G of the Government of Cochin Act, 1938 and the provisions of 1906 Cochin Hindu Religious Institution Act, Devaswoms under the ruler of Cochin except, Poornathrayeesa temple at Thrippunithura and Pazhayannur temple which were retained by the Ruler of Cochin, were vested under the direct control of CDB (these temples are under CDB now). The Cochin Devaswom Board was established on the basis of the Covenant and TCHRI Act, 1950. The formation of the CDB was a landmark in the history of Devaswoms in Cochin. The administration of Koodalmanickam temple, Irrinjalakkuda, another major temple in the Cochin region, was entrusted with a Committee as per the Koodalmanickam Devaswom Act 1971.

Administration of Koodalmanickam Devaswom

Koodalmanickam Devaswom is a very ancient religious institution in the erstwhile Cochin state. Ward and Conner in their *Geographical and Statistical Memoir of the Survey of Travancore and Cochin States* refer to this temple. The earliest historical reference to Koodalmanickam Temple is found in a stone inscription attributed to the Chera king Sthanu Ravi Varman dated 854 AD, donating a vast extent of land to the Temple. Some historians believe that the original temple was a Jain shrine dedicated to Jain Tirthankara Bharatheshwara, later the temple was converted into a Hindu temple during Brahminical upsurge. The management of the temple was vested in a body called the *Yogakkars*, but this right came to be subsequently vested with the *Thachudaya Kaimal*, appointed by the King of Travancore and the right was recognised by the treaties between Travancore and Cochin in 1765 and 1805. For the better management of the temple, the King of Cochin, Rama Varma issued a proclamation in 1917; accordingly a scheme had been drawn up, exempting the temple from Cochin Hindu Religious Institutions Act, 1906.

Soon after the formation of Kerala state in 1957, the King of Travancore surrendered his powers in the administration of Koodalmanickam Devaswom except the power of nominating Thachudaya Kaimal. The Government of Kerala appointed a Committee to entrust the administration of the temple in place of the ruler of Travancore through Koodalmanickam Devaswom Proclamation (Amendment) Act of 1957. Through this amendment, the government took an initial step to control the administration of the temple. In 1971, through the 26th amendment of the Indian Constitution, the Privy Purse was abolished and the claim of Thachudaya Kaimal in the Koodalmanickam temple administration too ceased. In the same year, the government formulated a scheme of administration for the temple in order to save it from the mismanagement of Thachudaya Kaimal. Thus, Koodalmanickam Temple Managing Committee came into existence.

Temple Administration in Malabar

Prior to the formation of the Kerala state, Malabar was a part of the Madras Presidency from the year 1800. So Madras laws were applicable for the administration of the temples in Malabar since 1817. As most of the temples in Malabar are private institutions, the scope for governmental interference was only minimal. Malabar temples were under the purview of Madras Endowments and Escheats Regulation VII of 1817 enacted by the British. This law was the first of its kind for giving the Hindu religious institutions in Malabar a statutory basis. Hindu population hailed this enactment as a protector and preserver of the properties of Hindu Religious Institutions (GoK, 1964: 34-35). The regulation laid down administrative machinery for temples in Malabar.

The role of the British Government in the administration of temples created dissatisfaction among the Christian Missionaries. They demanded a total withdrawal of the government from temple affairs. Accordingly, in 1841 the Madras Government instructed the Board of Revenue to refrain from temple administration and sent a report to the Government of India that a total withdrawal was done in the Madras Presidency. As per the decision of the *Court of Directors* of the East India Company, the control of temples was not effectively implemented till 1863 (Jayashanker, 1999: 21). As a result, the temples were dissipated and properties misappropriated by the persons in management. In 1863, the Hindu Religious Endowment Act was passed by the Government of India which replaced the earlier regulation of 1817. The Religious Endowment Act XX of 1863 enabled the Government to divest itself of the administration of endowments, marked the first step towards democratisation of the Temple administration (Aiyangar, 1931: 56). But the Act did not make any provision for adequate supervision and control of the management of temples.

Mismanagement and misappropriation of temple funds by the trustees continued and it was felt that a legislative enactment was absolutely necessary for their management. The Madras government made several attempts towards this but failed (GoK, 1964: 35-36). In 1922, a Bill, Madras Hindu Religious Endowments Bill, 1922 was moved in the Madras legislature to codify the law, but couldn't make the statute. In 1927, the Madras Hindu Religious and Endowments Act was made according to which the Madras HRE Board was constituted. The Act was modified in the following years, in 1928, 1929, 1931, 1934, 1935, 1938, 1939, 1944 and 1946 (Jayashanker, 1997: 16). After independence, the Madras state passed an Act to consolidate the laws relating to Hindu Religious Endowments named as Madras Hindu Religious and Endowments Act of 1951 which replaced the Act of 1927 and it came into force in the Malabar region; the Act is in force even today with amendments. With the State Reorganisation in 1956, the Malabar District and Kasargod Taluk became the part of the newly created state of Kerala. In 2008, through an amendment in the Madras Hindu Religious Endowment Act, Malabar Devaswom Board was formed for the temples in Malabar. While majority of temples in Travancore and Cochin were under the control and supervision of the state, the temples in Malabar region are free from such control and they remain under the management of hereditary trustees or *uralers*.

Formation of Malabar Devaswom Board

The creation of a Devaswom Board for the Malabar temples was a long-demanded one, but it became a reality only in 2008. In 1959, K. Govindankutty Menon, a member in the Legislative Assembly of Kerala demanded an administrative set up for Malabar temples in order to put an end to the mismanagement prevailed in their administration (KLA, 1959, March 13: 1365). K. Kelappan in 1968 appealed the Union Minister about the urgency to improve the conditions of Malabar temples and also the living conditions of the employees therein. As per the instructions of the Government of India 'Malabar Devaswom Bill' was drafted in 1975 by the State Government. But nothing took shape in pursuance to the said Bill (Re: Temples, 1994).

In 1987 and in 1991 the demand was again raised. In 1987, Malabar Temple Employees Association submitted a memorandum to the Government of Kerala demanding a Devaswom Board for Malabar temples (KLA, 1987, July 31: 28). In 1995, the Government of Kerala appointed a Committee headed by V. V. Vijayan, former Commissioner of TDB for preparing a draft for the uniform administrative system for Malabar temples. The Committee recommended a three-member body for the administration of Malabar temples, two members to be nominated by Hindu members in the legislature and one by the High Court (Malayala Manorama, 1996, November 27). Malabar Devaswom Board was formed in 2008 on the basis of 1994 High Court verdict. The Court issued directions to the Government of Kerala and the Hindu Religious and Endowment Department to develop a scheme for temple administration in Malabar and a unified board for all the regions viz. Travancore, Cochin and Malabar on the lines of the recommendations of Kuttikrishna Menon Committee and Sankaran Nair Commission. The verdict of the Court is a historical one and a milestone in the administration of Devaswom Board temples in Kerala. Justice K. P. Balanarayana Marar issued 13 directions regarding this.

Administration of Guruvayur Devaswom

Popularly known as the *Dwaraka of South India*, the Guruvayur Sree Krishna temple is one of the most famous temples in Kerala. It is the second biggest temple in South India in terms of revenue, next to Thiruppathi. William Logan mentions that Guruvayur temple was not a major temple in Malabar during the time of his writing *Malabar Manual*. According to him one of the major temples during the period was the temple of Thirunavaya in Ponnani Taluk (1887:190). Guruvayur temple was subordinate to the famous Siva temple at Thrikkanna Mathilakom until it was desecrated by the Portuguese. According to M R Raghava Varier, a reputed historian, the first reference to Guruvayur can be seen in *Kokasandesam* written in the 14th century (Myriad, 2016: 9). There is also a reference about a place called Kuruvayur in Tamil literature.

The temple was originally managed by seventy two Namboothiri families. The Zamorin, the ruler of Malabar, recognised them as the trustee of both Thrikkannamathilakam and Guruvayur (Myriad, 2016: 9). The Temple which was under the control of the Zamorin Raja was not plundered or destroyed by the Dutch because they did not want to hurt the feelings of the Zamorins (Seth, 2009: 29). It is interesting to note that Tipu Sultan and his aide Haidros Kuttee Moopan evinced great interest in the affairs of the temple. Hidros Kuttee who was in charge of Guruvayur seems to have made under the orders of Tipu Sultan, an annual grant to the temple for the conduct of daily *poojas* and offerings. Subsequently, the British authorities too accepted this obligation, exempting certain temple lands from assessment and authorising the use of the proceeds from them for the affairs of the temple (Menon, 1962: 615).

Like many other temples in Malabar, the Guruvayur temple had hereditary trustees, Zamorin Raja of Calicut and *Karanavan* of the Mallisseri Illom. Disputes between them over the *ooranma* rights were legally settled by the Madras High Court in 1889. In 1916, the British Government took over the administration and placed under the control of Court of Wards of Madras (Kurup, 2014: 33). In 1926, the Madras Hindu Religious Endowments Act was enacted and a scheme for the administration of the temple and its properties were settled accordingly. In 1927, the administration of Guruvayur temple was handed over to the Zamorin from the Court of Wards; then the total income and expenditure was not more than one lakh rupees (Kurup, 2014: 81). A group of devotees filed a petition before the duly constituted Hindu Religious Endowments Board complaining mismanagement of the affairs of the Temple by the hereditary trustees. The Board started enquiry which finally resulted in a scheme of administration being settled for the temple under section 63 (1) of the Act. The scheme recognised the hereditary rights of the Zamorin Raja and denied the rights of *Karanavan* of the Mallisseri Illom in the day-to-day administration of the temple.

The District Court of Southern Malabar restored the hereditary rights of *Karanavan* of Mallisserry Illom which was reaffirmed by the Madras High Court later. In 1970, an unfortunate fire incident happened in the temple which was enquired by Gangadharan Thampi Commission appointed by the government and the Commission pointed out prolonged neglect of the temple without proper maintenance and timely repairs. The report also unveiled the gross negligence on the part of those in-charge of the administration and management of the temple. It was an eye-opener to the mismanagement of the temple administration. Subsequently, the government took over its administration through an ordinance of 1971; the Guruvayur Devaswom Managing Committee was constituted; Zamorin Raja of Calicut was the Chairman and *karanavan* of Mallisserri Illom, the Vice-Chairman. Later the Ordinance was replaced into an Act which was challenged by the hereditary trustees before the Kerala High Court in 1971, claiming infringement of their fundamental rights under Articles 19, 25 and 26 of the Constitution. The Kerala High Court struck down this and a new Act was introduced for Guruvayur temple administration in 1978.

Devaswom Reforms Commissions

Lack of unified law, the existence of hereditary trustees, land encroachment, pathetic conditions of temples, poor wage and service conditions of employees, corruption and such grave issues were rampant in Devaswom administration from the very beginning. In the pre-independence period, several committees were appointed to study and propose reforms in Devaswom administration in the state such as Devaswom Separation Committee, Temple Entry Enquiry Committee etc. In the post-independence period also, a series of enquiry committees can be seen appointed by various agencies for studying different aspects of temple administration. The first among these was K. Kesava Menon (DIG of Police) Commission in 1950 to inquire into the Sabarimala fire incident. Though the Report was not published at first due to security reasons, later the government was compelled to publish it in 1957.Even the Union Government itself was eager to make uniformity in the administration of religious institutions throughout the country. In the 1960s, Religious Trust Bill was introduced in the Parliament for common legislation applicable to all religious institutions. But the Government failed in this move due to the dissolution of Lok Sabha (GoK, 1984: 8). The government of India appointed C. P. Ramaswamy Aiyar, former Dewan of Travancore as an Enquiry Commission. The Commission in its report of 1962 recommended the need of uniformity in legislation to temple administration at the state level. But no serious action has been taken by the Central Government on this report.

At this juncture, the Government of Kerala appointed a High-Level Committee under the Chairmanship of K. Kuttikrishna Menon, former Advocate General of Madras in 1961 to consolidate Devaswom laws in the state. The Commission in its Report recommended 108 suggestions; the creation of an *Apex Board* for all Devaswoms in the state was the most important among them. Two Commissions were appointed by the State Government, one in 1973 under C. R. Krishnamoorthy to enquire into the financial position and financial management of TDB and another in 1974 under G. Bhaskaran Nair to study the financial position of CDB. Like the previous Commission Reports, the fate of these reports was also to lay in the cold storage of Government Secretariat.

In 1983, the Government appointed K. P. Sankaran Nair, former Law Officer of TDB to study the nature of government control over its administration and to consolidate Devaswom laws. The Commission submitted its Report in 1984 with 40 recommendations which are considered as valuable guidelines for temple administration in Kerala. No action has been taken on the recommendations so far. In 1990, High Court of Kerala, fully realising the improper and inefficient administration in the two leading Devaswom Boards, TDB and CDB, like financial indiscipline and mismanagement of temple, appointed a High Power Commission headed by V. Ramachandran, former Chief Secretary to the Government of Kerala. The Committee submitted its Report on 30th August 1990 with suggestions such as de-politicisation of temple administration, de-recognition of trade unions in the Board with outside politicians and so on.

In 1995, the then UDF Government appointed V.V.Vijayan, Commissioner of TDB to study about temple administration, submitted Report to the Government recommending a unified administrative law for all Devaswoms in the state and separate administrative set up for temples in Malabar. The Kerala High Court in 2007 appointed a three-member High Power Commission with Justice Paripoornan as Chairman to inquire into the charges of corruption, misappropriation of public funds mismanagement, maladministration, nepotism and proven incompetence and indiscipline in the administration of the TDB. The Committee submitted its report with 79 suggestions for the better functioning and management of the TDB.

In 2017, Government of Kerala appointed a Law Reform Commission headed by K. Gopalakrishnan, the first President of MDB to study reforms in the Malabar Devaswom Laws. The Committee recommended drastic changes in the Devaswom Laws applicable to Malabar temples and proposed a draft Act, the Malabar Hindu Religious and Charitable Institutions and Endowments Act 2017, but no action has been taken by the Government so far. Thus, it is a fact that the interest of the government in appointing Commissions cannot be seen in implementing their suggestions thereby occurring wastage of public fund. Though Hindu organisations are frequently demanding the implementation of commission reports, the government turned a deaf ear. This may perhaps due to the suggestion of depoliticisation of temple administration, nomination of believers in Devaswom Boards and so on by these reports that are not preferred by the governments in power.

Role of Judiciary in Temple Administration

Judicial intervention has definitely played its role in the administration of Devaswoms in the state. It is a fact that it was due to the timely intervention of the Court that paved the way for many a reforms in the arena of administrative set up of the Devaswoms. Judiciary often acted as a saviour of devotees against the malpractices like corruption, mismanagement, misappropriation that are rampant in temple administration today. As per Devaswom statutes, the High Court has the power to interfere and supervise Devaswom Board administration. At the High Court level, there is a separate *Devaswom Bench* for the speedy disposal of temple related issues. The Chief Justice of the High Court appoints two judges- usually one junior and one senior- to the Devaswom Bench which sits twice weekly to hear matters for all public temples in the State. In order to combat corruption, ombudsman mechanism was also introduced in Devaswoms by the High Court of Kerala. The High Court enjoys the power to appoint Devaswom Commissioners from the panel submitting by the respective Devaswom Boards in the state. Likewise, the Court appoints an officer to coordinate the activities of various government departments during *Mandalam Makaravilakku* festival in Sabarimala Temple.

The Act brought forth for controlling the administration of Guruvayur temple, Guruvayur Devaswom Act of 1971 was invalidated by the KHC on the ground that it is an infringement of religious freedom guaranteed in the Constitution. The verdict was a warning to the government to interfere on temple administration in the state and it is considered as the *Magna Carta* of Hindu religious freedom. In 1990 and 2007, the High Court appointed two High Power Commissions to study various administrative issues prevalent in TDB and CDB. The High Court of Kerala appointed Krishnan Unni Commission in 2003 for enquiring the irregularities in Guruvayur Devaswom (C.K. Rajan, 1994). When mishaps happened due to stampede in 2000 and Pullumede Tragedy in 2011 at Sabarimala, the Government of Kerala sought the help of eminent jurists, Justice Chandrashekhara Menon and Justice M. R. Hariharan Nair and appointed them as Enquiry Commissions.

The KHC in its verdict in 1990 observed that the nomination of non-believers to Devaswom Boards as members is detrimental to the interests of temples and insisted that only believers in God and temple worship should be nominated. The Court also upheld the voting rights of Hindu Ministers and Hindu MLAs through another verdict irrespective of their faith in God subject to the condition that only believers should be appointed as members in the state Devaswoms. Similarly, the Supreme Court had to intervene in cases like appointment of non-Brahmin priests in temples under TDB in 1993 and 2002 pronouncing that the eligibility of a person in the appointment as priest should be on merit and not by birth or pedigree (Adithyan, 2002). Similarly, various judicial verdicts become landmarks in the cases of formation of the MDB, administration of Sree Padmanabhaswamy Temple, entry of women in Sabarimala and so on. Thus, it can be seen that when the policy options became failures, judicial activism emerged as the saviour of devotees.

Administration of Sree Padmanabhaswamy Temple

Sree Padmanabhaswamy Temple is one of the leading temples in Kerala belonging to the erstwhile Travancore royal family which is not coming under the authority of Devaswom Boards, so the study excluded its administration. However, there are provisions in the Travancore Cochin Hindu Religious

Institution Act, 1950 (Chapter III Section 18 to 23) for the administration of the temple. An Advisory Committee for the administration of the temple as per Section 20 of the Act has not been constituted so far because of the expected political interference in the advisory body, as the king afraid of (GoK, 1984: 51). Rs 6 lakhs (revised into 20 lakhs in 2004) has been earmarked annually to the temple as per Article 290 A of the Indian Constitution and the Covenant. The administration of the temple was performed by the two bodies, *Ettarayogam* and *Sabha,* the former took care of temporal matters other than spiritual in the bygone days. *Ettarayogam* was in charge of the maintenance of temple traditions then. The King never participated in the deliberations of the *Ettarayogam*, only supervised its functioning (Menon, 1983: 421-424).

The temple was the wealthiest institution in the state as it maintained treasury containing money and a large collection of precious jewels and stones. It possessed extensive landed properties also. According to Samuel Mateer, the temple could even lend to the government a large amount of money (1871: 181). The main cash income to the temple treasury was almost the regular donations made by members of the royal family whenever they visited the temple. The Yogam maintained, controlled and supervised treasury management; the treasury could be opened only in the presence of the members deputed by the Yogam (Menon, 1983: 425-26). Shesiah Sasthri in his *Administration Reports for 1873-74* stated that it has a government of its own unconnected with the state (Aiyyer, 1998: 639).

After the *Grand Dedication* of Travancore to Lord Sri Padmanabha by Marthanda Varma in January 1750, he and his successors ruled the state as *Sri Padmanabha Dasas.* Marthanda Varma ousted the Yogam from the temple administration and took over it with its properties by himself. Thereafter, the temple properties became intermixed with the properties of the State. The state patronised the temple until the time of the integration of the two States (Menon, 1955: 196). After the integration, the temple received an annuity for its maintenance as per Article 290A of the Constitution. The Government of Kerala has no control over the administration of this royal temple.

Report of the High-Level Committee for the Unification of Devaswom Laws (1964) recommended for the constitution of an advisory committee for Sree Padmanabhaswamy Temple. It is necessary not only for satisfying the statutory requirement, but also for the proper administration of the temple without giving any room for complaint (GoK, 1964: 66). Sankaran Nair Commission recommended a complete restructuring of the administrative system of the temple without affecting the hereditary rights of the royal family in the temple administration. An officer not below the rank of a Government Secretary who should be a believer in god and temple worship may be appointed to monitor the day-to-day administration of the temple. The Commission also suggested forming a temple Advisory Committee consisting of devotees for advising the King in temple administration (GoK, 1984: 53-54).

Recently, conflicts over the administration of the temple resulted in a litigation before the Court. The High Court in its verdict favoured governmental control in the model of Guruvayur Devaswom; the Supreme Court stayed the order of the High Court on an appeal by the royal family and appointed an *Amicus Curie*. Putting an end to a nine-year dispute, the Supreme Court in 2020 upheld the rights of the erstwhile royal family of Travancore in the administration and management of Sree Padmanabhaswamy temple. Putting an end to a nine-year dispute, the Supreme Court on Monday upheld the rights of the erstwhile royal family of Travancore in the administration and management of Sree Padmanabhaswamy temple. As per the Supreme Court direction in July 2020 a committee was constituted for temple administration with the Thiruvananthapuram District Judge as the chairperson to take care of the daily temple administration. The administration includes a nominee of the royal family, the chief thantri (priest) of the temple, a nominee of the state and a member nominated by the Union Ministry of Culture. The committee is entrusted to protect the treasures and properties of the temple, one of the richest in India.

Private Temples in Kerala

Varadhachari has made a distinction between public and private temples in his *Hindu Religious and Charitable Endowments.* While private temples are the places of worship for the members of particular families, public temples are dedicated to the public for worship (Prakash, 2006). In Kerala, there exist enormous private temples including local shrines, *kavus,* family *kovils* etc., besides the temples bearing the authority of Devaswom governing bodies; their exact number is not available. K. P. Sankaran Nair Commission in its report (1984) stated that around 500 such temples existed in the Travancore part alone controlled by *uralers*, *karakkars* etc., (GoK, 1984: 22). Some of them receive grant from Devaswom Boards. Guruvayur Devaswom spent an amount towards temple renovation grants to private temples every year. Devaswom acts stipulate certain provisions to take over these private temples if any laxity or corruption prevails in their administration.

Private temples generally having selfish interests, their managers have a notion that if these temples become profitable the government will unnecessarily interfere and take over them (Jayashanker, 1997: 257). Private temples lack any sort of governmental interference over their administration. Some of them are well managed and attract large number of devotees to its fold. Attukal Devi Temple, Thiruvananthapuram, Oachira Parabrahma Temple, Chakkulathukavu Temple in Alappuzha District, Mannarassala Nagaraja Temple at Haripad, Kumaranelloor Devi Temple at Kottayam District etc., are prominent private temples in Travancore area. Private temples are managed by private trusts, family groups, Hindu organisations like RSS,VHP, KTPC and caste organisations like SNDP Yogam, NSS, Yogakshema Sabha. Service conditions of employees in private temples are miserable so as there is no unified pattern of regulation for them. The study excluded private temples and their issues owing to lack of political interference or state control over their management and a definite pattern of temple administration.There are about 35 Gauda Saraswatha Temples belonging to another category of private temples. These temples prohibit the entry of other castes and meant exclusively for Gauda Saraswatha Brahmins only (Jayashanker, 1997: 21).

The employees in the private temples are not organised and there are no special rules or regulations for their salary and service conditions. In 1997, in the KLA, Babu Divakaran raised a submission regarding the plight of private temple employees and urged the government to take over the administration of these temples in the state when a uniform Devaswom Board come into force (KLA, 1997, December 22). Again in 1999, he introduced a private Bill in the Assembly, *Kerala Private Devaswom Employees Welfare Fund Bill* in which he proposed a welfare board for employees of private temples. According to him, there are more than one lakhs private temples, big and small, existing in the state in which over five lakhs of employees are working in different categories (KLA, 1999, December 17).

S. Jayashanker in his study *Temples of Kerala* surmised five important features from the past for the functioning of temples in the state. The first is during the period from1810-1820; when under the influence of the British, temple lands were taken over by the government that shattered the authority and influence of temples on society and polity. Second is the Mysorean invasion and later rebellions destroying, plundering and desecrating temples in Malabar and Cochin. Thirdly, the Marxian atheist philosophy indoctrinated large sections of people to become disbelievers of temple worship. Its impact is more pronounced in the Malabar region. Fourthly, Devaswom

Boards became a politicised institution and their inefficient management of temples observed by the High Court of Kerala further delinked their old importance. Lastly, the impact of Agrarian relations Act 1969 struck the backbone of the temples (Jayashanker, 1997: 20).

Thus, in a nutshell, the history of temple administration in Kerala has come across different landmarks from 1750 (*Thrippadidanam*) up to the present. First one is the taking over of the administration of temples by the state in 1811 during the period of Col. Munro. Formation of separate Department for Devaswom in 1922 was the second development and the temple entry proclamation of 1936 is the third one. Fourth is the formation of Devaswom Boards as per the Covenant of Travancore and Cochin integration in 1949. The outcome of the state reorganisation that resulted in a rearrangement of Devaswoms in South Travancore region is the next one. With this, the splendid temples like Kanyakumari, Sucindram, Thiruvattar, Padmanabhapuram etc. were transferred to Kanyakumari Devaswom Board. Sixth is the formation of Guruvayur and Koodalmanickam Devaswom Managing Committees through respective Devaswom Acts in 1971 and the seventh is the formation of Malabar Devaswom Board in 2008 on the basis of the historical verdict of the High Court of Kerala in 1994 and the last is the formation of Kerala Devaswom Recruitment Board in 2015 which is an innovative step in the history of temple administration. Thus, we can see that the administration of temples in the state passed through different stages and entered into new areas of concerns. The need for analyzing the elaborate administrative structure of the Devaswom Governing Bodies is *sine qua non* for the better understanding of the concerns the temple administration in the state face.

2

Temples and Governance

Temple Administration

Cambridge Dictionary defines *administration* as the arrangements and tasks needed to control the operation of a plan or organisation. Administration can be classified into public and private and the concept of temple administration covers both of the two aspects. By temple administration, it is visualised in looking after all temple functions, planning all the activities and handling every possible situation in a most noble manner, commensurate tradition with socio-politico-economic climates of emerging modernity (Shukla, 2013:42). Like any other institution temple administration also includes wide range of activities which includes planning, organising, staffing, recruiting, financing, budgeting, training etc. Temple Administration is not a new concept as from the ancient times temples were administered by different agencies known in different names.

As an organisation, the administration of Devaswom governing bodies in the state is well-defined and well-structured. The administrative structure can be broadly classified into financial, personnel, managerial and social welfare administration. There are two types of employees in Devaswom administration- employees under the establishment section and temple employees. Financial management devices like budgeting and auditing are there and annual publication of administration reports and budgets are regular processes as in the case of any other organisation. Service conditions of temple employees are different and their working hours are depending upon the daily rituals of temples. A well-structured bureaucratic administrative pattern based on the principles of hierarchy is prevalent in temple administration. Sufficient staff is appointed to carry out the work related to temples according to service rules, staff pattern, service conditions etc. Their salary and service conditions are similar to those of the State Government employees. Devaswom Manuals, Rules and other statutes are applicable to the Devaswom employees. Temple Management Committees are constituted and functioning on the basis of provisions of respective Devaswom Acts and its orders are executed by subordinate officials. At the Government level, there exists a monitoring mechanism for regulating temple administration.

As much as temples and their administration in the state are concerned their administration and ownership became the bone of contention that was associated with power in the locality. Kesavan Veluthat considers temple as an instrument for strengthening the power structure of kings. He classified temples in to two types, royal temples and those that formed the nucleus of agrarian settlements (2009: 72). A land-based power structure relation existed during the medieval period. The socio-economic systems developed by the *uralers* and *karalars* have existed for a long time in Kerala. In the course of the conflict for the ownership of temples, the management of several of them became disorderly and so the state had to assume their administration through the exercise of its paramount *melkoima* right (Tampi, 1941: 129). In the agrarian scene, these changes gradually altered the prevailing land ownership structure and created favourable conditions for the emergence of Brahminical landlordism in Kerala.

The vast accumulation of wealth and property in the hands of Devaswom authorities was a standing menace to the tranquillity of the state. The important Devaswom synods afforded a safe asylum to malcontents and law breakers (Aiyer, 1931: 54). Each Devaswom had a territorial jurisdiction which was called the *sanketham* and all matters, civil, social or religious were adjudicated and executed by the *yogam* consisting of *uralers.* Devaswoms owed no allegiance to any sovereign. On the contrary, Kings were compelled to pay penalty for breaches of the customary laws of *sankethams*. Technically each breach was called *sankethams azhikal* (Raja, 1932: 97).

In some cases, a synod of priests managed the temples. Temple synods were a source of standing menace to public security and good government in the tenth century of the Malabar Era (Aiyer, 1998: 636-37). The synods exercised judicial and executive power over *sanketham* lands owned by them, exercised authority over the rulers. The existence of such a sacrosanct and superstitious force in the country was a Damocles' sword over the throne (Aiyer, 1931: 54). In 1729, Marthanda Varma introduced measures to check the influence and power of these priestly classes. During his time, Travancore history is resonant with struggle between the state and Devaswoms. He initiated a bold action to curb the excessive powers of the *yogam* or council of the temple as he was aware of the grave pitfalls from the experience of *Ettarayogam* of Sree Padmanabhaswamy temple (Gouri Lakshmi Bayi, 1998: 22).

Under Maharaja Marthanda Varma, the process of centralisation of administration took place in Travancore and subsequently, Dewan Velu Thampi proposed the confiscation of temple property to the government. These states of affairs coupled with a desire to confiscate the enormous wealth of the temples prompted the British authorities to take over their administration. In the post-independence period, Devaswom Boards were created as autonomous bodies for the management of temples in the state. Though these bodies are envisaged as autonomous in nature, active state intervention is often can be seen in their working. A uniform pattern of administration of temple is an imperative one, provided the persons entrusted with the work are honest and have a say in the administration of temples as they are the beneficiaries and are responsible for sustain them (Jayashanker, 1997: 257).

Even before the formation of the state of Kerala in 1956, comprising of erstwhile princely states of Travancore, Cochin and Malabar of the Madras Presidency, Devaswom Boards were there for the administration of temples in Travancore and Cochin. Being the part of Madras Presidency, temples in Malabar were supervised by the HRCE Department. The socio-political reforms introduced in the state of Kerala after its formation, made drastic changes in the fundamentals of temple administration also. One of the significant developments in this regard happened in 1971 when Koodalmanickam temple and Guruvayur Sree Krishna Temple, major temples in Cochin and Malabar regions were brought under the control of the State. With the 26th amendment to the Constitution of India 1971, *Privy Purse* was abolished and thus the nominal right of the King over temple administration in Kerala ceased to exist; the right was transferred to democratically elected government.

Devaswom Administration in Kerala

Department of Revenue (Devaswom), Government of Kerala

Devaswom governing bodies are designed as autonomous institutions, but some sort of political control wields by the State Government over them. A Minister-in-charge of Devaswom affairs at Cabinet level is there to co-ordinate Devaswom administration in Kerala. In the Revenue Department, there is a separate section to handle Devaswom affairs headed by the Principal Secretary, Revenue (Devaswom) and an Additional Secretary under him. The Department is functioning under the direct control of the Minister-in-charge of Devaswom. The Department is acting as a link between the Devaswom Committees with the Government. All the five

Devaswom governing bodies in the state are functioning under the supervision of the Devaswom Department.

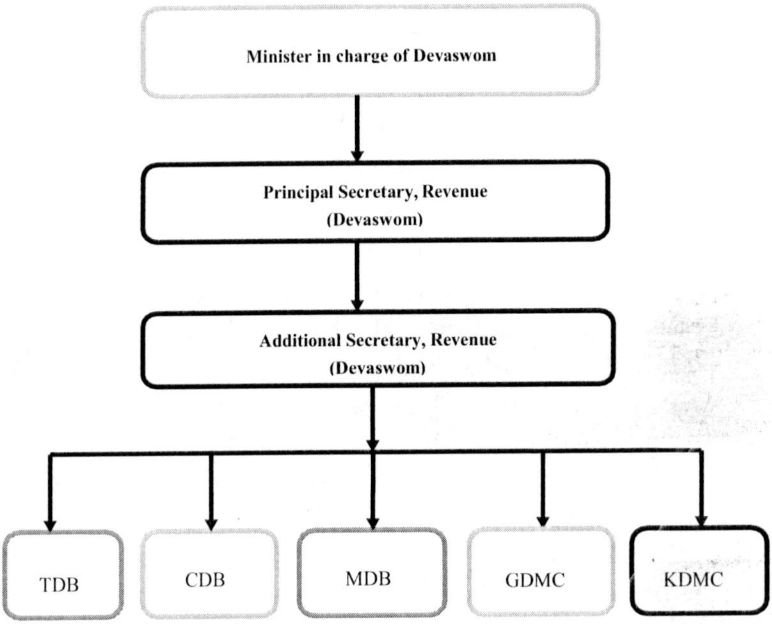

Fig. 2.1: Hierarchy of Devaswom administration in Kerala.

Without studying the organisational structure of Devaswom governing bodies, the study of temple administration in Kerala seems futile. There is no uniformity in the laws and rules for temple governance, classification of temples, income and expenditure, auditing of accounts, temple grants, statutory contributions, wage structure and service conditions for temple employees, corruption check mechanisms etc for the Devaswoms in the state.

Travancore Devaswom Board (TDB)

Travancore Devaswom Board is perhaps one of the leading institutions in the state as it manages the largest number of Hindu religious institutions. The temples once under the control of the Devaswom Department in Travancore along with their movable and immovable properties and the sovereign rights were transferred to the TDB during the process of state integration in 1949; thus thousands of big and small temples came under its management. Presently, two categories of temples- Scheduled and PD Devaswoms exist under the TDB. 96% of temples under the TDB are Scheduled Devaswoms. Besides spiritual administration, the Board runs educational institutions, institutions for the promotion of temple arts, heritage studies and arts and architecture.

The TDB was constituted in 1949 on the basis of an Ordinance which was replaced by an Act, Travancore Cochin Hindu Religious Institution (TCHRI) Act (Act XV) of 1950. The TCHRI Act provides a three-Member Board including the President and two other Members; the President and one Member are nominated by the Hindu Ministers and one Member from the Scheduled Caste/ Scheduled Tribe category is elected by the Hindu MLAs. In the 1950s, Pattom Thanu Pillai, a doyen in the state politics questioned the rationality of the rule of three men in the TDB having an asset of sixty to seventy lakhs at that time (TCLA, 1950: 1546). The Board is supposed to be an autonomous body and there is no provision for any interference by the government in its day-to-day affairs, but the involvement of the government in power is a usual practice in its administration.

Functions of the Board

The Board is entrusted with a wide range of powers categorised as obligatory and non-obligatory. The former is statutory, relating to temple affairs and the latter is non-statutory, relating to non-devotional aspects. It is the obligation of the Board to maintain temples in good condition administer Devaswoms in accordance with the recognised norms, work for the educational, social and cultural advancement and economic betterment of the Hindu community and provide expenditure for customary religious ceremonies. Running of educational institutions, marriage halls, shopping complexes etc., are included in the second category. Approval of temple expenses, policy decisions such as training, norms for employees' transfer and placement, approval of budgets etc., are decided by the Board. A Devaswom Recruitment Board is there for recruiting employees to the Devaswom services. The Board issues proceedings and rules for temple administration as per Section 17 of the TCHRI Act 1950.

The administration of the Board is categorised into two sections; Establishment and Temple Section. The Establishment Section is again divided into three major departments of administration, Finance and Maramath. Correspondingly, the employees under the Board are also categorised into administrative employees and temple employees. The affairs relating to temple rituals are managed by the Temple section Temple employees are classified into priesthood and helping class. The priesthood class can be broadly divided into *Tantris* and *shanthikkars* (Chief Priest and Head Priest). In any matter connected with temple rites and rituals, the words of *Tantris* are final. Apart from the Chief Priest and the Head Priest, there is another group of temple employees known as *Kazhakakkars* who are closely associated with the day-to-day affairs in a temple. They are also classified as *kaaraanma* and *non-karanma.*

There is a Secretary who is the chief administrative officer of the Board Secretariat and convener of the Board meetings. Secretary supervises all departments and issues directions in their administration, receiving directions of the Board and all official papers to the Government, High Court and high dignitaries. All circulars and instructions of the Board are signed by the Secretary (TDB, 2004: 164). He should prepare the minutes of the proceedings of the Board meetings and submit them to the Board's approval. He communicates all decisions of the Board to the Devaswom Commissioner in the Devaswom Department. The Board has separate departments of Accounts, Maramath (works), Sabarimala, Thiruvabharanam, Law, Vigilance, and Cultural affairs.

Devaswom Department

The functions of the Devaswom Department are planning, preparation of administration reports, personnel administration, office administration, legal matters, public relations etc. Devaswom Commissioner is the executive officer of the Devaswom Department (TDB, 2004: 64). In 2018, through an amendment in the TCHRI Act, a provision was made that the post of Devaswom Commissioner may be from an officer not below the rank of Deputy Devaswom Commissioner or an officer not below the rank of Joint Secretary of the government on deputation. This step to appoint Joint Secretary of the Government as Commissioner can be viewed as an attempt to tighten the governmental control over TDB administration.

Organisation of Temples

For administrative convenience, temples under the Board are grouped into Devaswom Districts, Devaswom Groups and Sub Groups. Devaswom Sub Groups are classified into six grades; first, second, higher, special, administrative grades and Sabarimala group. Such a classification is based on the income and the grade may change in every five year. There are four Devaswom Districts; Thiruvananthapuram, Pathanamthitta, Harippad and Vaikom under the control of Deputy Devaswom Commissioners. Devaswom Districts are divided into 20 Groups under the supervision of Assistant Commissioners and a separate group for Sabarimala that includes Sabarimala, Pamba and Nilakkal Devaswoms headed by an Executive Officer in the cadre of Deputy Devaswom Commissioner. In addition to the Executive Officer, there is a Special Commissioner for Sabarimala appointed by the High Court to co-ordinate and monitor all activities during the period of pilgrimage. Groups are again divided into 282 Sub Groups under Sub Group Officers.

Temples under the TDB are grouped into three grades; Grade I, Grade II and Grade III depending not on the basis of income but on temple rituals, customs and importance. At present, there are 1248 temples under the control of the Board including 236 Grade I temples, 479 Grade II, 481 Grade III and 52 PD temples. 18.91 % of temples under TDB belong to Grade I category, 38.38 % are Grade II, 38.54% Grade III and 4.17% constitute PD temples,Temples under TDB are arranged on cluster basis under four Devaswom Districts, 21 Groups and 282 Sub-Groups. Among the four Devaswom Districts, Thiruvananthapuram District is the biggest one consisting of 84 Sub Groups with 406 temples

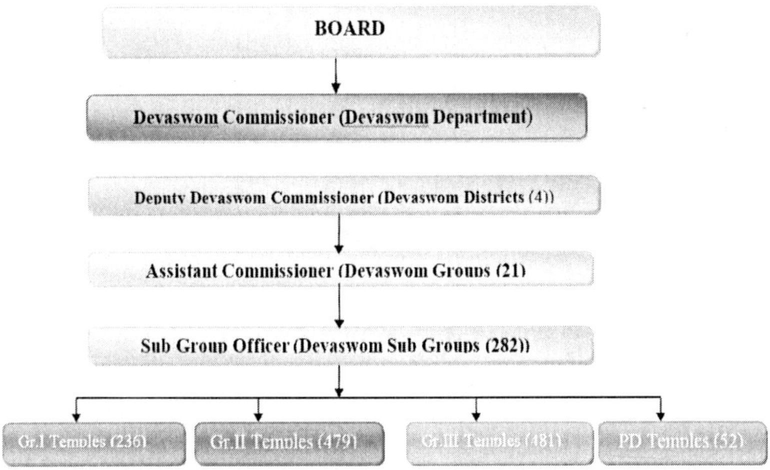

Fig. 2.2: Hierarchy of temple administration in TDB.

With regard to the number of Grade I and Grade III temples, Thiruvananthapuram District is the top, covering 32.53% of total temples under TDB. Pathanamthitta District is in the second position consisting of 310 temples, covering 23.08% of temples under its control. Pathanamthitta is the top in the number of Grade II temples; Harippad is comparatively the smallest District under the TDB comprising of 241(19.31%) temples. Sabarimala Group is the top in terms of income under the TDB.

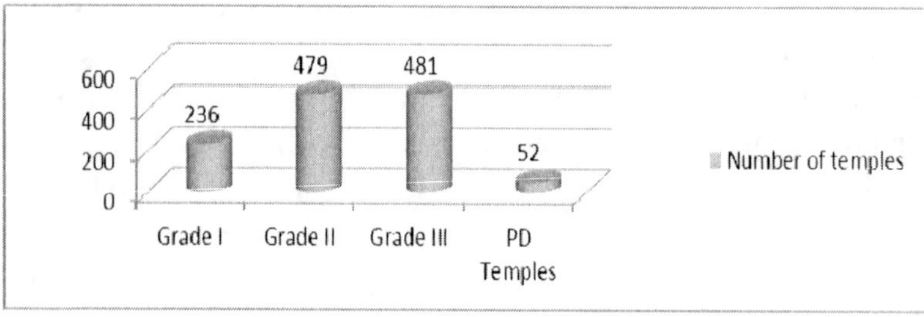

Fig. 2.3: Grade-wise list of temples under TDB

Table 2.1: Grade- wise list of TDB temples

Sl. No.	Grade	Number of temples	Percentage of total temples
1.	Grade I	236	18.91 %
2.	Grade II	479	38.38 %
3.	Grade III	481	38.54 %
4.	PD Temples	52	4.17%
Total		1248	100%

Source: Data compiled from 'Travancore Devaswom Board Temples' (2012), TDB, pp. 1-4.

Table 2.2: Grade-wise and District-wise list of temples under TDB

Devaswom District	No. of sub groups	Gr I	Gr II	Gr III	PD	Total temples	Percentage of total temples
Sabarimala group	3	2	1			3	0.24%
Thiruvananthapuram	84	65	115	209	17	406	32.53%
Pathanamthitta	64	56	142	99	13	310	24.84%
Harippad	65	56	110	73	2	241	19.31%
Vaikom	66	57	111	100	20	288	23.08%
Total	**282**	**236**	**479**	**481**	**52**	**1248**	100%

Source: Data compiled from 'Travancore Devaswom Board Temples' (2012), TDB, pp. 1-46.

PD Devaswoms

The Personal Deposit Devaswoms (PD Devaswoms) constitute a separate group of temples under TDB; supposed to be financially autonomous. The PD Devaswoms are unincorporated religious institutions which came under the government management and control at different times and under varying circumstances (Pillai, 1996: 559). Their accounts of receipts, expenditure and balance are not merged in the general Devaswom accounts but are maintained separately and have personal deposit accounts in treasuries (GoK, 1929: 106). The conditions of many PD Devaswoms are pitiable due to inaccessibility of Devaswom fund. The PD Devaswoms have

Table 2.3: Number of PD Devaswoms under TDB (Devaswom district-wise)

Devaswom districts	Number of PD temples	Percentage
Thiruvananthapuram	17	32.69
Pathanamthitta	13	25
Harippad	02	3.85
Vaikkom	20	38.46
Total	**52**	100

Source: *Data compiled from 'Travancore Devaswom Board Temples' (2012), TDB, pp.1-46.*

to sustain with the income from their landed properties. But their existence has become very difficult owing to the land legislations (GoK, 1964: 25). The only remedy to overcome this crisis is the conversion of these temples into Schedule Devaswoms. So, the Board decided to convert them as Scheduled Devaswoms.

Financial Administration

Administration of finance is one of the most important elements of an organisation. Without effective mechanisms to prevent fraudulent practices in financial administration, no organisation can achieve success. In order to keep up financial security, the Board has an Accounts Officer who is solely responsible for the proper maintenance, compilation and audit of all the accounts of the TDB. He systematically maintains accounts and audit relating to the receipts and expenditure of the department and prepares the annual budget. Section 33 of the TCHRI Act gives power to the Board to prepare a budget showing the probable receipts and expenditure of the incorporated and unincorporated Devaswoms and Hindu religious institutions under the management of the Board.

Devaswom Fund

Devaswom Fund comprises annual statutory government contributions (annuity), devotees' offerings, income from landed properties, commercial complexes, marriage halls etc. The unspent balance of each year shall be added to the Devaswom Surplus Fund (Section 26 of the TCHRI Act) administered by the Devaswom Commissioner. The surplus fund generally utilised for purposes like maintenance of temples, the appurtenant properties etc. Besides, the TDB maintains Sabarimala Improvement Fund, Bus Fund, Education Fund, Pension Fund etc

Revenue and Expenditure of TDB

The income of the Board includes annual government contribution, income from temples, rent from various sources like shopping complexes, elephants etc. Income from Sabarimala constitutes the backbone of TDB's revenue. Among the Board temples, only 61 are self-reliant temples (4.8%) and the remaining 1,187 temples are functioning with the fund generated from these 61 temples. Sankaran Nair Commission Report in 1984 pointed out that one-tenth of the annual income of TDB was spent for the establishment charges; to meet the salary bills of employees, allowances paid to the Board members etc. (GoK, 1984: 282).

After the state reorganisation when leading temples like Sucindram, Thiruvattar and 448 temples were transferred to Madras state, the income of the Board was affected considerably. Then steadily the expenditure began to exceed the income from 1958-59 period; the reasons may be the huge expenditure incurred because of the increase in number of employees, revision of scale of pay and allowances of the employees and the steady rise in the price of commodities (GoK, 1974: 10). A remarkable development in the history of the TDB is the enhancement of government contribution from Rs 46.5 lakhs to Rs 80 lakhs in 2004.While examining the expenditure statement of the Board it can be seen that the Board spent about 20% of its total income for the administrative establishment charges and about 40% towards the expenses for Scheduled Devaswoms. Corresponding to the increase in income, expenditure is also increasing due to the rise in establishment expenditure, price of commodities, DA etc. The administrative expenditure of TDB has been considerably increased in proportion to the increase in its revenue. The income from Sabarimala constitutes about 35- 46% of the total income of the TDB. But after the Supreme Court verdict on women entry, there happened a considerable decline in the income from Sabarimala temple.

After the Supreme Court verdict there happened a heavy decline in the income of Sabarimala temple. While the total income of Sabarimala in 2017-18 was Rs 272.74 crore, it is declined to Rs 180.18 crores in the year 2018-19; evidently, this shortfall affected seriously the financial stability of the Board. The income from temples under the TDB in general was also considerably declined. Media reported that *kanikka* boxes of temples under the TDB received white papers written *swami saranam* instead of currency. In 2019, the state budget earmarked an amount of Rs 100 crore for the TDB considering the temporary fall in the revenue of Sabarimala temple that has been affected the functioning of Devaswom Board temples

(GoK, 2019: 62). But the amount has not been fully disbursed so far even in the midst of the heavy financial crisis the Board faces (Janmabhumi, 2019, October 12). The income of Sabarimala includes income from offerings, *kanikka*, sale of *appam*, *aravana*, parking fee, auction, petrol pump etc.

Table 2.4: Income from Sabarimala temple under TDB-2006-2016

Year	Income from Sabarimala	Total income of TDB	Sabarimala's Share in the total income of TDB
2006-07	83,56,74,335	182,38,07,818	45.82%
2007-08	83,00,95,772	178,75,61,307	46.43%
2008-09	113,23,04,525	256,60,60,321	44.12%
2009-10	128,78,85,858	273,82,61,972	47.03%
2010-11	127,42,50,756	321,20,74,173	39.67%
2011-12	152,32,68,220	398,04,09,014	38.26%
2012-13	163,83,63,093	449,81,40,701	36.42%
2013-14	170,24,20,211	479,19,55,758	35.52%
2014-15	220,22,30,742	544,20,92,601	40.46%
2015-16	217,76,31,983	572,81,74,664	38.01%
2016-17	236,35,66,551	630,88,73,883	37.46%

Source: Data collected from Sabarimala Executive Office of TDB.

Temple Advisory Committees

Administration without the active participation of the people at every stage is bound to result in undemocratic practices and uncontrollable bureaucratic domination (Mathur, 1991: 30). Kuttikrishna Menon Commission (1964) suggested associating the religious-minded people of the locality in the management of the temples (GoK, 1964: 110). The High Power Commission 1990 also suggested that the effective participation of local committees is essential for the proper functioning of the temples restoring it to its original glory and splendour (KHC, 1990: 39). So, in order to ensure the participation of local people in temple administration, the TDB introduced an innovative step to constitute advisory committee system in all the temples under its control. The members of advisory committees are selected from the panel suggested by the concerned Assistant Devaswom Commissioner.

Trade Unionism in TDB

Devaswom employees are organised under different trade unions; sometimes their activities affect the serene atmosphere of the temples. The historic agitation of temple employees in the 1960s had its repercussions in state politics. Major political parties have their own trade unions in the TDB. In 1990, High Power Commission Report suggested some restrictions over the trade union activities of Devaswom employees. Subsequently, the TDB issued guidelines for recognising a single union for Devaswom employees by conducting a referendum Accordingly, a referendum was held in 2005, CITU affiliated Travancore Devaswom Employees Confederation got recognition. After this, two referendums were held and the Travancore Devaswom Employees Front of the Congress Party got recognition twice. With regard to the grievances of employees, the Board discusses only with the recognised union.

Table 2.5: Service organisations in TDB

Sl. No.	Union	Affiliated union	Party identity
1.	Travancore Devaswom Employees Front	INTUC	INC
2.	Travancore Devaswom Employees Confederation	CITU	CPI(M)
3.	Travancore Devaswom Employees Sangh	BMS	RSS
4.	Travancore Devaswom Board Staff Organisation	AITUC	CPI
5.	Travancore Devaswom Employees union	UTUC	RSP

A Division Bench of the KHC in 1990 directed the TDB to take necessary action to curb the trade union activities among temple employees and political interference in the Board as their activities posed disturbances to the serene atmosphere of temples. This was questioned by the left trade unions on the ground that these measures will weaken the bargaining power of the employees and urged the government to make necessary legislations to protect the freedom of association of Devaswom employees (Kerala Kaumudy, 1990, November 17).

On the basis of the recommendations of the High-power Commission that there should be only one service association in each Board and all category-wise unions and unions with outside political leaders as office bearers should be de-recognised (KHC, 1990: 75), the TDB took steps accordingly. A notification was issued stipulating that the associations should frame a bye-law and regulations in consultation with the Board and that there should be provisions for grievance redressal suitable to the calmness, serenity and discipline ordained by Hindu religious faith and without resorting to direct action and strike. The Board decided to conduct referendum and the association which secure maximum percentage of votes had to be granted recognition. Referendum would be valid only for five years.

The renovation and the reconstruction of temples are being systematically carried out by the Maramath Department headed by the Chief Engineer and two Divisional Engineers. Krishna Moorthy Commission and Kainikkara Padmanabha Pillai Commission recommended for the abolition of the Maramath Department and that the work could be entrusted to the state PWD. There is a Vigilance Department functioning to help the Board to eliminate corruption from administration, consisting of two Vigilance Officers of the rank of Assistant Commissioner. Vigilance division is conducting enquiry regarding corruption, misappropriation, theft, misuse of funds, corrupt practices, irregularities in *Kanikka* verification etc. In 1990, the Department has completely restructured and one police officer was deputed as the Chief Vigilance and Security Officer. In order to coordinate the cultural activities, there is a Cultural Affairs

Department under the supervision of Cultural Director. Sri Chitra Central Hindu Religious Library was opened at Trivandrum in 1936 with a view to promote liberal religious education among the masses (GoK, 1938: 229). Krishna Moorthy Commission noted several complaints regarding the issue of books, lack of proper cataloguing system and card indexing system in the library (GoK, 1974: 134). At present, the library is in good condition but the public is not utilising its resources properly. There are hordes of rare Sanskrit monographs that can be utilised by research scholars. It seems that if the library be located in the premise of Devaswom Head Office or any major temple, the resources may be utilised extensively. The Board is publishing a religious and cultural magazine, *sannidhanam*. The *Kshethra Kala Peedom Academy* came into existence in 1982 within the sacred premises of the ancient historic and great Mahadevar temple at Vaikom. Under the management of TDB there are 4 aided colleges, 3 self-financing colleges, 4 Higher Secondary Schools, 8 High Schools, 5 UP Schools, 5 LP Schools and 4 Central Schools.

It is rightly observed by K. P. Sankaran Nair Commission that with the interference of the state in temple administration, the golden period of temples ended (GoK, 1984:74). Such governmental interference became instrumental in alienating the devotees from temple administration. In spite of several pitfalls in its functioning, the contributions of TDB in the socio-cultural, economic, spiritual and political spheres of the state are really commendable.

Cochin Devaswom Board (CDB)

The Cochin Devaswom Board is one among the two Devaswom governing bodies formed for the first time in Kerala for the administration of the Hindu temples. The area covering 16 Taluks in the Districts of Ernakulum, Thrissur and a portion of Palakkad and a small portion of Malappuram constitute the erstwhile Cochin state. Going to the pages of history, it can be seen that the temples in the kingdom of Cochin were administered largely by *uralers*, feudal lords etc. When Col. Munro became the resident of Cochin (1812), the King entrusted him with the work of surveying the temples in the state and the report brought to light the pathetic conditions of the temples due to inefficient administration. Consequently, majority of temples in the state were brought under the control of the government.

After the integration of Travancore-Cochin states in 1949, the CDB was created for the temples in the erstwhile Cochin State. The Cochin Devaswom Board which was formed on 1st July, 1949 is one of the oldest and smallest (in terms of number of temples) Devaswom Boards in Kerala managing only 403 temples. The CDB is functioning as per the provisions of TCHRI Act XV of 1950. The Kerala Land Reforms Act of 1969 paved the way for losing considerable landed properties of temples in Cochin also. To compensate with, the government provided interim relief to the Board, but it was inadequate and many temples under the Board fell into financial crisis. Later several of them overcame the financial crisis with the help of offerings from the devotees.

The Board consists of three Members including the President and they hold office for a period of two years. Among the three Members, two including the president are nominated by the Hindu Ministers. One Member is nominated by the Hindu MLAs from SC/ST category. The President chairs the meetings of the Board. The Board appoints a Secretary who shall be the convener of the meetings of the Board and shall also be responsible for the proper functioning of the day-to-day administration of the Board. The first Board was constituted in 1949 with T.S. Narayana Aiyer (retired Chief Justice of Cochin), the nominee of the King of Cochin, K. Balakrishnan Marar and P. K. Devar (Members of Legislative Assembly), nominees of Hindu MLAs and Hindu Ministers respectively. The right of the King to nominate a Member was later delegated to Hindu

Members in the cabinet. Ernakulam was the headquarters of the CDB which was later on shifted to Thrissur, the cultural capital of Kerala.

The Devaswom Act provides a wide range of powers to the Board in matters of temple administration like; to oversee whether the regular traditional rites and ceremonies are performed promptly according to the prevalent practices; to monitor the working of administrative staff and employees and also employees concerned with religious rites; to ensure proper maintenance and upliftment of the Hindu religious institutions; to provide proper facilities to the devotees in major temples. Devaswom Commissioner is the Chief Executive Officer of the CDB. He executes all orders of the Board and submits reports to the government once in three months about the working of the Board (74 A of the Act). When the tenure of one Board expires and a time gap happens to assume charge by another Board, the gap is filled by appointing an officer, not below the rank of a Principal Secretary to the Government who believes in god and temple worship as the Chief Commissioner to perform duties of the Board.

Temples under the CDB

The 403 temples under CDB are classified as A, B, C and D Grades based on the criteria like income, importance, daily rituals etc. There are 43 A Grade, 76 B Grade, 255 C Grade and 29 D grade temples. Out of 403 temples, 284 are low-income temples (C and D grade temples). Only 43 temples are self-reliant that constitute merely 10.66 % of the total temples.

Table 2.6: Classification of temples under the CDB

Sl. No.	Grade	Temples	Percentage
1	A	43	10.66%
2	B	76	18.86%
3	C	255	63.28%
4	D	29	7.2%
Total		403	100%

For the administrative convenience, temples under the CDB are arranged in to 5 Groups including Chottanikkara Special Group.These groups are again divided in to 63 Sub-Groups dispersed in 16 Taluks covering four Districts Thrissur, Palakkad, Ernakulam and Malappuram. Among the five groups Thrissur is the biggest group that includes 18 Sub Groups and 126 temples. Thrippunithura is the smallest group with only 63 temples under its control. The financial aspects of each Devaswom are handled by these groups. Thrissur has greater number of temples (284) and Malappuram has the least number; only one situating in Ponnani Taluk under Thrissur group (see Table IV.14). 70.47% of temples under the CDB are in Thrissur district where the headquarters of the Board is located.

Table 2.7: Group and Sub Group-wise arrangement of temples under the CDB

Sl. No.	Name of Group	Sub Group Devaswoms	No. of temples
1.	Chottanikkara	1	1
2.	Thrissur	18	126
3.	Thiruvilwamala	14	114
4.	Thiruvanchikkulam	18	98
5.	Trippunithura	12	64
	Total	**63**	403

Table 2.8: District-wise classification of temples under CDB

Sl. No.	Districts	Number of temples	Percentage
1	Malappuram	01	0.25%
2	Palakkad	46	11.41%
3	Thrissur	284	70.47%
4	Ernakulam	72	17.87%
Total		403	100%

Chottanikara, Kodungalloor, Thriprayar, Vadakkumnathan, Tripunithura and Thiruvillwamala temples are the major temples under the CDB. In terms of income, they are the top five temples. Chottnikkara temple is the top among the 403 temples and Chottanikkara is grouped into a separate Group under the CDB.Apart from these temples, a large number of private temples known as *Ooranma Temples* otherwise known as *Vazhipaat Devaswoms* which get grants from CDB (Jayashanker, 1997: 17).

The administration of the CDB is hierarchically arranged into various offices, from the Board at the top to the temples in the bottom.

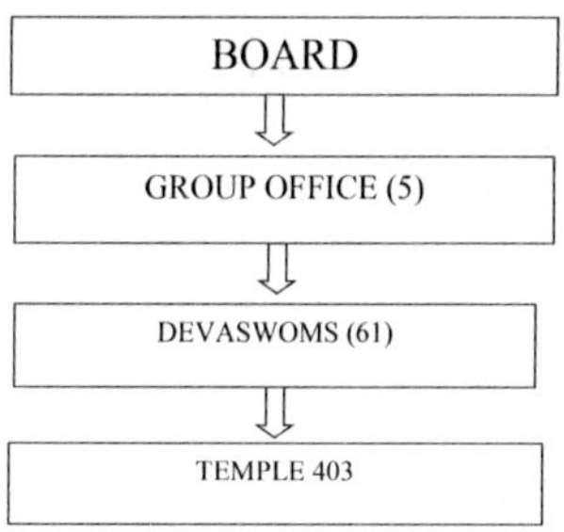

Fig. 2.5: Organisational structure of CDB

Financial Administration of CDB

Major sources of revenue of the Board are income from temples and temple lands, rent from buildings, elephants, utensils, interest from fixed deposits and annuity (CDB, 2014: 16-17).

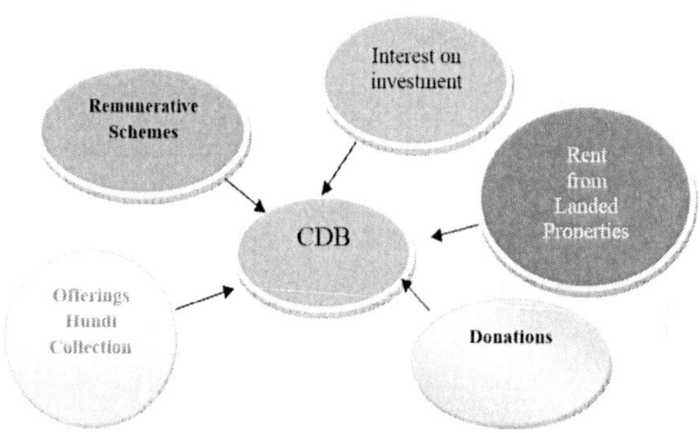

Fig. 2.6: Sources of income of CDB

Devaswoms in Cochin once possessed extensive landed properties and the income from these properties constituted one of the major sources of their revenue. Following the acquisition of temple lands by Diwan Col. Munro in 1812 and the land reforms of Left Governments in Kerala, great deprivation happened to the temple lands that badly affected their economy. 25,000 acres of temple land of Incorporated Devaswoms were taken over by Munro in 1812 (GoK, 1984: 24) and later 20,000 acres belonged to Unincorporated Devaswoms were taken over by the then governments. 60,000 acres of land under the possession of the Cochin Devaswom Board had been lost due to the land legislations of the Government of Kerala. To compensate the loss of land and thus its revenue, the government allocated an annuity of Rs 4.5 lakh as compensation to the CDB (GoK, 1984: 25). It is estimated that 97 acres 46 cents of Devaswom land has been found encroached; out of which 8 acres 45 cents has been brought back.Thus, the income from land revenue has been adversely affected due to the various land enactments of the government. It is found that only a handful of temples under CDB can meet their own expenses now. Proportionate to the increase in income, expenditure is also increased.

The major source of income of temples under the CDB is the collection from hundial and *vazhipadu* offerings. The income from temples constitutes 45% of the total income of the Board and around 15 to 20 percentage of the total income of the CDB is from *kanikka* offerings by the devotees. The CDB expends huge amount for providing salary, pension and other allowances to its employees. It is notable that the employees under the Board are provided with salary at par with the state government employees. The main items of expenditure are establishment charges, *pathivu* charges, land revenue assessment, purchase and repair of vessels, ornaments, law charges, *maramath* and petty constructions and repairs and contingencies (GoK, 1968: 330). Accounts of the Devaswom are audited by internal audit wing of the Board as well as the state audit wing. The CDB spends crores of rupees under the heads of salary, honorarium, TA/DA to Board members. A considerable amount is expending towards constructions, repairs and maintenance of educational institutions under the Board.

Temple Advisory Committees

The *Kshetra Kshema Samithies* (Temple Advisory Committees) are constituted in all the temples under the CDB to advise the Board for the proper functioning of temples. These are purely advisory bodies and not statutory; they cannot interfere with the administration of temples. It is stipulated that the TACs of the temples under the CDB should consist of at least 17 members including women, SC/ST members, Devaswom Manager and representatives of temple employees. Members should be believers in god and temple worship. Major temples like Chottanikkara, Thiruvilwamala, Kodungalloor, Vadakkumnatha temple, Thrippunithura and Thriprayar have 22-member TAC in which the Group Assistant Commissioner is a member. It has a period of two-year tenure. One of the major drawbacks is the political influence in the constitution of the advisory committees.

Trade Unionism

The CDB has granted organisational freedom to its employees subjected to certain restrictions as per the order of the High Court on the basis of High-Power Commission Report (1990). For implementing the recommendations of the Court, the CDB has to conduct referendum in every five years among the employees through secret ballot. The first referendum was held in 2007 for recognizing approved unions. Every political party has their own trade unions in the CDB. Cochin Devaswom Employees Congress, a pro-Congress association of employees got recognition in the last referendum in the CDB (see Table IV.19).

Table 2.9: List of service organisations of the CDB employees

Sl. No.	Name of Union	Affiliated Political Party
1.	Cochin Devaswom Employees Congress	INC
2.	Cochin Devaswom Employees Organisation	CPI(M)
3.	Cochin Devaswom Employees Sangh	RSS/BJP
4.	Cochin Devaswom Employees Federation	CPI

The Board has implemented several welfare schemes for its employees, salary and other benefits at par with the state government employees, pension fund for giving retirement benefits to the employees etc. (GoK, 1972: 363). In order to curb the evil practices exist in the administration of Devaswoms, a Vigilance wing has been constituted as per the recommendations of the High Power Commission Report of 1990. Vigilance and Security Officer is in-charge of the Vigilance Department that enjoys the power of supervision in the counting of hundi boxes in temples, inspect Devaswom counters, enquire cases of allegation against employees etc. (CDB, 2014: 148). The Cochin Devaswom Board promotes cultural activities too. The famous *Thrissur Pooram* is associated with cluster of temples under the aegis of Vadakkumnathan temple of the CDB, started by the then ruler of Cochin, Sakthan Thampuran in 1798 (Census, 2011: 4). The Board publishes a magazine named *Kshetra Darsanam*. The CDB manages three educational institutions, 2 colleges, 1 higher secondary school, aided by the Government of Kerala. Sree Kerala Varma College, Thrissur is one of the reputed higher education centre in Kerala under the management of the CDB. In addition to this, the Board is also managing Padasala Sanskrit High School, Thekkegramam at Chittur in Palakkad district.

Several Commission Reports put forward valuable suggestions and recommendations to improve the administration of the CDB. The High-Power Commission appointed by the High Court of Kerala in 1990 suggested the following major recommendations (KHC, 1990: 45-72):

(a) Temple employees should be believers in temple worship as non-believers cannot be having any interest in temple administration;

(b) Subgroup officers and accountants should be given orientation in temple administration;

(c) A systematic programme of refresher courses should be conducted for all supervisory and administrative staff both in the administration (accounts, budgeting, expenditure control etc) as well as in matters relating to temples;

(d) Temple Advisory Committees should be properly constituted duly recognised and actively associated with the temple administration;

(e) There is the need to encourage *mathapadashalas* in temples to educate the younger generation towards Hindu religion and customs;

(f) A complaint register should be kept in all temples to invite suggestions and complaints by devotees which should be seen by inspecting officers and appropriate action be taken;

(g) A single service organisation for employees;

(h) The creation of a separate Vigilance Department under a Deputy Superintendent of Police, so that independent enquiries could be conducted on complaints and disciplinary action be taken.

Several of these recommendations were implemented by the CDB.

Malabar Devaswom Board (MDB)

The temples in Malabar for a long period were administered by the Hindu Religious Charitable Endowments (HRCE) Department under the direct control of the State Government on the basis of Madras Hindu Religious and Charitable Endowments Act 1951. Here the temples were treated as separate entities or single units with a distinct administrative right; temple income is non-transferable and the salary to the employees is paid by the respective temple authorities from their own funds. The salary and other emoluments of the employees of each temple will be disbursed depending on the income of the temple they work. The HRCE Department had only a supervisory role.

The formation of Malabar Devaswom Board is a landmark in the administrative history of Malabar Temples. The Board was constituted as per the provisions of the Madras Hindu Religious and Charitable Endowments (MHRCE) (Amendment) Ordinance 2008. The Amendment Act 2008 provided that the Hindu public religious institutions coming under the purview of Madras HR &CE Act XIX of 1951 and the jurisdiction and control of the erstwhile Hindu Religious and Charitable Endowments (Administration) Department, Kozhikode are to be administered by the Malabar Devaswom Board. The MDB has only a supervisory role over the administration of temples; as such temples are administered directly by their Trustees. The Trustees consist of hereditary and non-hereditary members appointed by the Board.

There is no provision of pooling of temple fund into common fund of the Board as the temples are treated as separate entities. But there is a provision that the temples should donate a portion of their income to the management fund of the MDB. The Board acts as a supervisor to monitor the utilisation of temple funds for the interest of temples which ensures transparency also. The Board or the government has no power to take away or transfer of temple revenue for other purposes.

Constitution of the Board

The MDB is composed of 9 Hindu Members of whom one shall be a woman, one shall be a person belonging to SC and one shall be a person belonging to ST. Of the 9 Members, 7 including the women and Members belonging to SC and ST shall be nominated by the Hindus among the Council of Ministers and the other 2 Members shall be elected by the Hindu MLAs. As per the provision of clause 7 subclause 5 of the MHRCE Act, the Hindus among the Council of Ministers shall nominate a Member as the President of the Board. The Members of the Board are nominated or elected for a period of 2 years. The Act stipulates certain qualifications for membership in the Board in Section 7B that he/she should be a permanent resident of the Malabar area, professes Hindu religion, a believer of temple worship and completed the age of 45 years in the case of male Members and 60 years in the case of female Members. A person has been elected or nominated as a Member should take an oath before the Commissioner of the Board stating that he is a person professing Hindu religious rites and is a believer of God and temple worship (Section 7C). Resignation letter of a Member should be addressed to the Government Secretary incharge of Devaswom Department. The President and Members of the Board shall be entitled to receive monthly honorarium and TA as payable to the class I officers of the government. The headquarters of the MDB is at Kozhikode.

In Malabar, all temples are private institutions and lack of coordination among them becomes a major problem. Majority temples in Malabar area are depending upon the government aid and only very few temples are self-reliant. The low income temples have to depend on government grants for their existence. But many a times due to the negligence on the part of temple trustees regarding non-submission of audited statements causes delaying of government grants. It is the duty of the Board to ensure proper maintenance and upliftment of temples, to establish and maintain proper facilities in the temples for

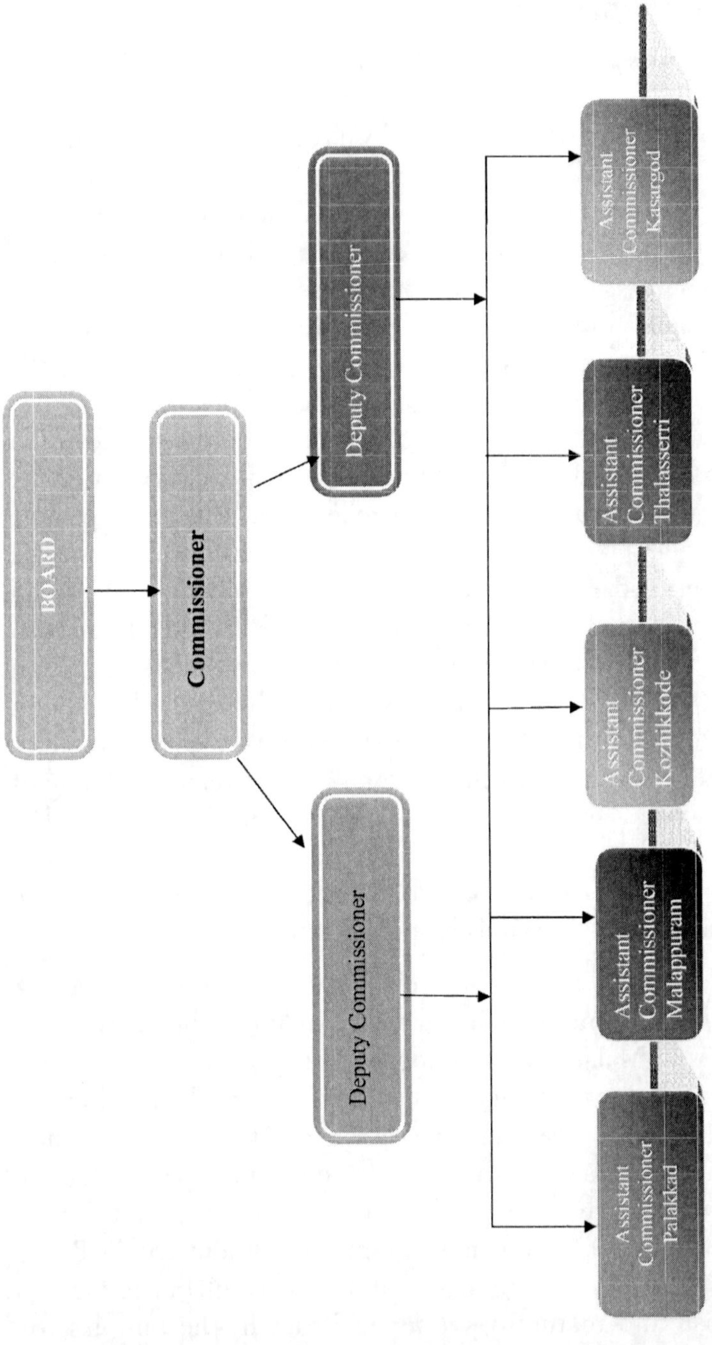

Fig 2.7: Organizational structure of MDB

devotees and supervise the working of the Area Committees. The Board has the authority to fix and regulate the service conditions and pay structure of the officers and employees of the temple from time to time and to supervise its implementation. A Welfare Fund Scheme is maintained by the Board for the benefit of the temple employees. The MDB has the power to take over the direct management of any temple on the basis of unconditional request of the trustees.

In the hierarchy of administration there is a Commissioner as the head of the bureaucratic set up. He may be an officer not below the rank of a Joint Secretary to the Government and a believer in God and temple worship for a term fixed by the Government as per section 8C (1) of the Devaswom Act. He shall also function as the Secretary and the Executive Officer of the Board who shall implement all decisions of the Board. He should submit reports regarding the working of the Board once in every three months to the government. The Board has the power to appoint Deputy Commissioners, Assistant Commissioners and such other officers and staff necessary for discharging its functions. There are no permanent employees under the MDB; the employees worked in the erstwhile HRCE Department, employees from other department on deputation basis, employees appointed through Employment Exchanges and temporary employees are working in the MDB.At present, various posts in the MDB has been filled by the Devaswom Recruitment Board.

There are three Standing Committees: (a) Finance and Resource Mobilisation, (b) Work, Development, Environment and Establishment and (c) Temple Arts and Devotional Services. The Board shall nominate one Member each as Chairman of the Committees. The duties and responsibilities of the Standing Committees shall be specified by the Board. Section 13 (1) of the Devaswom Act stipulates the composition of the Area Committees. Accordingly, every Area Committee shall be consisted of 7 Members appointed by the government and one Member is nominated as the chairman of Area Committee. The Act established a hierarchy of officers; the Commissioner, Deputy Commissioner, Assistant Commissioners and Area Committee for temple administration in Malabar.

Temple Advisory Committees

Temple Advisory Committees are constituted in all temples for ensuring adequate participation of Hindu devotees in temple administration. Duly constituted Temple Advisory Committees shall be approved by the Board. Every temple Advisory Committee shall consist of 9 members; 1 member each from among the trustees of the temple, the chief Priest, Scheduled Castes/Scheduled Tribes community, woman, 4 other members and the Executive Officer of the temple. Members except trustee and chief priest shall be nominated by the Board from among the locally residing Hindu persons having interest in the affairs of the temple. Every Temple Advisory Committee in its first meeting shall elect a member of the committee as its Chairman. Executive Officer shall be the Convener-cum-Treasurer of the Committee. Committee shall meet at least once in every month and quorum for a meeting shall be five. The Committee shall take special care in maintaining the existing customs and practices of each temple.

Annual Contribution to the MDB

Every religious institution under the Board shall pay to the Board annually such contribution not exceeding 5% of its income as may be prescribed, in respect of the services rendered by the Board and their officers and for defraying the expenses incurred on account of such services. And also pay audit fees annually to the Board not less than one thousand rupees, such sum further not exceeding one and half percent of its income as the Commissioner may determine.

Malabar Devaswom Fund

A Malabar Devaswom Fund is constituted as per Section 81 of the MHRCE (Amendment) Act 2008 including contributions payable by the religious institutions, grants and loans from the government, grants and donations from public, the money realised from time to time by the sale of movable properties, profits and interest from investments of funds of the Board and all other income receive by the Board.

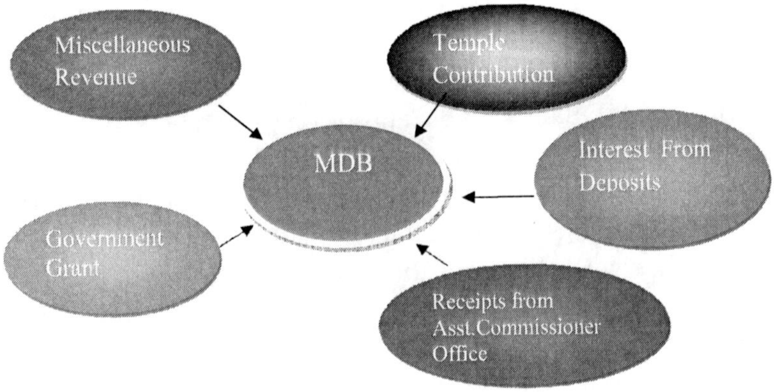

Fig. 2.8: Sources of income of MDB

The Trustees of every Hindu religious institution shall keep regular accounts of all receipts and disbursements. The audit reports should be sent to the Area Committee, if the institution is subjected to the jurisdiction of such a committee and to the Commissioner in other cases. The Auditor shall specify in his report all cases of irregular, illegal or improper expenditure or failure to recover money or other property due to the religious institution or loss or wastage of money or other property thereof caused by neglect or misconduct (Section 73 of the Act). In the financial sphere, MDB's position is entirely different from the other Devaswom governing bodies in the state. While the income from temples is pooled in to a common Devaswom fund in other Devaswom Boards, there is no provision for such a pooling of fund in MDB. Actually, the MDB has no power to control over temples in financial matters. In other words, the MDB has no financial autonomy. Unlike the TDB and CDB, the MDB is not a full-fledged Devaswom Board as there is not a single temple under its direct control. The major source of income of the MDB is government grant and contributions from temples.

The expenditure of the Board includes only the expense for providing salary and bonus to its employees, providing TA/DA and honorarium to Board President and Members, office expenses, telephone charges, legal expenses, pension contribution and medical reimbursement and so on. In addition to this, the MDB distributes renovation grants and maintenance and repair expenses to temples. The Board keeps regular accounts of all receipts and disbursement. All accounts of the Board should be audited annually by the Director of Local Fund Audit in accordance with the provisions contained in the Kerala Local Fund Audit Act, 1994. The Board may deposit its fund in any of the nationalised banks, Cooperative Bank or Government Treasury or invest the same in any security of the State Government or the Government of India (Act 2008, Section 81 B). As stated earlier, there is no common pooling of temple fund in Malabar and so the leading temples are having huge amounts as fixed deposit savings. At the same time majority temples in Malabar area are facing financial crisis to meet even their daily expenditure. These low-income temples have to depend on the financial assistance from the Board to meet daily rituals and providing salary to their employees. Temple employees get a nominal amount as salary in these temples.

Temple Renovation Grant

Majority temples in Malabar are functioning on the annual grant by the government. The State Government provides a renovation grant every year to the Board. This amount is distributed to selected temples based on their requirement for renovation. The grant is released in three stages; in the initial stage, 30% of the grant is released after obtaining a bond from the temple. The remaining 60% is released only after obtaining utilisation certificate of the first instalment and the balance 10% is released only after filing the completion certificate (KLA, 1999, July 21: 112). Temples belonging to low income status (C and D grade temples) spend 30% of the temple fund for salary purposes, but as this is not enough, the remaining portion is allotted by the Board from the management fund to meet the expenditure (KLA, 2004, July 28: 115). Public temples, private temples and temples belonging to SC/ST people are given financial assistance. Every year, the MDB invites application from temples and the temple authorities submit the application to the Divisional Assistant Devaswom Commissioner. Prior to the formation of the MDB, the State Government provided financial assistance to the HRCE Department for providing salary to temple employees. Even after the formation of the MDB, the practice of distributing grants to temples has been continuing. The MDB distributes annually grant to the needy temples under their jurisdiction. The government grant to the MDB is steadily increasing every year. The MDB is distributing 10 to 15% of the grant to the private temples and 10% to the temples owned by SCs/ STs as per government guidelines (KLA, 2009, September 16: 49). Special emphasis is given to C and D Grade temples whenever the renovation grants are to be released by the government (KLA, 2010, July 28: 237).

The State Government in 2016 had approved the Report of K. Jayakumar (a senior IAS Officer and former Chief Secretary to the Government of Kerala) Committee appointed for studying the pay and service conditions of the Malabar Devaswom Board employees. The Report has recommended for fixing annual income slabs for providing grant to disburse the salary of employees. Temples which are eligible for grant would be grouped as those with an annual income below Rs 5 lakh, up to Rs 15 lakh and above Rs 15 lakh. The Devaswom

Board should give grant to meet the salary expenses of temples with annual income below Rs 5 lakhs. The temples in the category of Rs 5 to 15 lakhs have proposed to fix at 70:30 to ease the burden of the temples. Temples having annual income between Rs 15 lakh and Rs 25 lakh should be given 50 percent of the expense as grant. The eligibility of employees should be fixed on the basis of the order issued in 2009 (The Hindu, 2016, March 4).

Temples under the MDB

The temples under the MDB are classified into Special Grade, Grade A, B, C and D temples according to their annual earnings. It is a fact that about 76% of the temples belong to D grade. Among the total of 1345 temples under the supervision of the MDB, 23 temples are special grade temples; 50 A grade temples, 129 B grade, 122 C grade and 1021 D grade temples.

Table 2.10: List of temples under the Malabar Devaswom Board (Grade-wise)

Sl. No.	Division	Sp grade	A Gr	B Gr	C Gr	D Gr	No. of temples
1.	Kasargod	7	8	32	35	133	215
2.	Thalasserry	5	11	22	27	154	219
3.	Kozhikkode	2	8	26	28	152	216
4.	Malappuram	6	6	16	7	318	353
5.	Palakkad	3	17	33	25	264	342
	Total	**23**	**50**	**129**	**122**	**1021**	**1345**

Most of the revenue rich temples in the Malabar region are being controlled by hereditary trustees who are not willing to any revenue sharing mechanism. While figures for individual temples are not available, Kadambuzha temple in Malappurm District is considered as the richest temple under the MDB. Sources at the MDB say that there has been at least a 30% increase in revenues annually. Majority of temples under the MDB are D Grade temples whose annual income is below 3 lakhs.

From the table below we can surmise that only a few temples in Malabar are high income, self-reliant temples and the majority temples are struggling for their existence. Grant-in -aid system is to some extent subsisting them. But negligence from the part of temple authorities in submitting utilisation of grants received creates delaying of further release of grants which cause hardships to those who depend on temples for their subsistence.

Table 2.11: Grading criteria and percentage of grade temples under MDB

Sl. No.	Grade	Grading Criteria (annual income)	Number of temples	Percentage
1.	Special Grade	75 lakhs and above	23	1.71%
2.	A Grade	25 to 75 lakhs	50	3.71%
3.	B Grade	10 to 25 lakhs	129	9.6%
4.	C Grade	3 to 10 lakhs	122	9.07%
5.	D Grade	Up to 3 lakhs	1021	75.91%
	Total		**1345**	100%

Table 2.12: District-wise list of temples under MDB

Sl. No.	District	Number of temples
1.	Kasargod	89
2.	Kannur	282
3.	Wayanad	47
4.	Kozhikkod	162
5.	Malappuram	272
6.	Thrissur	45
7.	Ernakulam	02
8.	Palakkad	446
	Total	**1345**

The temples under MDB are scattered in almost 8 districts of northern Kerala, mainly in Palakkad, Kannur, Malappuram and Kozhikkod districts.

In order to encourage an academic initiative to promote temple art forms, the proposal to establish a Temple Art Academy under the direct control of MDB was firstly mooted in 2011. The aim of the Academy is to revive temple art forms including *ashtapadi*, *sopana sangeetham*, classical music, instrumental music and dance forms to propagate the culture and tradition of the state. For this purpose, the MDB obtained 20 acres of land at Madayi Bhagavathi temple. A sum of Rs 50,00,000 was allocated in the 2012-13 budget for this purpose. The academy was formally inaugurated in 2015 by the then Devaswom Minister. In 2017-18, the State Government allotted an amount of 5 lakhs in the budget for the Academy.

The restructuring and revamping of the admnistrative machinerry of the Devaswom administration in Malabar is under the consideration of the government. For this purpose the Left Government in Kerala has recently appointed a Law Reform Commission to study all administrative issues prevailing in Malabar temples. The earlier Commission Reports like Sankaran Nair Commission of 1984 suggested a thorough change in this regard. Sankaran Nair Commission suggested certain recommendations like the need of a uniform Devaswom law for Hindu religious institutions in the state including Malabar temples, to find out the details of encroachments on temple lands, to ensure minimum wages to temple employees, constitution of Temple Advisory Committees, termination of trustees' right who commit offence or administrative inattention or misappropriation etc. (GoK, 1984: 30-31).

Malabar Devaswom Law Reforms Committee

The Government of Kerala appointed a Legal Reforms Committee headed by K. Gopalakrishnan, the first Chairman of the MDB to study and recommend reforms in the administration of temples under the MDB. The major recommendations of the Commission are:

(a) The management of temples should be entrusted to the Board rather than with the Trustees;

(b) The right to appoint employees and the power of disciplinary action against them should be vested with the Board rather than the Trustees;

(c) The income from all the temples would be brought into a consolidated account and distribute to all temples according to their need;
(d) Daily rituals in temples, festivals, maintenance work and construction work be vested with the Devaswom Board;
(e) The right to distribute pension and gratuity to temple employees shall also be vested with the Board;
(f) The disbursal of salary to temple employees, executive officers and administrative staff shall be done directly by the Board;
(g) It shall be the Board to determine the number of employees in temples and associated institutions and to make appointments;
(h) The government shall continue providing grants to temples (GoK, 2017: 39-41).

The Commission also recommended forming of a Malabar Devaswom Tribunal and Malabar Devaswom Finance Corporation for fostering economic prosperity of temples in Malabar (GoK, 2017: 28). The Law Reform Commission in its Report recommended taking over more than 1000 private temples in Malabar region, including the temples under the Zamorin Raja, former rulers of the Calicut Kingdom. The Law Reforms Commission submitted to the government a draft act named as the Malabar Hindu Religious and Charitable Endowments Act, 2017 along with their Report. The proposed act specifies all power to the Board rather than the Trustees. A nine-Member Committee besides the President is proposed and among them, three Members and the President are to be nominated by the Council of Ministers and remaining Members shall be elected by the Hindu MLAs (GoK, 2017, Appendix: 3-41).

The MDB today confronts with several dilemmas in its functioning. Scarcity of employees is a major problem. All temples are private institutions in Malabar and lack of coordination in temple administration is a problem there. The MDB is exercising only a supervisory control to see that the temple funds are used for the beneficial interest in a proper, transparent and lawful manner. Majority temples in Malabar area are depending upon the government aid and only very few temples are self-reliant. But the government funding delayed several times due to the negligence on the part of temple trustees regarding the submission of audited statements to the government in proper time.

Guruvayur Devaswom Managing Committee (GDMC)

The reputed Sree Krishna temple at Guruvayur is one among the leading temples of South India in terms of income and fame. Hereditary Trustees; Zamorin Raja of Calicut and *Karanavan* of Mallisserry illom were the administrators of the temple and their administration proved unsatisfactory. When a mishap due to fire incident occured there in 1970, causing havoc to the temple, the Enquiry Commission, Gangadharan Thampy Commission pointed out to the utter and prolonged neglect that the temple had to face in maintenance and timely repairs from the part of temple authorities which ultimately led to the disaster. The Report disclosed the mismanagement of Guruvayur temple administration and ultimately the Government of Kerala took over its administration.

The Government of Kerala took over the administration of Guruvayur temple through an Ordinance which became an Act in 1971. As per the Act, Guruvayur Devaswom Managing Committee was constituted for the administration of Guruvayur Devaswom. This Act was challenged before the Kerala High Court by the hereditary trustees. The Act was amended in 1972 which again came to be challenged in the Kerala High Court. Subsequently, a Bench of five Judges of the Kerala High Court struck down the said Act in *Krishnan Vs. Guruvayur Devaswom Managing Committee* case (Tharamel Krishnan, 1978). As per the provisions of Guruvayur Devaswom Act 1978, Guruvayur

Devaswom Managing Committee was re-constituted consisting of three permanent members and six political nominees of the Hindus among the Council of Ministers. Hereditary Trustees, the Zamorin Raja, the *Karanavan* (for the time being, from the Mallisserri Illom at Guruvayur) and *tantri* of the temple (ex-officio member) are the permanent Members and the six nominees include a representative of the employees of the Devaswom and not more than five persons of whom one shall be a Member from Scheduled Caste, nominated by the Hindus among the Council of Ministers who are having interest in the affairs of temples. The Committee in its first meeting elects one of its Members as the Chairman.Every member shall take an oath in the name of God before entering into the office. Through the nomination of 6 Members out of a total of 9, the government can always implement its decision in an easy walk over. The Guruvayur Devaswom is functioning on the basis of Guruvayur Devaswom Act, 1978 and Guruvayur Devaswom Rules, 1980.

In 1999, the Government of Kerala issued an Ordinance that curtailed the term of office of the Guruvayur Devaswom Management Committee from four to three years (Mathrubhumi, 1999, June 3). Again in 2001, through another amendment the term of office of the GDMC has been reduced to 2 years. The Bill also proposed to limit the voting right of Hindu MLAs and Ministers, only to those who have faith in God and temple worship (The New Indian Express, 2001, December 7). It shall be the duty of the Committee to arrange for the proper performance of the rites and ceremonies in temples, provided facilities for the proper performance of worship, ensure the safe custody of the funds, valuable securities and jewellery and the preservation and management of the properties vested in the temple etc.

The decisions regarding religious or spiritual matters of the temple are completely left to the discretion of the *tantri*. The Managing Committee or the Commissioner or the government cannot involve in decisions regarding religious or spiritual matters of the temple. The State Government interference is limited to the administration of Devaswom Committees only and in religious matters, the state cannot interfere. Major decisions regarding temple administration are carried out by the Devaswom Committee. There is a Commissioner of Devaswom appointed by the government, an officer not below the rank of Secretary to the Government who profess Hindu religion and believes in temple worship and he shall hold charges and exercise the powers and perform the functions of the Committee till the vacancy in the Committee is filled up.[44] All the Commissioners so far appointed in the Devaswom were IAS officers. He has to exercise remote control from Thiruvananthapuram over the working of Guruvayur Devaswom (KHC, 1993: 187).

The Administrator is the head of the administrative machinery of the Guruvayur Devaswom Department appointed by the Devaswom Committee from among the panel of names furnished by the Government of Kerala. He shall be an officer of the government not below the rank of Deputy Collector. Coming to the powers of the Administrator, he shall be the Secretary to the Committee and its Chief Executive Officer and shall subject to the control of the Committee and the powers to carry out its decision in accordance with the provisions of the Act. Appointment of officers and other employees of the Devaswom shall be made by the Devaswom Recruitment Board as per its guidelines.

There is a Finance Department headed by the Chief Finance and Accounts Officer (CFAO), the second highest executive officer in the Guruvayur Devaswom who has come on deputation from Accountant General's Office. This system was started in 1989 at the request of the Managing Committee for getting trained the staff of the Finance Department. The budget of the Guruvayur Devaswom is prepared by the Devaswom Committee and presented to the Commissioner and sends a copy of the approved budget to the government. This ensures transparency in the accounts and prevents possible irregularities in the Devaswom fund. The local Fund Audit Department of Government of Kerala has a division in the Devaswom office for auditing the accounts of the Devaswom. It is headed by the Joint Director with other 13 personnel. Under Section 26 of the Act, the Commissioner shall send a copy of every audit report to the Committee. If any irregular, illegal or improper expenditure or of failure to recover loss of money or waste of money or other property thereof, caused by neglect or misconduct noticed by the auditors and specify in their report the Committee has the power to take proper action in this regard.

Devaswom Act stipulates that the revenue of the temple should be deposited in the government treasury that was started from 1978 onwards. Investments of the Guruvayur Devaswom include *Vazhipadu* and endowment deposits, pension fund deposits, security deposit and work deposit. Kuttikrishna Menon committee in its Report stated that no misappropriation of Devaswom funds has been brought to their attention, but Devaswom funds are not properly utilised (GoK, 1964: 64). The Devaswom has 10 *keezhedams (minor temples)* under it. As per the information collected from the Devaswom there are 687 permanent employees. Besides, several employees work on ad hoc basis also.

Major source of Devaswom revenue are revenue receipts, income from offerings, investments, lands, guest houses, publications etc. The income from *kanikka* (the metal cash box) is one of the major sources of income of the Guruvayur Devaswom which constitutes 16 to 25% of the total income. As there are no receipts given in return to the offerings, there is no way to ascertain the exact amount of cash deposited in the cash boxes (Madhusoodhanan, 2010: 105). Allegations are there regarding the malpractices while accounting the collections from hundies. There are chances of not recording all the contents of the *bhandarams (hundies)* in the official ledger account books. A Public Interest Litigation (PIL) was filed in the High Court of Kerala to evolve a suitable mechanism for accounting the income from the hundies. The Court appointed a Committee in March 2002 which included two nominees of the Court, the Manager of the bank which receives the cash deposits, one official from the Vigilance Department of the state, a nominee of the devotees, and one of the employees of the Devaswom. After this, receipts from the *bhandarams* have gone up considerably.

Guruvayur Devaswom is providing financial assistance to private temples in the state. Guruvayur Devaswom manages a first-grade College, one High School and an English medium School. Sree Krishna College was taken over by the Guruvayur Devaswom in 1976 (GDMC, 1977: 3). The Devaswom manages a library and a reading room that was started during the time of Zamorin Raja in 1945. The library contains 24000 books including thousands of Hindu religious books. Besides these, the Devaswom also manages hospitals, mural study centres etc.

A thorough change is needed in the administration of Guruvayur Devaswom as mentioned by various Commission Reports. Politicisation of administration, corruption, misbehaviour of temple employees etc., are widespread in the administration of Guruvayur Devaswom also. Political nomination in the Devaswom Committee creates so many issues and the High Court of Kerala issued directions in this regard. K. P. Sankaran Nair Commission also pointed out the elimination of practices like nomination of the representatives of political parties in the Devaswom Management Committee. The Commission recommended to suspend the existing Devaswom Management Committee and suggested to constitute a Temple Advisory Committee with Zamorin Raja, Namboothiri of *Mallisserri illom*, temple *tantri* and six non-official members. A senior Hindu officer who has belief in God and temple worship should be appointed as Administrator (GoK, 1984: 42- 43).

In 1993, a letter written by C. K. Rajan to one of the Hon'ble Judges of the High Court of Kerala, Justice Paripoornan, alleged serious irregularities, corrupt practices, mal-administration and mismanagement prevalent in the administration of Guruvayur temple. On the basis of the letter, the High Court appointed S. Krishnan Unni, District Judge, officiating as the Director of Training at the Commissioner to make an enquiry on the various aspects highlighted in the said complaint. The Commissioner has filed fifteen interim Reports and the final Report in two volumes to the Court (KHC, 1993). In 2014, Kerala Government appointed N. Krishnan Nair, former Judge in the Kerala High Court to study Devaswom reforms and suggest appropriate amendments in the Devaswom Act (KLA, 2014, July 10: 161).

Major recommendations of the Krishnan Unni Commission (1993) are the following:

(a) Zamorin Raja, *Karanavan* of *Mallisserry Illom* and *tantri* may be excluded from the Managing Committee in order to relieve them from the burdened duties of Managing Committee Members. The Committee should seek the advice of *tantri* on all religious rites. The representative of employees may also be removed from the committee;

(b) Devaswom Committee Members should not associate with any political party or communal organisations, the nomination of politicians to the Managing Committee should be avoided;

(c) Devaswom Commissioner must be a retired Judge of the High Court; IAS officers are not competent as they are often silenced by the political patronage of the government. This will give independence, dignity and autonomy to the Devaswom;

(d) Enhance the term of Managing Committee to 4 years.

(e) All temple staff should be properly trained in the fundamentals of Hindu religion;

(f) The temple must start institutions for the training *Acharaks*;

(g) Computerisation of all accounts of Devaswom should be made;

(h) All money of Devaswom should be deposited in the Government Treasury; money should not be deposited outside Guruvayur;

(i) Recruitment to Devaswom and related institutions must be fool-proof, a Recruitment Committee may be constituted;

(j) The conduct rules for Devaswom servants and rules regarding disciplinary proceedings be framed, a District Judge be deputed and posted as Law Officer and disciplinary authority in the Devaswom who will have exclusive authority to deal with matters of discipline of the Devaswom servants;

(k) The employees should have only one association and all other unions based on political lines should be banned;

(l) Devaswom is an autonomous institution, concerned only with the interests of the deity and the devotees. Though the government may have control over it, it is better that it is not to be subordinated to government (KHC, 1993: 135-206).

Several radical suggestions were put forward by the Commission are not implemented by the government and the Devaswom Committee so far. Enhancement of the term of the Devaswom Committee to four years is a major suggestion of the Report, but the government has not accepted it so far. The suggestion for removal of hereditary trustees from Devaswom Committee is not an accepted one due to their role in the spiritual affairs. The proposal for the removal of representative of employees in the Board is an imperative one in the special circumstances of Devaswom as so many complaints against them. Guruvayur Devaswom is generally considered as a model administrative system that is highlighted by the Court in the Sree Padmanabhaswamy temple case. Malabar Devaswom Reform Commission's recommendation to merge Guruvayur Devaswom to the MDB creates concerns.

Koodalmanickam Devaswom Committee

Koodalmanickam temple is an ancient and most sacred Hindu temple in Kerala dedicated to *Bharata*, the younger brother of *Sri Rama*, situates at Irrinjalakkuda in the erstwhile Cochin state. The temple is famous for its architecture, carvings in stone, round shaped *sanctum sanctorum*, mural paintings, *koothambalam*, impressive gateway, etc. The temple had also been an important centre of nourishment of Kerala's temple arts like *Kathakali*, *Koothu*, *Koodiyattom* and *Thullal*. It became a witness for several socio-political movements like that of the renowned *Kuttamkulam* Agitation of 1946 and thus became historic in the social renaissance of Kerala.

Role of Thachudaya Kaimal in Administration

The ruler of Cochin was the overlord of Koodalmanickam temple. He assigned the task of supervising the customary repairs of the temple to the ruler of Kayamkulam The architect of Kumara Kurup was specially entrusted with the work and Kurup was came to be called as Tachudaya Kaimal in around 1341- 42 AD (Nair, 1998: 153). The melkoima right of the King of Kayamkulam made Thachudaya Kaimal the authority over the Koodalmanickam temple administration. Later the King of Travancore had conquered Kayamkulam princely state and staked his claim in the temple. The relationship between Travancore and Cochin began to be strained during the time of the fourth Kaimal in 1868 as he obeyed only the orders of Travancore King and neglected that of the King of Cochin.

The conflict between the Government of Travancore and Cochin over the issue of management of Koodalmanickam temple had finally been referred to an arbitrator appointed by the Madras Government in 1880. The arbitrator J. C. Hannyngton repudiated the contention raised by the Government of Cochin (Pillai, 1996: 495). The Cochin Government temporarily took over the administration of the temple in 1912 on the death of the then Thachudaya Kaimal and placed under the supervision of Dewan Peishkar (GoK, 1913: 12). Later there arose disputes between the Governments of Travancore and Cochin regarding the removal of Thachudaya Kaimal in the event of mismanagement of temple affairs. Finally, a compromise was arrived through the intervention of British paramount power and a scheme of management was devised. The Koodalmanickam Proclamation was issued by the ruler of Cochin, Rama Varma Raja on 30th November, 1917 in accordance with the terms agreed to between Travancore and Cochin for the management of income and properties of the Devaswom. A scheme for the management of temple was enacted under the full control of Thachudaya Kaimal. The rights, privileges and duties of Kaimal were laid down in Schedule A of the Cochin Proclamation 1917 (GoK, 1964: 254). Till the end of British paramountcy in India, the British resident was the controlling authority. Later this was transferred to the King of Travancore and eventually to the State Government.

A drastic change in the administrative structure of the Koodalmanickam temple occurred in 1957 when the King of Travancore expressed his willingness to surrender his powers in the temple administration except for his power of nominating Thachudaya Kaimal. Koodalmanickam Devaswom Proclamation. Amendment Act was passed by the government in 1957, accordingly the controlling authority of the temple may be appointed by the government from time to time (Devaswom Act 1957, Section 3 (b)). By the government notification dated 26th April, 1958 one of the members of the

Board of Revenue was appointed as controlling authority (GoK, 1964: 255). With the abolition of Privy Purse in 1971, the princely order was abolished and the rights and claims of Thachudaya Kaimal too were lost in the administration of Koodalmanickam temple. Further, in 1971, the government formulated a scheme of administration for the management of the temple so as to save the temple from the mismanagement of Thachudaya Kaimal. Koodalmanickam Devaswom Ordinance was issued accordingly. As per provisions of the Ordinance the government constituted a managing committee for Koodalmanickam Devaswom; the Thachudaya Kaimal as its Chairman. On 12th April, 1971, a Bill passed by the legislature that replaced the Ordinance. The Devaswom Managing Committee consists of the Administrator, the Commissioner HRCE (Administration) Department, the President of Cochin Devaswom Board, District Collector of Thrissur and four persons professing the Hindu religion nominated by the government (Act, 1971, Section 4(1)). The Act was amended in 1976 incorporating the provision for reducing the number of members of Devaswom Committee so as to minimise the administrative expenditure of the temple. Thachudaya Kaimal was removed from the post of Chairman of the Committee and a provision was inserted that the District Collector or an officer not below the rank of the Deputy Collector may be appointed as the new Chairman and a Deputy Tahasildar as the new Administrator. Thachudaya Kaimal became an official Member in the Committee and five non-official government nominees were to be included.

Fifteen years after the enactment of Devaswom Act in 1986, the Koodalmanickam Devaswom Kshema Samithi filed a case in Kerala High Court against the legal validity of the Act. The Advocate General informed the government that there is a possibility of the Court to declare that act as invalid. So the government decided to frame a new Act for the administration of Koodalmanickam temple on the same line as Guruvayur

Devawom Act 1978. The new Act made provisions for representation of temple thantri, temple employees and of Scheduled Castes and Scheduled Tribes in temple administration.

In 2007, a new Devaswom Management Committee was constituted as per the provisions of section 4(1) of the Koodalmanickam Devaswom Act, 2007. Accordingly, the Devaswom Committee consists of a person nominated by the government from among the tantries of the temple as ex-officio Member; a representative of temple employees and not more than five persons having interest in the temple of whom one shall be an SC or ST (Act 2 of 2007, Section 4 (1) a-c). The Members of the Committee in its first meeting elect one of the Members as the Chairman.

Duties of the Devaswom Committee

As per Section 10 of the Koodalmanickam Devaswom Act, 2005, it shall be the duty of the Committee:

(a) To arrange for the proper performance of the rites and ceremonies in the temple and the subordinate temples subject to the customs and usages in accordance with the scale of expenditure specified in Schedule I of the Koodalmanickam Devaswom Act 1971;

(b) To arrange proper facilities for the worshippers;

(c) To ensure the safe custody of the funds, valuables, jewellery and preservation and management of the properties of the temple;

(d) To ensure maintenance of order and discipline and proper hygienic conditions in the temple and for the proper standard of cleanliness and purity in the offerings made therein;

(e) To make provision for the payment of suitable emoluments to the salaried staff of the Devaswom; and

(f) To do all such things as may be incidental and conducive to the efficient management of the affairs of the Devaswom and for the facilities of the worshippers.

In the Koodalmanickam Devaswom, the income and expenditure statement since its formation are not properly maintained. They are kept only for the purpose of the audit. Local Fund Audit department audits Devaswom accounts. There is no Vigilance Department in Koodalmanickam Devaswom. There are eleven *keezhedoms* (sub-temples) and 51 employees including temporary employees work under Koodalmanickam temple. Offerings from the devotees are major sources of income of Koodalmanickam Devaswom. There is no separate staff for surveying temple land; vast acres of land were encroached from time to time, so it is not possible to assess the nature of encroachment. A part of the temple land was allotted to the Christ College and other government institutions to facilitate development activities around the region (Dauhashanti & Paanchajanyaa, 2017, March 29). But no documents are available as proof to this land alienation in the Devaswom office. The temple is getting annuity of Rs 8,17,646 from the government for the land alienated (about 3551 acres and 78 cents of land).

Administrator of Koodalmanickam Devaswom

The Administrator is appointed from among the panel of names furnished by the government as per Section 14 (1) of the Act, who is an officer not below the rank of Under Secretary or Deputy Collector who professes the Hindu religion and believes in temple worship. He is the Secretary to the Committee and the Chief Executive Officer who has powers to carry out the decisions of the Committee in accordance with the provisions of the Act. As a full time officer of the Devaswom he/she shall not be undertaken any work not connected with his office without the permission of the Committee. Salary and allowances of the Administrator shall be paid out of the Devaswom funds (Act 2007, Section 15 (2)).

Section 17 (1) of the act stipulates powers of the Administrator:

(a) The Administrator shall arrange for the proper collection and credit of the offerings made in the temple;
(b) The power to incur expenditure not exceeding five thousand rupees to meet unforeseen contingencies during the interval between two meetings of the committee;
(c) Power to appoint all officers and employees of the temple;
(d) Administrator should maintain a register containing the details of gems, jewels gold and other valuables (Rules, 2008, Section 12).

Budget of Koodalmanickam Devaswom

The Committee in every financial year submits to the Commissioner a budget estimate of the receipts and expenditure of the Devaswom for the following financial year. Every such budget should make adequate provision for:

(a) The scale of expenditure for the time being in force;
(b) The due discharge of all liabilities of the Devaswom;
(c) The construction, repair, maintenance and renovation of buildings connected with the Devaswom; and
(d) The maintenance of working balance (Act 2007 Section 21(1) (2)).

The Commissioner sends a copy of the budget approved by him to the government. The Committee incurs expenditure out of the funds of the Devaswom for the following purposes:

(a) Maintenance including repairs and reconstruction, management and administration of the temple, its properties and the temples subordinate to it;
(b) Training of *archakas* to perform religious worship and ceremonies in the temple and temples subordinate to it;

(c) Medical aid, water supply and other sanitary arrangement for the worshippers and construction of building for their accommodation;
(d) Promotion and propagation of the tenets and philosophy associated with the temple;
(e) To give any grant or contribution to any poor home or other institutions established and maintained for the benefit of the persons mainly belonging to the Hindu religion;
(f) The construction of buildings connected with the affairs of the Devaswom; and
(g) The making of any kind of donation to any religious institution.

As per the Section 23 of the Koodalmanickam Devaswom Act, a temple fund was constituted which shall be vested in and be administered by the Committee. The fund shall consist of the income derived from the movable and immovable properties of the Devaswom, contribution by the government either by way of grant or by way of loan, all recoveries under this Act, any other gifts or contributions made by the public, local authorities or institutions.The Committee should annually submit a report on the administration of the affairs of the Devaswom to the government (Rules, 2008 Section 10 (3)). The administration report should contain the details of the execution of the Act, the income and expenditure; the amenities arranged for the devotees, the construction works undertaken, festivals conducted, financial position, the administration of the subordinate temples and other institutions under the management of the Devaswom etc.

K. P. Sankaran Nair Commission recommended for the immediate abolition of the post of *Thachudaya Kaimal* and the temple administration and funds should be transferred to the CDB. Several defects were pointed out in the administration of the temple. Careful preservation is needed for the temple and its architecture, precious ornaments and gold (GoK, 1984: 45-46). The tenure of Koodalmanickam Devaswom Managing Committee is three years.

Melsanthi of the temple is a hereditary post and *tantri* of the temple is the same as the *tantri* of Sree Padmanabhaswamy Temple, Thiruvananthapuram. Trade union politics is not seen in this Devaswom and there is only a single union which is independent of any political affiliation, Koodalmanickam Temple Employees' Union.The Administrator of the Devaswom is appointed on deputation basis. Shortage of administrative staff, high expense on temple rituals, low income and illegal encroachment of temple lands are the major issues faced by the Devaswom today. At present the Devaswom commissioner of Guruvayur Devaswom is in-charge of the Koodalmanickam Devaswom. The Guruvayur and Koodalmanickam Devaswom have certain similarities in the Board and other administration.

The Devaswom has no right to change the priest and *tantri* of the temple. There are 11 *keezhedoms* under the Devaswom which are not self-reliant. There is no need for a separate Temple Advisory Committee due to the presence of a seven-member Managing Committee for the administration of the temple. Chairman and Managing Committee receive no monetary benefits including TA/DA from the Devaswom fund. The Devaswom income is remitted in the Koodamanickam Devaswom Fund and invested in nationalised banks and treasury accounts. The Devaswom administrator stated that the daily collection in the Koodalmanickam temple is around Rs 50,000. Thus, the temple got Rs 15,00,000 per month as revenue, thus in a year the revenue from temple becomes Rs 1,80,00,000.The temple owns 1279 acres of land of which the temple complex is situated in an extent of 9.50 acres (Jayashanker, 2006: 539).

Koodalmanickam Devaswom is suffering from serious drawbacks such as shortage of finance, shortage of employees, wide range of encroachment of temple lands etc. The temple revenue is very low compared to the high-income temples under the TDB.The presence of a seven-member Devaswom Committee for such a low-income temple is highly incompatible as it is intended only for protecting the political interests of the party in power. Sankaran Nair Commission pointed out the merger of this Devaswom to the CDB which is relevant and the need of the day. The presence of large number of local people in the festival committee of the temple signifies the necessity of an Advisory Committee for temple governance.

Devaswom Administration: A Comparative Analysis

The chapter examined the organisational structure and personnel, financial administrations of various Devaswom governing bodies in the state separately. For preparing the study, the data used is mainly primary, collected through interviews, personal visits to various Devaswom offices and major temples. The details of income and expenditure of the Devaswom governing bodies are collected from Devaswom offices, administration reports and budgets. In this context a comparative analysis seems necessary which is imperative for understanding the pros and cons of the existing diverse administrative set up for temples.

Classification of Temples

The study found out no uniform pattern for the classification of various Devaswom Board temples in the state. When the temples under the TDB are classified into four as Grade I, II, III and PD temples, that under the CDB are arranged into grade A, B, C and D and the MDB temples are grouped into Grade A, B, C, D and Special grade temples. In the case of Guruvayur and Koodalmanickam Devaswoms such a classification is not seemed necessary as these Devaswoms are set up for the administration of particular temples and only some minor temples (*keezhedoms*) are attached to them. Majority of temples under various Devaswom governing bodies are not self-supporting.

Table 2.13: Comparative analysis of classification of temples under the TDB, CDB and MDB

Board	Grade I/ Grade A	Grade II/ Grade B	Grade III/ Grade C	Grade D	Special Grade/ PD Temples	Total
TDB*	236	479	481	-	52(PD)	1248
CDB	43	76	255	29	-	403
MDB**	50	129	122	1021	23	1345
Total	329	684	858	1050	75	2996

*Temples under TDB are classified as grade I, II, III and PD temple
** MDB temples are classified as special grade temples grade, A, B, C and D grade temple.

Each Devaswom governing body has a few major temples as revenue generators and the rest have to depend largely on these prospered temples for their survival, except with the MDB where the absence of common pooling of fund system, unlike TDB or CDB, creates problems for the survival of low-income temples. Out of a total of 2996 temples under the control of all the three Devaswom Boards in the state, 329 are Grade I or Grade A temples and 23 temples under MDB are special grade temples. Thus, in total 352 nos. are self-supporting temples under all the three Devaswom Boards that constitute only 11.74 % of the total temples. Guruvayur and Sabarimala temples are the top in terms of income.

Comparing the annual yield from the public sector undertakings with that of the temples under various Devaswom managements in the state, the Times of India daily- published a report in 2012 which reveals that while the 42 public sector undertakings together make a revenue of Rs 200 crore a year, the four Devaswom bodies (except Koodalmanickam) can boast of having Rs 1,000 crores in total as annual revenue. The Guruvayur Devaswom is the richest Devaswom in the state followed by Travancore, Malabar and Cochin. According to unofficial estimates, Guruvayur Devaswom alone possesses assets worth Rs 2,500 crore and makes about Rs 400 crores in both cash and gold annually (Times of India 2012, September 4). This fact indicates the necessity of proper and effective supervision over Devaswom administration. The intervention of the High Court of Kerala on the Audit Reports of Devaswoms helps to some extent to maintain transparency in financial transactions of the Boards.Comparing the three Devaswom Boards in Kerala in terms of their income, TDB occupies the position of the highest earner; no surprise it manages more number of temples including Sabarimala, the second temple in the state in terms of revenue, the first being the Guruvayur temple.

Composition of Devaswom Boards

Disparities can also be seen in the composition of members in various Devaswom Governing Bodies while comparing them. When the TDB and CDB, the two major Devaswom Boards in the state possess only three members each for them, the other three Devaswoms, the MDB, GDMC and KDMC have more members, 9, 9, and 7 respectively. More number of members in Devaswoms incurs huge expenditure for them.

The prevailing laws for Devaswom administration in the state are mostly out-dated. Though the terms 'Travancore', 'Cochin' and 'Malabar' ceased to exist after 1956, the Devaswom Statutes in Kerala still refer to these terms. Likewise, the temples of Malabar are ruled according to the Madras Hindu Religious and Charitable Endowments Act, 1951. Even after the separation of Malabar from the state of Madras, the Act continued to be in force till now. It is a fact that when the state of Tamil Nadu was formed, the word 'Madras' in the Madras Hindu Religious and Charitable Endowments Act was substituted by 'Tamil Nadu' by the Tamil Nadu Adaptation of Laws (Second Amendment) Order, 1969 for the State of Tamil Nadu. When the name

'Madras' was changed as 'Chennai' appropriate amendments had been made to all enactments as per Tamil Nadu Act 28 of 1996. But the Government of Kerala who is the custodian of Devaswoms here did not take any action to amend the Devaswom Statutes suitable to the circumstances of Kerala (Ramesan, 2006: 7). Even after six decades of our state formation, the government is indifferent to the Hindu religious institutions for having religious enactments of Kerala touch. Lack of uniformity in Devaswom laws is another crucial issue that the administration of temples faces. In Kerala, the system of Board administration is prevailing for the temples in which the responsibility is jointly exercised by a number of individuals with an indirect governmental control.

Table 2.14: Composition of Devaswom Governing Bodies

Board / Committees	Nominated	Elected members	SC/ST Representation	Women	Employees representation	temple Advisory Committees	Permanent Members (hereditary)	Total membership
TDB	2	1	1	0	0	0	0	3
CDB	2	1	1	0	0	0	0	3
MDB	7	2	2	1	1	1	0	9
GDMC	6	0	1	0	1	0	3	9
KDMC	7	7	1	0	1	0	0	7

Source: Data compiled from various sources.

Table 2.15: Various Devaswoms at a glance

Status	TDB	CDB	MDB	KDMC	GDMC
Year of formation	1949	1949	2008	1971	1971
Members	3	3	9	7	9
Division/ groups	4	5	5	Nil	Nil
Tenure	2	2	3	3	3
Districts covered	5	4	7	3	2

(*Contd...*)

Classification of temples	Gr I, II, III PD	A, B, C, D grades	special Grade A, B, C, D	Main temple and Keezhedoms	Main temple and Keezhedoms
Employees	3000	2000	6000	50	600
Temples	1248	403	1345	12	11
Colleges	4	2	Nothing	Nil	1
Higher Secondary Schools	4	Nothing	Nothing	Nil	1
High Schools	8	1	Nothing	Nil	1
UP Schools	5	Nothing	Nothing	Nil	Nothing
L.P Schools	5	Nothing	Nothing	Nil	Nothing
Central School	4	Nothing	Nothing	Nil	1
Other Institutions	Temple art Academy Attingal & Vaikom, Institute of Art and Architecture at Thrissur, Heritage Museum at Kottarakkara	Ayurveda Hospital, Nelluvai		Nil	Vadya Vidyalayam, Mural Institute Padana Kendra, Hospital

The chapter analysed the organisational structure of Devaswom governing bodies, the biggest social as well as religious institution in the state. Existence of diverse administrative set up for the temples in the three regions of the state, Travancore, Cochin and Malabar has created manifold issues in their administration. Unlike in other South Indian states where there are centralised administrative patterns for temples, Kerala lacks such a system for the governance of her temples. Existence of five Devaswom Governing Bodies involves huge administrative expenditure including expenses towards Board members and Chairman. 28 elected/nominated members including five Chairmen in these bodies incur huge financial liability to the temple fund. Besides, several anomalies exist in the administrative side, corruption, politicisation, mismanagement, favouritism, trade unionism among employees etc., are also rampant in the administration of Devaswoms.

In order to curb corruption from temple administration Ombudsman mechanism prevails in TDB and CDB. Proposal for a Devaswom Tribunal for retaining the encroached temple land is under the consideration of the State Government. Establishment of an independent Board for Devaswom recruitment is an innovative step in temple administration. Each Devaswom Board is having a few temples as income generators and the other temples are surviving on the income from these temples. Absence of effective control of MDB over temples in Malabar creates a lot of issues such as lack of common pooling of temple funds, wage disparity among temple employees, mis-utilisation of grants etc. Land Reforms affected the revenue of the temple considerably. There are leakages of temple revenue due to negligence in the part of temple authorities. A common Devaswom law for the whole temples in the state is a panacea for the evils exists in the Devaswom administration.

3

Temple Administration: Issues and Concerns

Temples are conceived as holy and spiritual hubs of the society; but their administration is always confronted with several grave issues which are mostly political and economic rather than spiritual or religious. Mismanagement of temple affairs is not a rarity. It is the diversion of temple funds and fraudulence on the part of temple trustees which prompted the government to interfere in temple affairs. Subsequently, in 1811 the government took over temples and their assets and made them government property. Later, in the post-independence period when the government started nominating Members to various Devaswom Boards in the state as part of democratisation of temple administration, politicisation of temples became almost completed. Successive State Governments nominated politicians to temple governing bodies. Entry of politics and politicians into temple affairs has generated several issues such as corruption, mismanagement and misappropriation of funds, politicisation of administration, favouritism, nepotism and other essential evils of parochial politics in the temple administration. This chapter analyzed the major issues in the administration of Devaswom Board temples in Travancore, Cochin and Malabar areas. Temples act as a unifying factor among the Hindus. Though they once promoted caste-based polarisation by segmentalising large section of people who had to observe pollution rules, due to the ceaseless efforts of reformers, the gates of temples were thrown open to all devotees. Today temples become centres of common worship integrating all Hindus beyond the boundaries of caste.

Political Issues

Politicisation of Temple Administration

Politics involves compromise and adjustment; substantive policies are based not only on merit and reason but on influence and competing interests as well. What is formally rational is not always politically rational (Rudolph, 1984: 61). Theoretically, a secular state should be totally abstained from religious activities. But in Kerala, the secular government actively involves in the affairs of temples, both temporal and spiritual. Political control over Hindu religious institutions by a secular state had become a highly debated issue in state politics since the 1950s. The formation of *Hindu Mahamandalam* (1950), perhaps the first Hindu consolidation movement in the state became a stage for protest against the politicisation of Devaswom administration. Mannathu Padmanahan, the first President of the TDB and R. Sankar, the nominated Member to the Board, were expelled from their positions under the pressure of Christian groups in the Congress party. Thus, they were the first victims of politicisation of Devaswom administration in the state. After two decades, with the abolition of Privy Purse, the nominal right of the King over temple administration came to an end and his rights to nominate Members of Devaswom Boards were delegated to the Council of Ministers. This led to the process of total politicisation of temple administration.

Politics is a competitive enterprise; its purpose is the acquisition of power for the realisation of certain goals and its purpose is one of identifying and manipulating existing and emerging allegiance in order to mobilise and consolidate positions (Kothari, 2004: 4). The evils of corruption, nepotism, favouritism misappropriation of funds etc., are the direct results of this politicisation process. Trade unionism in Hindu religious institutions is a rare phenomenon which became the backlash of the politicisation process happening in the administration of temples. Today, most of the members of Devaswom Boards are having political backgrounds; some of them were active politicians in the past. Even non-believers are being appointed in the temple governing bodies. These measures actually make Devaswom administration a political affair and the temples have become fertile grounds for political malpractices (GoK, 1984: 21). As mentioned earlier, discussions regarding the politicisation of temple administration began from the 1950s. When in 1950, the Hindu Religious Bill was placed before the first session of Travancore-Cochin Legislative Assembly (TCLA), fiery discussions happened on the issue of political control over Hindu Religious Institutions. Pattom Thanu Pillai questioned the rationality of the Bill and demanded that the internal administration of religious institutions should be left to the owners or beneficiaries of temples (TCLA, 1950, April 5: 1543-44). According to him, even the Gods in our temples have been made pawns in the political chessboard of the Congress Party. Thus, he sowed the seeds of the temple liberation movement in the state.

In 1955, Travancore Cochin Hindu Religious Institution (Amendment) Bill was introduced in the first session of the Assembly and during the discussions on it, Kalathil Velayudhan Nair, NSS leader and a member in the Assembly, pointed out the discrepancies in the election of members to Devaswom Boards; members of the Legislative Assembly are not even familiar with the details of candidates; but only their political background. So, members with political background should be debarred from contesting elections to the Board and also it is pertinent to make restrictions on giving voting rights to political activists (TCLA, 1955, January 29: 122-23). While participating in the Guruvayur Devaswom Bill, in 1978, Seethi Haji, leader of IUML made an interesting and thought provoking statement in the KLA. He asked the House how the election to the Devaswom bodies would be conducted if, by some miracle, there happened to be an Assembly sans any Hindu MLA (KLA, 1978 March 2: 1821).

State governments in power have often made amendments in Devaswom laws for implementing their political agenda. The left political parties are generally viewed as atheists and hence, in order to avoid them from securing seats in the Devaswom bodies, the Congress Government in 1984 made a dramatic move. As majority of the Hindu MLAs of that Assembly belonged to the left front led opposition party, the government brought in an amendment to the Devaswom laws by which it was made mandatory that the voters (Hindu MLAs) should produce a signed declaration that they were believers in God and temple worship, to become eligible for casting votes in the election to Devaswom Boards. The Congress Government thought that the declaration would force the Left Hindu MLAs keep away from voting and that would lead to an easy walk over for the Congress candidates. This amendment kick started a series of amendments in the Devaswom laws until the High Court in 1989 made in its judgment that all Hindu MLAs, irrespective of their faith in God and temple worship, are eligible for voting to Devaswom Boards. The Ministers and MLAs may be atheists; even then they could exercise this right, but they have to nominate only believers to Devaswom Boards after the Court pronouncements and recommendations of High Power Commission Report (1990).

The various Commissions appointed by the State Government and the High Court of Kerala for suggesting Devaswom reforms have strongly recommended de-politicisation of temple administration. Kuttikrishna Menon Commission in 1964 recommended a Central Apex Board as the ultimate authority over temples which would be free from all sorts of political influence or pressures. The Central Board should consist of persons absolutely free from politics and one essential qualification of the members should be that they have faith in Hindu religion and temple worship (GoK, 1964: 104-105). In 1974, while enquiring the financial position of TDB, C. R. Krishnamoorthy Commission in its Report suggested that the Board system may be replaced and a Commissioner may be appointed as in the case of Tamil Nadu, under HR &CE Act, 1950 for ensuring efficient management of temples. If for any reason, it is still considered necessary or desirable to have a Board for the temple administration; it is desirable that the members should be selected on the basis of qualification and competency rather than their political background or party affiliations or for any reasons of the community which they belong to (GoK, 1974: 132). In 1983, the representatives of various Hindu organisations in the state submitted a memorandum to the then Governor P. Ramachandran, one of their demands was the liberation of Devaswoms from the clutches of politicians. As a result, the government appointed K. P. Sankaran Nair Commission to study and submit a report on Devaswom administrative reforms in Kerala. The Commission recommended the de-politicisation of temple administration (GoK, 1984: 86-87). The High Power Commission appointed by the High Court of Kerala in 1990 in its Report stressed the need for de-politicisation of the Board and recommended that persons associated with political parties should not be nominated as members. Eminent persons with proven integrity and are held in high esteem by the public should only be nominated as members (KHC, 1990: 69). Politicisation has polluted the atmosphere and there should not be political bargaining in temple premises.

It is significant that the Court has intervened occasionally in protecting Devaswom affairs from politicisation. In 1998, when the restructuring of Guruvayur Devaswom by the then LDF Government created a messy controversy in state politics, a devotee filed a petition in the Kerala High Court contending that the Devaswom Minister Viswanatha Menon, a Marxist and non-believer had no right to nominate members to the Guruvayur Devaswom Managing Committee. The KHC entrusted the then Education Minister and Janata Party leader K. Chandrasekharan, the only believer among the 15 Hindus in the 19-member State Cabinet, to nominate the Devaswom members (Pillai, 1988, May15).

Religious freedom without state interference is inevitable for a secular society. It is a severe injustice to the Hindu community that the secular state makes the temple a platform for political clashes and pressure game politics. Excessive political interference leads to mismanagement and malpractices in the administration of temples. This can be found especially in the case of appointment of staff in Devaswom services. Thus, the political control and politicisation of temple administration have become a controversial issue in the present state politics (Jayaprasad, 1992: 238). The temple politicisation process ultimately led to the Hindu communal groups to consolidate their power. Temple liberation movement organised by Hindu groups paved the way for the formation of Hindu front in state politics.

Politicisation in Devaswom administration is harmful not only to the temples but also its employees. The employees in Devaswoms are allegedly subjected to disciplinary actions on political reasons (KHC, 1993). Krishnan Unni Commission (1993) recommended that employees should have only one association and all other unions based on political basis should be banned from the services of Devaswoms. Such unions would create only group loyalties which are harmful to the interests of employees as well as Devaswoms, serving only the interests of those particular political groups. In the case of discipline of the Devaswom servants, politicisation had a very bad effect. Devaswom servants themselves own allegiances in certain unions over which political groups have influence. This resulted in wildcat strike on unreasonable demands and inconvenience to the devotees ultimately affecting the sanctity of the temple (KHC, 1993).

It is true that for the democratisation of the administration of any organisation, the role of political parties is essential. However, their intervention and power-sharing in Devaswom Boards reduced temple administration to one of politicking and political maneuvering. Excessive politicisation will create numerous issues in temple administration that may pose a challenge to the secular fabric of Kerala society. Hindu organisations raised slogans like "Hindu temples for Hindus" and "property of temples for temples" that often creates communal divide and imbalance in society.

Politics of State Control

The state-temple relationship is not similar in all the states of India; it varies according to the existing political and socio-religious scenario. Prevailing social, political and economic conditions became more important in determining the nature of the relationship between the state and the temple management (Pressler, 1988: 27). Almost all the temples in South India are in one way or the other, under the control of the state. When the Britishers proceeded to enact the Madras Religious and Charitable Endowments Act 1925 for regulating the administration of religious institutions of the major religions in the state, the Muslim and Christian communities protested. So, the government had to redraft the same excluding the religious institutions of Muslim and Christian communities and made applicable only to Hindus, renaming it as the Madras Hindu Religious and Endowments Act 1927 (Nayyar, 2019).

The Hindu Religious Endowment Commission headed by C. P. Ramaswamy Aiyar, appointed by the Central Government in 1962 recommended suitable legislation for the Hindu Religious Endowments in all states. But excessive political interference, particularly in the affairs of Hindu religious institutions created several grave issues in temple administration. In 1964, Kuttikrishna Menon Commission in his Report suggested that the ultimate authority regarding temple administration is to be entrusted with a statutory body rather than a department of the government (GoK, 1964: 168).

With regard to the state-temple relationship successive Ministers in-charge of Devaswoms expressed divergent opinions. In 1950, the then Chief Minister T.K. Narayana Pillai, while replying to a question in the United States of Travancore-Cochin Legislative Assembly (USTCLA), clarified that the state had no control over Devaswom Board or Devaswom Department (1950, January 21: 1744). In 1980, the then Devaswom Minister Krishnan stated in the Assembly that the Government had no power in Devaswom administration other than the power to nominate Members to Devaswom Boards (KLA, 1980, December 11: 141). A different opinion was expressed by the former Minister of Devaswom V. Viswanatha Menon, when saying that since the Devaswom Board Members are appointed by the elected representatives of the people, the government has a moral obligation to examine its income and expenditure (Mathrubhumi, 1987, September 23). In 2006, the then Devaswom Minister G. Sudhakaran stated that the State Government should not interfere in the internal (ritualistic) matters of temples but should interfere in the administration of temples (KLA, 2006, October16: 175). It is notable here that the LDF Government intends to intervene in temple affairs for ensuring financial accountability of the Board, particularly on the ground of financial assistance to the temples. But this interference is not justifiable to the Hindu outfits as they consider the grant from government as a part of its obligation enshrined in the covenant.

The judiciary occasionally interfered against the irrational interference of the state over Hindu religious affairs. In *Devaraja Shenoy Vs. The State of Madras* case, the Madras High Court quashed the Government Order to took over the administration of the Shri Venkataramana Temple in Mulki, South Kanara District as per the provisions of the Madras Hindu Religious and Charitable Endowments Act 1951 (Devaraja Shenoy, 1957). Similarly, the Madras High Court quashed the Government Order to take over the administration of Udupi Sri Krishna Temple and Shri Sabhanayagar Temple in Chidambaram (Shri Lakshmindra Thirtha, 1952). The Guruvayur Devaswom Act, 1971 was struck down by the Kerala High Court in *Tharamel Krishnan Vs. Guruvayur Devaswom Managing Committee* case (1978), on the grounds of violation of religious freedom and the verdict remains as a warning against the state interference over temple administration. In the light of the above verdict the Government of Kerala brought about amendments in the Koodalmanickam Devaswom Act in 2007 to the interest of devotees. Frequent legislative amendments on the Devaswom Acts clearly substantiate governmental intervention.

Recent verdicts of the Court limiting state control over temples can be seen as a relief to Hindu devotees as these satisfied their long cherished demand for liberation of temples from the clutches of politics. The Supreme Court in its historic verdict in 2014 regarding the administration of Chidambaram Temple ruled that even if the management of the temple is taken over by the government to resolve the evil of mismanagement, it must be handed over to the original trustees immediately after the evil is remedied (Ramesh, 2016). The temple would be managed by the priests and not by the State Government and the management by the state can only be for a limited period. The verdict of the apex court is a landmark in the history of temple administration and it is a warning to the state against interference in temple administration. Justice B. S. Chauhan and Justice J. Chalemeshwar ruled that 'small and silly mistakes' made by the trust cannot be grounds for the government to takeover temples on a permanent basis (Subramanian Swamy, 2013). Temples may be taken over for short periods to sort out problems. State control is an infringement on the autonomy of Devaswoms.

The KHC refused the plea of T. G. Mohandas to strike down various sections of the Travancore- Cochin Hindu Religious Institutions Act, 1950 alleging that the method of appointment of Devaswom members was undemocratic and a violation of the religious and administrative rights of the devotees. In October, 2018 the BJP leader Subramanian Swamy and T. G. Mohandas approached the Supreme Court seeking dismantle of Devaswom Boards in the state and the Court issued notices to the Travancore, Cochin Devaswom Boards and the State Government seeking their response in the matter; the case is still pending before the Court.

In the *Chidambaram* case of 2014, the Supreme Court expressed its concern over the failure of various State Governments in managing temple affairs and that the administration of religious places should be entrusted with devotees. Attorney General K. K. Venugopal also agreed to the view of the Court that there should be no state interference in the management of temples and said that the issue should be examined by the Court on 'how a government could take over the control of temples in a secular country'. He told the Bench that temples in Kerala including the famous Sabarimala temple, are also controlled by state sponsored Devaswom Boards. He raised the question, *how far could the government, in a secular state, control or manage a temple?* (The Times of India, 2019, April 8). The LDF Government's intervention in the Sabarimala issue created dissatisfaction among the major section of Devaswom employees. Moreover, the issue effected large scale erosion in the income of Sabarimala and other temples under the Board.

A sizable section of Hindu populace has resentment towards the state control over the administration of temples, its politicisation and trade unionism as these factors often affected the serene atmosphere of temples. The state control over the religious institutions of a particular religious community is definitely unjustifiable, especially in a secular state like India. It is unfair that while the religious institutions of other communities are largely left free for deciding the administrative affairs of their respective religious institutions, the Hindu temples alone are fettered in the matter. In order to escape from the allegations of direct control, the government formed autonomous Devaswom Boards for temple administration, but exercises indirect control over them. The secular state intervention on Hindu temples is not justifiable and the action would only help to destabilise temple administration in the state. The LDF government intervention on Sabarimala issue created dissatisfaction among large sections of Devaswom employees as well as devotees leading to a large-scale erosion of temple income.

Rights of Devotees or Worshippers

The worshippers of Hindu temples are often called beneficiaries. But they are not beneficiaries in the sense that they have any beneficial ownership in the endowment properties (Prakash, 2006: 564). Devotees make visits in temples regularly and make offerings, but the temple governing bodies never took a devotee centred approach. From the devotees' point of view, state control violates the religious freedom of large sections of Hindu population. They are denied the right to manage their own religious institutions. Temples are the highly influential institutions in the society and their growing influence due to fame and wealth is one among the reasons that evolved for governmental intervention.

Trade Unionism in Temples

Existence of trade unions for the employees working in religious institutions like temples seems paradoxical. Trade unions are, of course, abundantly found in industrial sectors. Generally speaking, trade unions are bargaining forces indulging in direct action methods like strike, dharna etc., for achieving their political objectives. But, no doubt, unlike in industrial and other service sectors, the concept of trade unionism in temples is unbecoming to their serene atmosphere. An interesting development in Kerala politics is that trade union activities are in high gear among temple employees including priests. It is the direct result of the politicisation of temple administration. A plurality of trade unions and their political affiliations have created disunity and disarray in temple administration. Their direct actions and radicalism have polluted the serene atmosphere of temples and badly affected the dedication of temple employees. There exists category-wise unions among Devaswom Board employees; most of them have conspicuous political affiliations. Sub Group Officers Association, Devaswom Officers Association, Temple Employee Union, Maramath Employees Association etc. are a few among them.

At the same time, viewing from the angle of the employees, some sort of union is a must for protecting their service rights. To a certain extent trade unions are essential for protecting the service conditions of employees. Because of the unionism, temple employees have got salary and allowances at par with the state employees.Whether it is a temple or an industry, no matter, the methods of strike of political parties would be the same. This is a common factor in industrial and service sectors. Such strikes are obnoxious in temple premises where devotees come seeking peace of mind and tranquility.The history of trade unions in the Devaswom Boards is significant in the history of the trade union movement in the state. With the formation of trade unions, the status of Devaswom Boards has been reduced to the level of a business establishment. The tussle between Devaswom Board management and employees and the overflow of trade unionism have further changed temple atmosphere similar to that of a bargaining market place (Jayaprasad, 1989: 272).

Temple employees are a special category and their nature of work and other conditions are entirely different from that of other organisations. Unlike in other services, temple employees are catering to the requirement of devotees who may visit the temple at any time of the day, and hence theirs is a spiritual work or service. Spiritual service is not a wage-earning one. Kuttikrishna Menon Commission pointed out certain features which differentiate temple employees from other sectors. There is no capitalist or employer-employee relationship in temples and Labour Laws are not applicable to them. Nature of work being spiritual, working hours, rules regarding holidays, overtime work etc. cannot be made applicable to them. Matters regarding temple services shall be taken up only with the *tantric* authorities. Matters relating to remuneration for temple work cannot be dragged to a Labour Tribunal. Things like abstinence of lady employees from temple work during monthlies are outside the scope of Labour Laws (GoK,1964: 134). Such privileges are part and parcel of temple customs which do not come under the purview of Labour Laws in the state.

Devaswom employees are categorised into Maramath employees, Board employees, Temple employees, Contingent employees etc. and so naturally a plurality of trade unions are there. But this plurality of unions created division among various categories and also sowed the seeds of hatred, disunity and conflict. It is sure that multiplicity of trade unions was a severe setback for the betterment of employee-employer relations (Menon, 1956: 6). The process of negotiation would have been smooth and expeditious if it were on one or two unions (Rao, 1986: 152).

After examining the pros and cons of trade unionism in temples, K. Kuttikrishna Menon Commission specified that it is against the spiritual atmosphere of the temple and should be prohibited (GoK, 1964: 134). Subsequently, Sankaran Nair Commission Report also suggested that the service associations of temple employees should not have any political relations and they should not indulge in any activities that affect the spiritual atmosphere of the temple; at the same time the temple employees may be provided with a systematic facility for redressing their grievances (GoK, 1984: 176). It is worth mentioning here that the administration of Devaswom Boards has been deteriorated to the level of a business establishment due to the presence of strong and highly politicised trade unions (Jayaprasad, 1992: 238).

The activities of trade unions like direct action methods in temple premises have created aversion among the devotees. The politicisation of administration as well as bureaucracy have resented by the people as it affects the spirituality of the shrines. RSS and other Hindu organisations who stood against trade unionism among temple employees, are now started their own trade unions in leading Devaswoms in the state. Through temple-oriented activities, the political parties try to reap political benefits, but the devotees' responses indicate their apathy towards the excessive politicisation process.There is a feeling among the devotees that trade unions with political affiliation are detrimental to the divine atmosphere of temples. They are actually bargaining forces by applying any means for achieving their goals. An effective legislation should be promulgated to exempt temples from the jurisdiction of Industrial Dispute Act, Trade Union Acts etc. for protecting the serenity of the temple atmosphere.

Trade unionism in temples is the direct result of politicisation of temple administration. All political parties have organised employees of temples including the priestly classes under their banner. Their direct actions and radicalism have affected the serene atmosphere of temples. Through the intervention of the KHC some sort of restrictions is imposed on them that become a great relief to the devotees. Commissions appointed for Devaswom reforms; Kuttikrishna Menon, Sankaran Nair, Paripoornan, Krishnan Unni and High-Power Commission Reports stressed the need for regulating trade unionism among temple employees. It is worth mentioning here that the administration of Devaswom Boards has been often deteriorated to the level of an industrial establishment due to the presence of strong and highly politicised trade unions. *Temples of Kerala* published by the Census Directorate, Kerala, suggests that trade union activities in temples should be strictly prohibited as they vitiate the serene atmosphere and affects dedication of the workers.

Economic issues

Corruption

Corruption is an age-old phenomenon, a deep-rooted evil and a universal malady afflicting each and every society in one form or another (Padhy, 1986: 1). Corruption-free administration of temples is a long-cherished demand of the devotees in the state, but in vain. It is *sine qua non* of the process of politicisation of temple administration. Everybody knows that the politician-criminal-bureaucrat nexus is responsible for unleashing the hydra-headed monster called corruption (Mohanan, 1998: 246).

Corruption is deep-rooted in the administration of Devaswoms in Kerala. Nominees of both the left and right political parties in the Devaswom Board are not exceptions. When allegations of corruption brought to the notice of K. R. Gouri, the first Minister in-charge of Devaswoms in Kerala, she expressed her helplessness saying that the government had no power to interfere in the issue (KLA, 1957, December 20: 9). Thus, the government was only an onlooker in the Devaswom administration of the state then. The gravity of corruption increased in the Devaswom Board when it entered into the field of managing educational institutions, thus the temple fund was begun to spend for non-devotional purposes. This led to mismanagement and malpractices in the appointment of staff to these institutions.

Transactions involving huge amount by the Devaswom Board often tend to corruption and misappropriation. Such an irregularity was reported by Local Fund Audit in their report in 1967-68 periods in the purchase of elephants for temples under the TDB. When the KHC held it as malafide, the government appointed K. Sankaran, former Chief Justice of Kerala High Court in 1969 to inquire into the allegations, but under the pressure of the TDB, government abolished the Commission before they completed their inquiry (GoK, 1974: 65). In 1992, another allegation happened when a huge amount was transacted as bribe for the appointments of various posts in the TDB. The nomination of a person facing vigilance inquiry as a member of the TDB in 1993 was another case which questioned the credibility of Devaswom Board. Financial irregularities were noticed several times as in the purchase of jaggery in 1995 and Devaswom appointments, construction works, auction of commercial complexes, transfer of employees in 1996.

The Devaswom Minister in the 12th Legislative Assembly, 2007 revealed that fifty Vigilance enquiries and thousands of department level enquiries were conducted on allegations of corruption in Devaswom Boards. Even the selection of the much-coveted post of the chief priest of Sabarimala is not free from allegations of corruption. An allegation of corruption for demanding fifty lakhs as bribe against the Board authorities in the appointment of the Chief Priest was raised in the KLA (KLA, 2007, July 4: 263). In the same year, the Devaswom Department disclosed that 1050 complaints received regarding the allegations of financial misappropriations, corruption and irregularities prevailed in all Devaswom Boards. These allegations were not only against employees of the Devaswom but also its Members. In 2008, the government ordered a Vigilance enquiry on the basis of a letter from Devaswom Minister into the allegations and it was handed over to the Devaswom Ombudsman. An allegation of corruption and nepotism against the President and a Member of the TDB for obtaining job for their close relatives and nine others in the Lord Krishna Bank and Union Bank by depositing crores of Devaswom fund in these banks. A writ petition was filed in the High Court against them (KHC, 2007: 30-31).

In 2007, the then LDF Government as a measure to prevent corruption in the temple administration made an amendment in the Devaswom Act by which reduced the term of the Board to two years, entrusted the KPSC with the appointments in Devaswom Service, provision for appointing enquiry commission when allegations of corruption and misappropriation are noticed in the administration (KLA, 2009, September 26: 115-16). These measures may not be fruitful unless the Board should be constituted with persons of high integrity and avoid nomination merely on political lines. Moreover, providing full autonomy to the Board is seemed as the only remedy to tide over the situations rather than governmental interference.

In the beginning, there was no systematic mechanism for recruitment of staff in temples and other institutions of Devaswom Boards. Vacancies were neither notified nor conducted any screening procedures and were filled through interviews and hence there were chances for malpractice and corruption in all postings. Corruption is still prevalent in the appointment of teachers and non-teaching staffs in the educational institutions of the Board. In order to curb these unhealthy practices, the LDF government in 2007 decided in principle to hand over the appointments of Devaswoms to Kerala PSC. This decision created controversies, various Hindu organisations including the NSS strongly condemned the move. When the next UDF government came to power, Devaswom Recruitment Board was constituted for ensuring a fair mechanism to select candidates to Devaswom services as per the provisions of Kerala Devaswom Recruitment Board Act 2015.

A feeling that Devaswom Boards are immersed in corruption is strong among the public. Lack of accountability to the thousands of devotees from the part of the Board and bureaucracy is a major flaw in the prevailing administrative system of temples. It is a matter of surprise that even if the KHC is closely monitoring the auditing and accounting system, corruption is still prevailing. This attitude is reflected in the field study conducted.

Corruption, mismanagement and misappropriation of fund are rampant in Devaswom administration. People from different walks of life have the notion that Devaswom Boards are fully corrupted. Frequently, there are having reports in the print and visual media regarding allegations of corruption in the Devaswom governing bodies. Corruption is alleged against the officials from the top to bottom of the administrative machinery of Devaswoms including the President and Members to the low-level employees. At times, Commissions are appointed to enquire into these allegations. Corruption is reported in various audit reports regarding recruitment, selection of *ad-hoc* employees, financial transactions, purchase, accounting of hundi collections, tampering of records, presenting bogus vouchers etc. The accused in these cases are usually protected by their political and trade union influences.The High Court of Kerala itself appointed three enquiry commissions to study the gravity of corruption and corrupt practices prevailed in various Devaswom Committees; one for the TDB, another one for both TDB and CDB and the third one for the Guruvayur Devaswom and their reports pointed out the existence of serious irregularities in temple administration.

Misappropriations of Funds

Effective utilisation of fund is a pre-requisite for the success of an organisation. Misappropriation and mismanagement of fund have been reported several times in the administration of Devaswom Boards. Instances of misappropriation of fund are levelled against both the members of Devaswom Boards and the employees. In order to enquire into the financial negligence and inefficiency of the TDB and CDB, the government appointed Krishnamoorthy Commission and Bhaskaran Nair Commission respectively for the above Devaswom Boards during 1973-74. Again, the High Court of Kerala appointed the High-Power Commission a couple of times, one in 1990 and the other in 2006 to probe into the financial misappropriations in the Boards.

The Travancore Cochin Integration Committee Report (Butch Committee), 1949 suggested that the Devaswom funds should be utilised for the benefit of the general public instead of spending on unnecessary things and non-essential religious ceremonies (GoK, 1949: 35). But, ignoring the above suggestion, the Board was going on with huge unnecessary expenses. The Travancore Cochin Hindu Religious Institutions Act, however, does not allow diversion of Devaswom funds for public purposes. The Act mentions that funds of the Boards should be utilised only for the upkeep and maintenance of Hindu religious institutions. At the same time, there are instances when the government transferred funds to its coffers to tide over financial difficulties. In 2014, *The Hindu* daily reported that the State Government made a move for transferring crores of rupees of the Travancore Devaswom Board to the treasury to salvage the government from financial crisis (2014, March 3).

Misappropriation of Devaswom fund is one of the major causes of the financial difficulties in temple administration. In order to check mismanagement of funds in Devaswom Boards, strict auditing is conducted at regular intervals. Illegal and irregular utilisation of funds violating Devaswom Acts and Rules have been reported by the Audit Department and submitted to the KHC. Several instances of misappropriation of Devaswom fund have been noticed in the audit reports of Devaswoms. In the audit report of TDB (1993- 94), certain financial irregularities have been pointed out like the deposit of surplus fund of the

TDB in *Can. Fin. Homes* shares in the stock market contrary to the provisions of the Act. During the audit of 1997- 98, it was found that a Sub Group Officer under TDB misappropriated Rs 1.31 lakhs received from auctions and devotees' offerings without issuing proper receipts (The Hindu, 2000, August 4). The High Court in June 1989 came down hard on the Cochin Devaswom Board for its failure to take strict actions when financial irregularities involving lakhs of rupees came to its notice. The President and members of the TDB were summoned by the High Court when its queries regarding the audit report concerned were not properly answered. The Court admonished the Presidents of the two Devaswom Boards for their incapacity to control the staff and made caustic remarks for not complying with the instructions of the High Court regarding Board administration (Nair, 1994: 226).

In 1997, Devaswom Finance and Accounts Officer in his Audit Report on Thiruvananthapuram Group Office found out series of irregularities like large scale misappropriation of Devaswom fund. Serious irregularities such as tampering of office records and bank passbooks, forgery of chalans, financial irregularities and irregular payment were noticed. Irregularities are also noticed in the financial transactions of Temple Advisory Committees attached to various temples under the TDB.

Serious financial manipulations were found in the accounts of Thiruvananthapuram Group office of the TDB in the 1992-96 period. An amount of Rs 10 lakhs were stolen by the officers from the PF, DA, Loan Recovery accounts by forging documents. Irregularities in the auction of shops, maramath works, bank deposits and other allegations of the mismanagement and misappropriation of funds are noticed in the Devaswom administration by the Local Fund Audit Department many a times. The officers who were found guilty of corruption remain in service due to political and other compulsions. The Board's ground for retaining these corrupt officials seems illogical; in many cases Devaswom Boards retained the employees who were involved in financial misappropriation cases merely because they refunded the loot. These actions are often criticised by KHC directing that the Board should not allow delinquent persons to continue in service merely because they are ready to return the stolen things. Consequently, in 2015 the Board issued an order stating that financial misappropriation cases should not be dropped on the basis of departmental action and recovery of loss and directed that criminal prosecution proceedings should be initiated against them (The Hindu, 2017, April 13).

Several irregularities are noticed in Sabarimala temple during the two-month long festival season. In order to avoid misappropriation and leakages of revenue at Sabarimala, counting and accounting of currency notes and sale of *prasadams* are closely monitored by Vigilance personnel. There are several instances of smuggling of currency and gold by counting staff on contract basis in collusion with the guards on duty. There are complaints about looting food items and black-marketing of *prasadams* (The Hindu, 2008, October 6). There is considerable leakage of revenue at various temples under Devaswom Board. There are many reported cases of receipt of costly offerings from devotees by temple staff without issuing proper receipts, misappropriation during accounting of hundi (cash collection box) collections etc.

The decision of the TDB to invest 150 crores in the Dhanalaxmi Bank's debenture bond from the Provident Fund of employees has become a controversial issue in 2019. For that purpose, the TDB prematurely closed 58 fixed deposits having a maturity value of Rs 152.18 crores. The Audit Department pointed out a serious case of misappropriation of fund that the investment was done without conducting a proper study on the risk factors. The Board has not ventured to explore any other alternative options than depositing in government treasuries that can earn more than 8% annual interest and are safer than the unsecured debentures of private banks

(The New Indian Express, 2019, April 27). When the case of investment in the debentures of Dhanalakshmi Bank came before the High Court, the TDB filed an interesting statement of fact that it was none other than Lord Ayyappa who advised them to go for the debentures as he saw in advance the impending financial crisis due to natural calamities and agitation over the entry of women in the temple. The TDB claimed that the investment was beneficial for the Board.

The existing TCHRI Act has no provisions to prevent the Boards from exercising powers arbitrarily or misuse their powers. But the Act empowers the High Court to surcharge the Board members for loss of Devaswom fund pointed out by the auditors. But this provision is quite ineffective as the members of the Board may not be even alive when the audit objections are finally disposed of (GoK, 1964: 57). The High-Power Commission recommended to complete the departmental enquiries in a time bound manner and the guilty to be punished.

The officers who were found guilty of corruption remain in service due to political and other compulsions. The Kerala High Court directed the Board that delinquent persons should not be allowed to continue in service merely because they are ready to return the stolen things. The Board in 2015 issued an order stating that financial misappropriation cases should not be dropped on the basis of departmental action and recovery of loss and criminal prosecution proceedings should be initiated against the culprits.

Certain financial irregularities have been pointed out in the audit report of TDB (1993-94) like the deposit of surplus fund of the TDB in the stock market contrary to the provisions of the Act. Financial misappropriations from the part of Devaswom employees including theft, forging documents, irregularities in the auction of shops, construction works, bank deposits and other allegations of the mismanagement and misappropriation of funds were detected. Besides these, there is a notion that huge administrative expenses are incurred due to the existence of five Devaswom governing bodies that involves huge financial liability on the temple fund. In 1973, Kerala Government appointed C. R. Krishnamoorthy Commission to study about financial irregularities in the TDB. The Commission in its Report commented that the Board is not working strictly in accordance with statutory provisions and there is no need for such a Board and even suggested reverting to the system prior to the setting up of the Board. All the above cases of corruption and financial mismanagement affected the credibility of Devaswom administration seriously.

Shortage of Finance

Financial indiscipline is one of the major drawbacks of Devaswom administration in the state. Majority of temples are not self-reliant. Each Devaswom Board has certain pockets of temples which constitute their source of income. Another source of income is the grant from government which is too meagre to satisfy their financial needs. The Boards spend huge amount for meeting establishment charges every year which is steadily rising due to the hike in the pay and allowances of employees. Misappropriation of funds, leakage of income, entertainment of non-remunerative schemes and the paucity of government grants etc., are the major causes of financial problems faced by the temple administration. The idea of the autonomy of the Devaswom Board is illusory unless it is accompanied by financial independence. These sources of income of the TDB are more or less inelastic. The working capital of the Board is the statutory annuity. One of the major sources of income of the Devaswom is the voluntary contributions from the Hindu public. Apart from these sources, the Board collects money by conducting special religious programmes in important temples.

In order to cut short the financial burden of Travancore Devaswom Board, Kainikkara Padmanabha Pillai Commission recommended the retrenchment of unnecessary posts in Devaswoms. There are allegations against the TDB that several new posts are unnecessarily created and existing ones are upgraded yielding to the pressure from the service unions. But the audit report of 1967-68 pointed out that some of the retrenched posts were subsequently restored on administrative grounds (GoK, 1974: 85-86). The TDB's revenue has recorded a steady increase due to escalation in the number of worshippers and their contributions and offerings especially in Sabarimala and in other popular temples under the Board. Even though there is an increase in the receipts, the Board finds it difficult to wade through because of unbridled expenditure on account of periodical revision of DA, pension, pay revision and implementation of new projects (TDB, 1996:1). Conditions of the CDB are also similar to that of the TDB. The annual revenue collection of various TDB temples, excluding Sabarimala in 2013 was Rs 75 crores while the Board had to spend an amount of 125 crore on employees' pension and for the day-to-day affairs of various temples (The Hindu, 2013, December 3). Serious laxity on the part of various government departments has been seen for non-repaying of fuel charges to the TDB. Media reported that various government departments are yet to pay up lakhs of rupees to TDB's petrol pumps at Pamba and Nilakkal. The Board has one lakh sale per day from these petrol pumps.

Devaswom authorities repeatedly clarified that the funds of the temples are utilised only for the purposes of the temples, including maintenance, repairs, and establishment charges and for temple rituals. The government have no authority to transfer temple funds for government functions as alleged by some Hindu outfits in the state. This propaganda badly affected the income of Board temples that may endanger even the existence of temples and their employees. With the women entry issue in Sabarimala, the situation became worse as reported by the Mathrubhumi daily that after September 28, 2018, the income from Sabarimala has been considerably declined.

The first four days' income of the temple after the verdict indicates this.

Table 3.1: First four days' income of Sabarimala after the SC verdict on women entry

Day	2017 (Rs)	2018 (Rs)	Fall (Rs)
Day 1	8.42 lakhs	4.83 lakhs	3.59 lakhs
Day 2	45.59 lakhs	19.30 lakhs	26.28 lakhs
Day 3	32.30 lakhs	17.51 lakhs	14.79 lakhs
Day 4	**36.58 lakhs**	**36.74 lakhs**	**15,800(excess)**

Source: Mathrubhumi English Edition 22nd October, 2018, retrieved from https://english. mathrubhumi.com

The income registered an all-time low position that has fallen by around 40 percent. In order to overcome the crisis, the government sanctioned a financial assistance of Rs 100 crores to the TDB in the State Budget of 2019, but the amount has not been completely released even before the next pilgrim season. The Supreme Court verdict on Sabarimala women entry and the decision of the Board not to file a review petition against the Court verdict resulted in the launching of a 'no-donation campaign' by various Hindu outfits. The campaign adversely affected the income of the temples under the Devaswom Board.

Inadequacy of Annuity

The temples in the state are functioning on the income from various sources including the government contribution (Annuity). Annuity to temples is an obligation on the part of the government as compensation for the properties taken over. The annuity provides by the government to various Devaswoms in the state prove inadequate. Annuity to TDB is an obligation of the government as a part of tripartite agreement among the rulers of Travancore and Cochin with the Union government. Temples of Cochin and Malabar receive annuity as compensation due to Kerala Land Reforms Act 1969.

In the case of Malabar, annuity provided to the temples is inadequate. The temples once possessed lakhs of acres of land including the forest land which may fetch crores as annual income. Due to the progressive land reforms, acres of land were lost to these temples, thus their income also. The Kerala Land Reforms Act provides for payment of the annuity as compensation. The annuity is not a concession, as considers by many, but only payment of the value of the commodities to which the Devaswoms are entitled. As the KHC observes, when the properties had already vested in the government, it only stands to reason that the Devaswoms should be paid the value of those commodities at the prevailing market rate. In other words, the annuity fixed by the government has to be periodically revised (In Re: Temples, 1994). Huge amount was pending in arrears to temples has been reported by the Revenue Minister; Koodalmanickam temple alone was to be paid 160 lakhs arrear up to 1999 (KLA, 1999, April 13: 77). The government in principle recognised the demand for revision by assuring 25% increase in every five years (KLA, 2001, March 7: 109-110).

But the conditions of temples of Travancore are different from that of Malabar and Cochin. The TDB receives an annuity of Rs 46.5 lakhs as per Article290A of the Constitution of India. The TDB persistently demanded for the enhancement of annuity in proportion to the rise in the price of commodities. In a case in the High Court of Kerala in 1973, Justice P. Subramaniam Potti observed that it was the obligation of the government to revise the annuity in a rational manner (GoK, 1984: 136). Former Chief Minister C. Achutha Menon stated that the secular government had no obligation to pay the grant to the institutions of a particular religion. Sankaran Nair Commission criticised the statement of the Chief Minister and stated that the grant was not a concession of the government, but a moral and legal responsibility of the government (GoK,1984, 134-35). In 1991, the TDB filed a petition in the High Court of Kerala praying for enhancement of annuity to the Board. In the petition, the Board did not mention how much enhancement the Board expected. After a long 55 years, in 2003-04, the government enhanced the grant to one crore as statutory contribution to the TDB. From this amount, 20 lakhs were for Sree Padmanabhaswamy Temple (KLA, 2004, July 21: 88-89).

Encroachment of Temple Land

Preservation of temple land from illegal encroachment has become a major task for Devaswom authorities in the state. It is estimated that considerable portions of landed properties of temples were encroached by private individuals including non-Hindus. The unassessed landed properties of the TDB are included in the Land Conservancy Act as guaranteed in Section 27 and 50 of the TCHRI Act 1950. But the landed properties of the CDB, though it also come under the purview of the TCHRI Act could not acquire this safeguard. In Malabar, thousands of acres of temple lands were alienated. The Agrarian Relations Act of 1960 deprived the Devaswoms of the right to resume the land given on lease and at the same time gave all facilities to the tenants to get the agreed *pattom* reduced through land tribunals gave a place to the ordinance in 1962. Kerala Tenants and *Kudikidappukars* Protection Act 1963 has given certain concessions to the tenants in the matter of paying up arrears. Subsequently, Devaswoms took a policy not to give their lands on lease but to arrange for the yield being taken departmentally.

In the 1960s, Kerala politics witnessed massive tenants' agitation in Malabar backed by the Christian Church and Communist Parties against eviction by the Devaswom authorities. 30,000 acres of private forest owned by Kottiyoor temple became illegally occupied by the migrant settlers (Chander, 1981: 120). Temple authorities decided to execute a super lease to Nair Service Society for a long 99 years by evicting the unauthorised occupants. Thus, started agitation by the evictees with the support of the Church and the Communists;

two opposing forces in the state brought together for a common goal (Nair, 1994: 130). An enquiry commission constituted by the Kerala Pradesh Congress Committee (KPCC) also recommended the inclusion of temple land under the purview of Agrarian Relations Act and to protect the interest of Devaswom tenants (KLA, 1962, March 14: 841). Meanwhile, the NSS obtained a favourable verdict from the Court, but finally decided to hand over the occupied land of Devaswom to the government (Sethunathan, 2015: 55).

Another incident of illegal encroachment of temple land was reported in 1966 at Lava Kusha temple, in the Pulpally village of Waynad district. The Devaswom authorities planned to evict the illegal occupants of temple land through special squads appointed for the purpose. But this move was resisted by the tenants with the support of the Christian Church and *Malanadu Karshaka Sangham;* the Communist Party provided support to them on human rights grounds. Subsequently, a massive eviction drive was started, but the temple authorities had to stop the eviction process as per the Government Ordinance. Thereafter, property rights were conferred on the occupants of the land as per the Kerala Land Reform Act of 1969. Accordingly, in 1975, 4837 occupants were assigned ownership titles by the competent authority. Nearly 59.29% of the beneficiaries were Christians, 36.80% were non-Tribal Hindus, 3.16% were Tribals and 0.75% were Muslims (Nambiar, 2005: 125). In *Temples of Wayanad District*, Jayashanker mentioned that prior to the Land Reforms Act the temple owned 14,999 acres of land, but that has been reduced to mere 15 acres (2002: 79). Such instances of massive land alienation can be seen while passing through the pages of history of Malabar temples.

Government of Kerala launched drastic moves to regain the encroached temple lands under various Devaswoms. Consequently, a Special Officer was appointed in 2000 to study and report all aspects relating to temple land encroachment in Malabar. Similarly, in 2007 various officers were appointed; a

Land Special Officer for the TDB, the District Collector of Thrissur for Guruvayur, Special Tahsildar under the Kerala Land Conservancy Act for the CDB and a Tahsildar and a Surveyor for Koodalmanickam Devaswom (KLA, 2010, July 28: 231-32). As per the report of *The Hindu* daily in 2010, more than 24,900 acres of land belonging to 353 temples under the Malabar Devaswom and more than 500 acres of land of 525 temples of the TDB had been occupied by various private parties. Guruvayur and Koodalmanickam Devaswoms also had lost 2.50 acres and 1 acre respectively. The extent of land lost to the temples under the CDB has not fully estimated (The Hindu, 2010, April 5). The move of the government resulted in the reclaiming of 6.12 acres of encroached land belonging to the TDB, 1.05 acres to Guruvayur, 3.35 acres to Malabar, 2 hectares to the CDB and 45 cents belonging to Koodalmanickam Devaswoms. Compared to the land alienated, the extent of regained land is meagre; but the initiative from the part of the government in this direction is a positive sign. In 2011, the then Devaswom minister stated in the Legislative Assembly that the government intended to form a land conservancy unit in the MDB to find out land encroachment of temples under their control (KLA, 2011, June 29: 230), but this has not been implemented so far.

In 2012, the KHC criticised the Revenue officials who committed malpractices in the records of Vadayambadi Palace temple land under the CDB. The temple once possessed 200 acres of land, now has only eight acres as per the report of the Land Revenue Commissioner. The KHC sarcastically remarked whether Parasurama would come to regain the temple land (Mathrubhumi, 2012, October 19). The route of *Thiruvabharanam* procession to Sabarimala between Pandalam and Perunad has been encroached by private individual that are testified by the revenue records. But due to political interference, the eviction process was delayed which was condemned by the Hindu organisations.

The government occasionally issued orders for the recovery of alienated temple lands, but none of them properly executed and led to several litigations. An interesting fact is that many of the temple trustees have no idea of the extent of their land. The alienation of land is ranging from a few cents to hundreds of acres. Many of the encroachers secured title deeds illicitly in connivance with the officials of Revenue Department (The Hindu, 2015, December 10). The gravity of encroachment of temple land, particularly in Malabar is very alarming. Both the temple authorities and the Revenue officials are responsible for such a massive intrusion to the Devaswom land. This laxity has led the impoverishment of Hindu religious institutions in Malabar which is actually deplorable. In contrast to this, the land belonged to the Hindu religious institutions in our neighbouring state of Tamil Nadu that was being cultivated by tenants, has been recovered through proper governmental action during the implementation of the Land Reclamation Development Programme. The recovered land was given back to the respective temples. Both the Government and Devaswom Boards are to a certain extent responsible for the alienation of temple properties. Setting up of a Land Tribunal as suggested by the Kerala High Court is the only panacea to deal with encroachments of temple land. Accordingly, the government decided to form a Devaswom Tribunal in 2016 and drafted a Bill to protect temple properties; but the Bill is not realised so far and remains in papers.

Challenges to the Welfare of Devaswom Employees

In the past, Devaswom employees faced a lot of issues such as low salary, poor service conditions and severe disciplinary actions. Often they had to work without proper salary. Promotions and other privileges were granted only to sycophants. Corruption and nepotism were rampant in Devaswom administration. The plight of Devaswom employees was addressed several times in the Assembly and the Court.

There were not any norms in the state to regulate the service conditions of temple employees. This resulted in illegal transfers and postings in the Devaswom Boards. Those employees who did not grease the palms of higher officials were indiscriminately transferred. The long cherished demand of temple employees under TDB was realised in 1989 by the constitution of a welfare fund for them.

The absence of a unified Devaswom law remains as the prime factor for remedying the ills existing in Devaswom employees' service conditions. Problems of temple employees in the state are not uniform as they are categorised variedly. Contingent staff is doing the same work, known by different names in different temples and even in the same temple. More than eighty designations are there for the contingent employees who form 80 percentages of the total Devaswom staff. While the temple employees of Travancore, Cochin, Guruvayur, and Koodalmanickam Devaswoms are paid salary at par with the state government employees, those under the MDB are still paid a meagre salary and there exist wage disparities. Though temple employees in the erstwhile Travancore and Cochin areas receive reasonable remuneration, those in Malabar area are getting only a pittance. In 1991, *The Hindu* daily published a news captioned "*A raw deal for temple staff*" highlighting the pitiable conditions of temple employees in Malabar. About 9000 employees altogether were working in temples under Malabar area and their salary was in commensurate with the income of respective temples they were working. Around 5% temples in Malabar were self-reliant at that time and the rest were fighting for their existence; the living conditions of the employees were even pathetic. The High Court interfered and issued directions in 1994 to form a Devaswom Board for Malabar temples and to revise emoluments of temple employees.

The formation of the MDB in 2008 has been hailed by the temple employees in Malabar as the second freedom declaration. The Board initiated radical changes in the pay structure and welfare schemes for the employees. In 2008, the Board decided to restructure the salary and service conditions of the employees including priests and appointed committee under the chairmanship of the Board President. Within one year of the formation of the MDB, the salary of the employees had been revised.

Temple employees under the TDB are dissatisfied over the government policy of intervening in the women entry issue in Sabarimala by violating temple customs. This paved the way for considerable reduction of income from Sabarimala and other temples under the TDB. Rs 100 crores offered by the government as a compensatory measure to the TDB in the 2019 budget has not been released so far (Personal Interview, 2019 d). The TDB's approach to temple employees are not cordial as many complaints are raised against the body checking practice prevailed in Sabarimala. The State Human Rights Commission issued directions to the TDB to end this barbarian approach. Allegation of transfer of employees as part of political retaliation is also prevalent in TDB (Personal Interview, 2019 d). Though several changes were effected in the service rules of temple employees since 1972, absence of a consolidated set of rules was a cause of concern to the Board. The Board has around 3,500 temple employees including the posts of priests, *kazhakam*, *thali*, watcher etc. and nearly 3,000 establishment employees of the TDB enjoy service benefits on a par with the government employees. The temple employees do not have the option to avail of half-pay leave.

The *karanma* employees (hereditary employees) who played a crucial role in the day-to-day administration of temples earlier, have to face serious service issues today like denial of the right to take leave without providing substitutes whose wages are to be paid by the employee himself. On the other hand, the rest of the employees are enjoying leave facilities provided that the wage of the substitutes is to be met by the Board itself. They are also lacking pensionary benefits. They approached the TDB with a request to revise their pay scales as the other employees, the Board refused their claim and so they approached the High Court. During the pendency of these petitions, the Travancore Devaswom Board had issued pay revision order and accordingly sanctioned DA/HRA and other benefits to *Karanma* employees.

Administrative Issues

Lack of Unified Devaswom Laws

One of the most important hurdles in the way of the smooth functioning of the Devaswom administration in Kerala is the absence of unified Devaswom governance. The effective coordination of the administration helps to attain uniformity in rituals and service conditions of temple employees, prevention of land alienation, fraudulence in the financial administration etc. It becomes a usual practice to appoint Commissions when any such issues arise, but not implementing their suggestions. Kuttikrishna Menon and K. P. Sankaran Nair Commissions have recommended a unified Devaswom administrative system, but no steps have been taken in this regard so far. Such a system is prevailing in the neighbouring state of Tamil Nadu and the administration of temples there is carried out by the HRCE Department of the State Government. But in Kerala temples are under various Devaswom governing bodies like Devaswom Boards and Devaswom Managing Committees; each of them is governed as per particular Devaswom laws.

The demand for a common law for temples was persistent even from the 1960s, two Commissions were appointed in 1962 and 1983 and draft Bills were also prepared, but in vain. A High-Level Committee under the chairmanship of K. Kuttykrishna Menon, former Advocate General of Madras, to go into the question of unifying the laws relating to the administration of HRI and Endowments in the state was appointed and the Committee in its report recommended a uniform law applicable throughout the state by repealing the acts then in force. Creation of an apex body for the administration of all Hindu Religious Endowments in the state was the Commission's major recommendation (GoK, 1964: 105). In 1977, C. M. Sundaram, PSP leader urged the government to make a law for coordinating the administration of all minor temples in the state in the low-income group and provide adequate salary to temple employees (KLA, 1977, August 5: 3230). In 1979 and 1980, the then Devaswom Minister stated in the Assembly that a uniform law for temples was under the consideration of the government.

The government appointed another Commission in 1983 headed by K. P. Sankaran Nair, the Law Officer of the Travancore Devaswom Board which suggested for the unification of the laws and to formulate a scheme for proper management of temples. The reports of both Kuttikrishna Menon and Sankaran Nair Commissions are gathering dust in the archives of the Government Secretariat. In 1985, K. G. R. Kartha of NDP, a political outfit of the NSS, urged the government to appoint a Special Officer to study the proposals for a unified Devaswom law for temples by Kuttikrishna Menon Commission and Sankaran Nair Commission Reports (KLA, 1985, July 23: 18).

The High-Power Commission Report in 1990 stressed the need for a unified law for improving the management, upkeep and maintenance of Devaswoms. The Commission proposed for the formation of a nominated board with special provisions for a few major temples. The Commission also proposed the extension of the Malabar system throughout the state. The aim behind the argument for common management under a board or boards was that with the help of a common fund, small temples with low income could also be looked after and that there would be a common pattern of administration for all temples. But it was pointed out that, though the aim is praiseworthy, in practice the proposed system might lead to a bloated bureaucracy, corruption and inefficiency in the management of temples (KHC, 1990: 68).

In 1994, the KHC directed the State Government to consider the formation of a Devaswom Board for Malabar temples and a unified Devaswom Board for the whole state. Again in 1996, the Court reiterated the demand on the lines of the recommendations of Kuttikrishna Menon and Sankaran Nair Commissions. Thus, the government appointed V.V. Vijayan, former Commissioner of the TDB as a Commission for studying the possibilities for Devaswom unification by the State Government which also stressed the need for a uniform Devaswom Board for monitoring all Devaswoms in the state. The TDB, however, opposed the move for Devaswom codification.

For the first time in the history of Kerala in 1997, the government initiated a major step to consolidate Devaswom laws in the state. The Bill proposed the creation of an apex board to supervise and control the administration of the Devaswoms consisting of the Presidents of three Boards, four members nominated by Hindu Ministers of which one shall be a competent person to act as full-time Member Secretary of the Apex Board (KHRCIE Bill 1997, Section 3 (1)-(a), (b)). The Bill contained provisions to tighten the bureaucratic and political control over Hindu religious institutions in the state. It was noted that in the proposed Bill, Hindu MLAs were excluded from section process of the Members to the Apex Board and right was conferred on the Hindu Ministers. As the Bill contained some controversial clauses, it had to be put on the back burner following public protest. Unification of Devaswom law is a Herculean task owing to the heterogeneous administrative set up prevailing for the temples. Historical reasons are behind the diversified administration for the temples in the state. Like the administrative set up existing for the religious institutions in other South Indian states, Kerala Government also should take appropriate action to coordinate and unify Devaswom laws existing in the erstwhile three regions;

Travancore, Cochin and Malabar that will certainly help to solve the grave administrative issues prevailing.

Lack of Proper Representation to Dalits in Devaswom Boards

Temples act as an icon of promoting collective worship of all sections of Hindus. Even after eight decades of the Temple Entry Proclamation, some sections of Hindus are denied adequate representation in the temporal and spiritual matters of temples. Social ostracism is still in force towards *Dalits* and *Adivasis* which keep them aloof from the bureaucratic, administrative and spiritual affairs of temples. They got the right to freedom of worship only in the later period of the 20th century. In the Devaswom administrative services, they got only meagre representation. Demographically these people constitute nearly 11 % of the total population and 20 to 25% of the total Hindu population.

For a long time, demands are there from various quarters for proportionate representation of Dalit communities in Devaswom services in the state. Dalit communities were excluded from temple-related jobs, including priesthood due to the orthodoxy of the *savarna* people. With the establishment of *tantric* school (Tantra Vidya Peedom, Aluva) in the 1960s, the non-Brahmins including Dalits were provided opportunity to acquaint with priesthood. In 1976, E. M. S. Namboothirippad urged the government to remove all barriers in the posting of *Harijans* as temple priests (KLA, 1976, February 25: 694). Later Dalit leaders and organisations sought proportionate share in the appointment of temple-related jobs including priesthood. *Pattikajathi Kshema Samithi* (Scheduled Castes Welfare Committee), a Dalit movement submitted a petition to the government demanding implementation of reservation for backward communities in the Devaswom Boards in the state.

The TDB decided for the first time to implement reservation for backward communities in 2006, as their representation in the Devaswom service was nominal (TDB, 2006). But the decision was delayed for years as it was challenged by the NSS in the High Court. In the state level review meeting of National Commission for Scheduled Castes (NCSC) in 2014, the representatives of Dalit communities brought to the notice of the Commission that despite government control, reservation was not implemented in the five Devaswom governing bodies in the state. With the formation of Devaswom Recruitment Board in 2015, the long-awaited reservation for the backward communities became a reality; 8% seats are reserved for SCs and 2% are for the STs, out of a total of 32% reservation for the backward classes.The government decided again to enhance the reservation to SC and ST communities 2% in 2019 that will be implemented shortly.

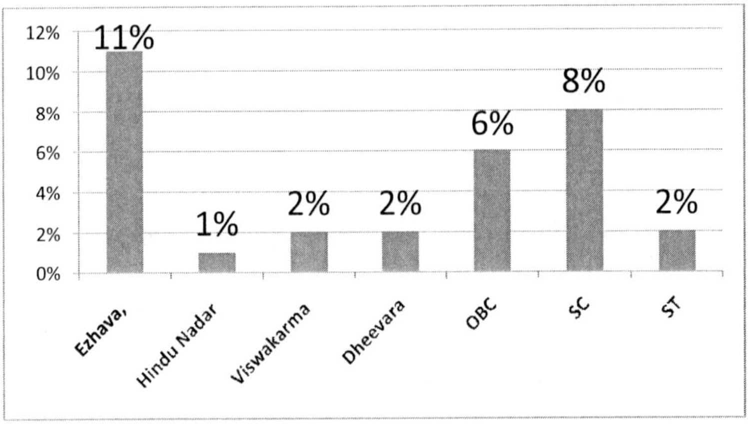

Source: Data collected from the website of Kerala Devaswom Recruitment Board.

Fig 3.1: Reservation for backward Hindus in various Devaswoms as per the norms of Devaswom Recruitment Board (2018).

The Dalits and Adivasis were given reservation in the governing bodies of Travancore and Cochin Devaswom Boards from 2007 after the amendment of TCHRI Act, though representation of these communities were there in the Board before. Guruvayur, Koodalmanickam and Malabar Devaswom governing bodies already possessed Dalit reservation from their inception. Representation of these communities is also ensured in the Temple Advisory Committees and Area Committees in the MDB. The demand of the Dalits for getting appointment in priestly duties is also a significant one like their representation in Devaswom governing bodies as well as in the administrative services. In 1995, the High Court and in 2002 the Supreme Court in their historic verdicts pointed out the necessity of appointing non-Brahmins including Dalits to become priests in temples. Years after the verdicts, 36 non-Brahmins including 6 Dalits were appointed by the TDB in 2017 during the observance of the 81st anniversary of the historic Temple Entry Proclamation. It was definitely a revolutionary step taken after 130 years of Aruvippurm Siva deity consecration.

Nomination of Non-Believers in Temple Administration

Who is a Believer?

Belief is a subjective and psychological idea that indicates the attitude of a person and so it is purely personal. While analyzing the administrative aspects of temples, belief in God and temple worship become yardsticks for the selection of members to various temple governing bodies. However, the idea of *belief* in God turn into a contentious issue here as it is difficult to define and differentiate a believer from a non-believer. While examining the procedure for selecting members to Devaswom Governing bodies, a pertinent question arises regarding the concept of *Hindu*. Only Hindu MLAs and Ministers are eligible for participating in the election to Devaswom governing bodies irrespective of their belief. However, the High Court of Kerala in 2005 held that the members of the Devaswom Boards should be believers in God and temple worship (Nair, 2005).

Shashi Tharoor in his book *Why I am a Hindu* stated in a different way that there are simply no binding requirements to be a Hindu, not even a belief in God (2018: 4). Earlier in 1950, Pattom Thanu Pillai questioned the rationality of atheist Hindu MLAs participating in the election of Devaswom Board Members in the Travancore Cochin Legislative Assembly (1950, April 5: 1548). In the same session, another member A. K. Pachu Pillai suggested an amendment of inserting the provisions that the qualification of a Member in Devaswom Board should be a believer in temple worship. But T. K. Narayana Pillai, the then Chief Minister rejected the amendment stating that it would divide the Hindu community into two sections - believers and non-believers (1950, April 12: 1645-46).

An interesting thing is that there is no reference regarding belief rather than being a Hindu in the principal Devaswom Act, the Travancore- Cochin Hindu Religious Institution Act 1950 (TCHRI Act) and in course of time the clause for *belief* has been incorporated. The Guruvayur Devaswom Act 1978 stipulates that the members nominated to the Devaswom Committee by the Hindu ministers should have interests in the temple and belief is not specifically mentioned. But the Koodalmanickam Devaswom Act, 2005 defines Hindu as a person who is a believer in God and temple worship. In the Madras Hindu Religious and Charitable Endowment Act (MHRCE Act) concerning the administration of Malabar temples also stipulates belief in temple worship as necessary qualification for nomination.

A sizable section of Hindu believers holds that Devaswom Boards should be ruled by true believers. The first inquiry Commission for studying Devaswom reforms in Kerala, the Kuttikrishna Menon Committee (1964) in its report suggested belief in temple worship as an indispensable qualification for becoming members of Devaswoms. Ever since in the history of Devaswom administration in the state, the term *belief* was firstly incorporated in the TCHRI Act in 1984 by the then Chief Minister, K. Karunakaran who was an ardent devotee of Lord Guruvayoorappan.

Certain curious customs as part of belief are existed in temple worship from ancient times. Some sections of people were excluded from temple worship earlier in connection with purity and pollution and due to the superstitious belief that the presence of these people would affect the spirituality of the temple as well as the sanctity or *chaithanya* of the deity installed in the temple. Even the Courts in Travancore considered the entry of *avarnas* in temples as defilement owing to the desecration of temple customs. In a case related to the entry of some Ezhava people in Kadakkavur temple in Chirayinkeezhu Taluk, Thiruvananthapuram District, the Court held that their entry was punishable as it constituted defilement of the temple (GoK, 1934: 35). It should be remembered that these are pre-constitutional developments in India. From the introduction of the Constitution, precedence is given to constitutional values rather than customs and traditions. The Supreme Court verdict of 2018 regarding women entry in Sabarimala is an instance for this fact. The ban on the entry of young women in the age group of 10 to 50 at Sabarimala is based on the belief that the deity is a perennial celibate and the conflict between belief and constitutional rights of citizens has resulted in agitations which had its imprints on the socio-political scenario of the state.

The concept of *believer* is a disputable and immeasurable one in the general framework of Hinduism. Webster's New World College Dictionary defines a believer as a dedicated follower or disciple, especially a person whose devotion to another, a cause etc. is blind or unquestioning. While the organised religions, Christianity and Islam stipulate certain pre-requisites for a believer, Hinduism does not instruct such qualities; belief in God and temple worship is not a pre-requisite as Hinduism accommodates even atheist schools of thought also to its fold. The admirers of *Charvaka* philosophy who did not believe in God were also included in Hinduism (Tharoor, 2018: 9). In an ecclesiastical perspective a true believer is a person who strictly adheres to religious doctrine. With regard to temple affairs a general perspective is that belief in God and temple worship are pertinent qualities of a true believer.

Atheism is a challenge to the concept of belief as it discards the existence of God. Atheism is the negation of theism. The prefix 'a' means without, so the term atheism means without theism. One who does not believe in the existence of a God or supernatural being is properly designated as an atheist (Smith, 1989: 7). Jayashanker in his *Temples of Kerala* stated that the political and socio-cultural movements of about four decades (1940-1980) particularly the Marxian ideology and the atheistic doctrines attracted a section of the people and it became a fashion of the day to refrain from worshipping in temples, then gradually happened a shift in the attitude of Marxian followers (1997:15). But the party insisted that the leaders should abstain from following religious beliefs and practices. Whenever they came to power there happened controversies regarding the nomination of non-believers to temple governing bodies. An established thing is that without the factor of belief it would seem impossible to make any approach to religion. Indeed, a religious person and a believer have become nearly synonymous terms (Prakash, 2006: 3).

Belief in God or temple worship has now not become qualifications for selecting a person to be a member in Devaswom Board; occasionally non-believers are also being appointed in the temple governing bodies. Inclusion of these people makes Board's administration largely a political affair. This practice has been questioned by many leaders from the inception of the Board itself. Doyens in Kerala politics like Pattom Thanu Pillai, Kalathil Velayudhan Nair etc., pointed out the discrepancies in the election of members to Devaswom Boards; the political background of the candidate alone become the eligibility to be a member. So, demands for barring members with political background from contesting election to the Board came to the fore. Whatever be the belief, a Hindu MLA can have the right to vote in the election to Devaswom governing bodies as the Kerala High Court pronounced in 1989, but the member to be considered should have faith in temple worship.

Controversies over Nomination

The nomination of non- believers in temple governing bodies is a controversial issue in state politics and no uniform opinion has evolved so far in this regard. Recommendations of various Commissions and landmark judgments of the judiciary reiterate the necessity of the appointment of true believers as Members in Devaswom administration. The political parties who have no faith in Hindu religion are also keen to nominate their nominees to various Devaswom governing bodies in Kerala. Voting rights of those who have no faith in God and temple worship is always a bone of contention. K. N. Gopalan, former President of Cochin Devaswom Board frankly admitted that he had no faith in Hindu religion and temples and stated that he was convinced that Hinduism was a decaying religion (GoK, 1964: 105). Kuttikrishna Menon Committee Report suggested that belief in temple worship should be the essential qualification to become the Members in Devaswom governing bodies as well as in the local Temple Advisory Committees (GoK, 1964: 110). In the sixth KLA, 1980 the Congress leader K. Karunakaran also demanded that temples should be entrusted with the believers. In 1989, Pandalam Palace Managing Committee Chairman, Rama Varma Raja observed that the temple administration should be entrusted with the believers and non-believers should not be permitted to meddle with temple affairs. In *Krishnan Vs. Guruvayur Devaswom* case, 1979, the KHC observed that the purpose of ensuring efficient and proper administration of the Devaswom would undoubtedly be better served by a compact Committee consisting of persons having faith in the deity and real interest in the affairs of the temple. Why those people who have no faith in temple worship crave for berths in Devaswom governing bodies is a relevant question raised from many corners (Personal Interview, 2018).

In 1984, the Congress Government for the first time made an amendment in Devaswom Acts through an Ordinance that only believers in God and temple worship should participate in the election to Devaswom Boards. A written declaration was also made compulsory for the Hindu MLAs in this regard. The leftist political ideology does not permit them to give such a declaration and hence they abstained from voting and thus the treasury benches could put their nominees in Devaswom Boards. The Ordinance was challenged by some Hindu members of the Legislative Assembly, but the Court rejected their petition. The government on the strength of the Ordinance reconstituted two Boards within a short period. The then Chief Minister K. Karunakaran remarked that the Bill was intended to entrust temple administration in the hands of believers in temple worship and God (KLA, 1986, November 27: 155).

In the year 1988-89, the then LDF government made two controversial moves, one to appoint a *Harijan* converted Christian to Guruvayur Devaswom Management Committee and the other to accommodate non-believers in Devaswom Boards through a notification. The notification was challenged in the KHC and the election process became quashed. In the judgment, the KHC observed that those who believe in God and temple worship should be nominated or could vote in the election for the Devaswom Boards (Muraleedharan Nair, 1990). Accordingly, in 1990, election to the TDB was set aside by the High Court. In order to overcome the verdict, the government amended the Devaswom Act (TCHRI Act) which redefined the term *Hindu*. According to the Act, Hindu means a person by birth or conversion into Hindu religion or one who professes the Hindu religion even if such a person does not believe in God and temple worship (GoK, 1991: 13). In 1993, the then UDF Government reinstated the voting rights of the believers in God and temple worship through an Ordinance in the TCHRI Act which was replaced by a Bill in 1994.

Again in 1998, through an Ordinance, the LDF Government enabled the non-believers to participate in the election to Devaswom Boards. The Ordinance was challenged in the High Court and the Court directed the State Government not to make any appointments to the vacancies of members to the TDB and CDB till the verdict of the Court. Again in 1999, an amendment in the Act was made which reinstated the voting rights of non-believers and insisted that the Members nominated to the Devaswom Boards should be Hindus who believed in God and temple worship. This amendment was challenged before the Court and the Court upheld the amended Bill and pronouncing that faith in God and temple worship are not essential for the Ministers, but, at the same time, the persons who are elected as Members of the Managing Committee should be a believer in God and temple worship. The Supreme Court upheld the verdict of the KHC in 2005. The management of the temple is primarily a secular affair; the state has the requisite jurisdiction to oversee the administration of a temple subject to Articles 25 and 26 of the Constitution of India. Differentiating matters relating to the worship of the deity and the management of the Devaswom, the Bench described as absurd in insisting that persons nominating the members to the managing committee should also believe in temple worship (M.P. Gopalakrishnan Nair, 2005).

Two veteran communist leaders E. K. Nayanar and M. V. Raghavan openly declared that they were not Hindus but firm communists (KLA, 1990, June 20: 127). But both of them took part in the Devaswom members' selection process. Leftist are generally non-believers, but they nominate their party men to various Devaswom governing bodies. Varkala Radhakrishnan, Speaker in the KLA in 1990, observed that MLAs are elected by both believers and non- believers. A left front MLA is elected by the voters by fully knowing that he is not a believer in God, but believers vote for him with the belief that he would protect the interests of the electorate (KLA, 1990, June 20:170).

In 2015, T. G. Mohandas, filed a writ petition before the High Court challenging Sections 4 (1) and 63 of the Travancore Cochin Religious Institutions Act, 1950 which allowed nomination of two Members each to the Travancore and Cochin Devaswom Boards by a Cabinet Sub Committee of Hindu Ministers and election of one Member each to the two Boards by Hindu MLAs. He sought to address the issue where devotees and those having deep-rooted faith have little importance or say in matters of temple administration. The petitioner sought a directive either to implement earlier Commissions' recommendations or to formulate a scheme for administering the temples with assured democratic participation of devotees (T. G. Mohandas, 2015). The concept of *belief* is personal and it is difficult to define a believer. In fact, the concept of *belief* is subjective and so immeasurable. From the viewpoint of a layman, a believer is one who is attached to religious dogmas, rites, rituals and temple oriented activities. The Communist ideology is generally against religious dogmas and so they are labelled as non-believers.

Development of Sabarimala Temple

Sabarimala temple is always a cynosure of the media as well as the public due to various reasons of socio-economic, political, ecological and spiritual importance. Besides corruption in administration, mismanagement, misappropriation of funds, lack of coordination among various governmental agencies in the temple, issues like problems in allotting forest land to the shrine, lack of infrastructure and proper sanitation, basic amenities to pilgrims, environmental issues etc., are also pertinent.

Table 3.2: Various Commission Reports on Sabarimala since the formation of TDB

Sl. No.	Committee Report	Appointing Authority	Chairman of the Committee	Published Year
1.	Enquiry Report of Sabarimala temple Arson Case	Government of Kerala	K. Kesava Menon	1957
2.	Report of the Committee on the Development of Sabarimala	Government of Kerala	Mahabala Rao. V	1985
3.	High Power Commission	High Court of Kerala	V. Ramachandran	1990
4.	Environmental Pollution Problems in Sabarimala	Legislative Committee on Environment	A.V. Thamarakshan	1998
5.	Commission of Inquiry on Sabarimala Stampede Tragedy	Government of Kerala	Justice T. Chandrashekhara Menon	1999
6.	Report of the Parliamentary Panel on Sabarimala	Lok Sabha	O. Rajagopal	1999
7.	Environmental Impact Assessment of Diversion of Forest Land at Sabarimala	KFRI	Dr. S. Sankar	2000
8.	The Precautions of Environment Problems in Sabarimala Pilgrimage	Legislative Committee on Environment (KLA)	George. J. Mathew	2002
9.	Human Problems and Ecology - Preliminary Report	Public Accounts Committee, Lok Sabha	Buta Singh	2004
10.	Sabarimala-Human Problems and Ecology	PAC, Lok Sabha	V. K. Malhotra	2005
11.	The Report of Sabarimala Pilgrimage and Development Programmes	Petition Committee, KLA	V. Surendran Pillai	2009
12.	Commission Report on Pullumedu Tragedy	Government of Kerala	Justice M. R. Hariharan	2011

A Study Report submitted by the Kerala Forest Research Institute (KFRI) in 2000. The SC verdict on 28th September, 2018 permitting the entry of women belonging to all age groups became sufficient to make the shrine a centre of attraction and the polity of the state calamitous. Sabarimala is one of the leading Devaswom Board temples in the state in terms of income and number of pilgrims. It is estimated that crores of pilgrims visit every year in Sabarimala during the two month long festive season. The influx of pilgrims creates environmental issues in the Periyar Tiger Reserve Area. Lack of basic amenities in the pilgrim centre is not solved fully, even though master plans are prepared and implemented by the TDB and the Government.There are at least a dozen reports on various administrative and environmental issues in Sabarimala temple revealed that the Devaswom Board should adopt a pilgrim-centred approach rather than a revenue-centred approach (KFRI, 2000). V. K. Malhotra Committee suggested for de-linking of Sabarimala temple area from the Periyar Wildlife Sanctuary and long-term development of the area in consonance with a Master Plan and the broader considerations of the ecology of the region (Malhotra, 2005: 42). The Committee stressed the need for setting up a statutory body for the administration of Sabarimala and a professional approach in the pilgrim management similar to that of the Vaishno Devi temple in the western Himalaya (Gaur, 2006: 69). The Report of the Environmental Committee of the Kerala Legislative Assembly suggested a master plan for Sabarimala to safeguard its serenity and sanctity. The Report also contained suggestions for providing basic amenities to the pilgrims without affecting the natural environment of the forest (KLA, 1998). The Committee however, noted that instead of constituting a high-level political body as suggested by them, only a coordination committee comprising of officials at the state level has been constituted by the Government of Kerala under the Chairmanship of the Chief Secretary, the President of the TDB and the representatives from different departments as members. Justice Chandrasekhara Menon Commission also recommended a statutory body for Sabarimala temple administration consisting of a representative of the State and Central Governments, Devaswom Board, Tantri, representative of the Pandalam royal family and three Hindus appointed by the Kerala High Court (KHC, 2000: 225-26). In 2008, for the purpose of introducing an effective administration for Sabarimala temple, the government authorised the then Additional Chief Secretary of Devaswom Department to draft an administrative system in the model of Tirumala Thirrupathy Devasthanam for Sabarimala temple. He visited the Tirumala temple and studied the system and submitted his report to the Government (KLA, 2008, June 26).

Sabarimala Development is possible only with the cooperation of various governmental agencies. Sankaran Nair Commission stressed the need for an integrated development programme to be implemented by the State Government with the cooperation of the TDB. The expenses of the programme should be included in the annual state budget (GoK,1984: 56). Dr Rajan Gurukkal, historian and former Member of the National Tiger Conservation Authority who has made several human-ecological studies and impact assessment of the developmental activities in respect of Sabarimala, has accused the TDB of considering Sabarimala only as a money-making site (Gurukkal, 2015).

Sankaran Nair Commission Report mentions about the irresponsible attitude of the TDB towards Sabarimala temple administration. The Commission suggested certain recommendations for the administration of Sabarimala temple. Major suggestions are the following (GoK,1984: 56):

(a) An interim administrative set up for Sabarimala temple is to be constituted. A Government Officer not below the rank of Additional Secretary should be appointed as Administrator on deputation basis. He should be a believer in temple and temple worship.

(b) An expert committee including Devaswom Board Members and representatives of various Government Departments should be constituted; representatives of *tantri* and Ayyappa Seva Sangham also should be included in it.

(c) A nine-member temple committee consisting of representatives of devotees, temple employees, *tantri* and Ayyappa Seva Sanghom shall be constituted for Sabarimala temple.

(d) Government should take necessary steps to provide adequate forest land to Sabarimala temple without any delay.

It can be surmised that separate administrative system as recommended by various Commissions for Sabarimala temple seems impracticable because the temples in Travancore depend on the income from Sabarimala for their survival. Effective co-ordination of various government departments under the aegis of the TDB is the only solution to the problems of the hill shrine. An eco-friendly and pilgrim friendly approach should be initiated from the part of Devaswom authorities and the Government for a durable solution to the development of the shrine.

Other Major Issues

Besides the various administrative issues relating to Devaswom governance stated above, certain issues are there affecting the stake holders' interests also reflected in the field study.

Alienation of Devotees from Temple Administration

Temple administration in Kerala is not a devotee centred one and allegations are there of ignoring the interests of the devotees. In a sense, they are alienated from the governance of temples and their role is only of the spectators and they are even ignorant about the administrative machinery of temples. As public institutions, Board temples are under the purview of Right to Information Act, but the devotees are not aware of these mechanisms. Actually the Board system bureaucratised temple administration in which devotees are treated only as their customers. Rate for offerings in temples are decided by the Board without considering the interests of devotees. Thus, a feeling is widespread among them that they are wholly estranged from temple administration.

A pilgrim friendly and devotee centred approach is a prerequisite for solving these issues. The visions of Sree Narayana Guru, Mannathu Padmanabhan and V. T. Bhattathirippad regarding the universalisation of temple worship can be accomplished only with the involvement of devotees in temple administration. The contributions of Temple Advisory Committees in ensuring devotees' participation in the affairs of temples are valuable, but their functioning is often not up to the level expected. Major Hindu organisations demand persistently for the disbanding of Devaswom Boards on the grounds of politicisation and corruption. T. G. Mohan Das and Dr Subrahmanyam Swamy, the Hindutva leaders approached the Supreme Court seeking abolition of politicized Devaswom Boards in the state; the case is still pending before the Court. Earlier the case was rejected by the Kerala High Court on the ground that the Court could not interfere in the issue.

The proverbial saying of 19th century British politician, Lord Acton that power tends to corrupt and absolute power corrupts absolutely is applicable in the case of Devaswom Boards in Kerala. Representatives of caste organisations and political parties who are appointed in Devaswom governing bodies often face allegations of corruption and mismanagement. In order to cope up with the situation, the government should explore an alternative model of administrative system by revamping Devaswom Boards, incorporating devotees' interests, free from politicisation as that of the other religious institutions in the state; then only the true spirit of secularism can be enjoyed by its citizens.

In short, administration of temples in Kerala encounters a lot of issues. Interference in the affairs of religious institutions by the state is an unusual practice in a secular structure. Corruption is rampant in the administration of temples even the KHC's intervention is there in financial matters. The issues concerned with the administration of temples in the state began from the very inception of Devaswom governing bodies. The state intervention in Devaswom administration, misutilisation of Devaswom fund, leakage of money, corruption, favouritism, politicisation, trade unionism among temple employees, lack of transparency in the recruitment process, wage disparities exist among temple employees in Malabar, shortage of annuity, lack of unified law for governance, encroachment of temple lands, pathetic conditions of temples etc. are the grave issues prevailed in the administration of temples. Complaints regarding alienation of devotees from temple administration, violation of religious freedom of Hindus etc. are also strong among the populace. When issues are raised, the governments appoint commissions and committees occasionally, but the laxity in implementing their suggestions invites criticisms from various corners as it involve both wastage of money and time. Even the major pilgrim centres like Sabarimala and Guruvayur temples are suffocated with unscientific development projects and lack of amenities to their pilgrims. The issues in consequence of the SC verdict lifting the ban on entry of women of all age group in the most reputed hill shrine at Sabarimala, the State Government measures to implement the Court verdict and thereby shattering the age- old customs prevailed at the temple resulted unprecedented protests from the believers that created repercussions in the state politics.

4

Women Entry in Sabarimala

Temple Entry

Women entry in Sabarimala temple and related controversies have created repercussions in state politics, especially after the Supreme Court verdict on September 28, 2018 allowing the womenfolk irrespective of their age considerations to enter into the temple. The issue created polarisation among the Hindu population that helped the Hindu organisations to amass great support and to stabilise their social base. Passing through the pages of history, it can be seen that once the social fabric of Kerala was filled with caste taboos that kept away the majority to enjoy even their Fundamental Rights. The downtrodden sections were forbidden from temple entry as part of Brahmanic hegemony, caste ostracism and pollution rules. Then the combined efforts of both *savarnas* and *avarnas* among the Hindu population made the stigma and discrimination ended through various temple entry enactments. The people of Kerala can have the pride that it is the first state in India that opened the doors of its temples to all Hindus for worship through the historic Temple Entry Proclamation. Even then, the right of temple entry is not unregulated or unrestricted; certain restrictions for temple worship prevailed for a very long period. In the *Narhari vs. B. N. Temple Committee* case, the SC in 1952 pronounced that the public had no right to enter the *sanctum sanctorum* of a temple when the deity is located (Prakash, 2006: 566). The right of entry of *sanctum sanctorum* of the temple was permitted only to the Brahmin community. Though some changes that can be termed as revolutionary, are being occurred like the appointment of non-caste priests in temples, that does not become wide spread and even now the Brahmanic hegemony continues in spiritual affairs.

Temple entry and related issues are widely discussed in Kerala for a long time. There are complaints still of denying temple entry to the downtrodden communities in certain temples in the state. Besides, restrictions imposed on the entry of non-Hindus in Guruvayur and women of a particular age group in Sabarimala created much controversy. In 2017, the then TDB Member and the Congress leader Ajay Tharayil raised the demand that non-Hindus also be allowed to enter in temples under the control of the Board for worship (The Hindu, 2017, September 9). K. J. Yesudas, the legendary singer has expressed intense desire to enter in the Guruvayur Sree Krishna temple, but is not allowed so far for being a non-Hindu, but Sree Padmanabhaswami temple authorities had given him permission to enter in the temple and he is a regular visitor of Sabarimala temple and sung the lullaby of Lord Ayyappan (*harivarasanam*). In certain temples like Sabarimala, some sort of restrictions is prevailing for women devotees for worship.

Sabarimala

Sabarimala is perhaps the only temple in the state promoting universal temple entry and common worship. Sabarimala temple is predominantly a male pilgrimage centre in South India, which does not discriminate its devotees on caste and religious lines (Roopesh, 2018: 12). Here the taboo is for the entry of women of a particular age group (10 - 50), but it is not the case of gender-based discrimination as it allows other sections of women for worship. Women entry issue in Sabarimala and the subsequent happenings becomes a landmark in the social and religious history of Kerala. An epitome of secular culture and a great centre of pilgrimage, Sabarimala temple attracts a large section of people from all over the state as well as neighbouring states to its fold. It is one of the greatest centres of pilgrimage in South India, managed by the TDB, a statutory body constituted as per the provisions of the Covenant during the time of Travancore- Cochin Integration. As far as women are concerned, those who have not attained the age of puberty and the menstrual cycle and those who are post-menopause alone should undertake the pilgrimage. Women in the age group of 10 to 50 years are prohibited in the shrine because the presiding deity is considered to be a *naishtika Brahmachari* (perennial celibate). Such a rare system of worship exists in Sabarimala temple alone in the country.

A group of historians are of the opinion that significant changes in the rituals have been undergone in the temple after the 1950 fire incident. The restriction on the entry of women was one such imposition. The ban was enforced under Rule 3(b) of the Kerala Hindu Places of Public Worship (Authorisation of Entry) Rules, 1965 (Jithesh, 2018). The TDB constructed a new temple after the fire incident and replaced a new idol instead of the broken idol of *Ayyappa* (Gurukkal, 2018).

The temple is located in a dense forest area on the banks of the holy river Pampa at Perunad Grama Panchayat in Pathanamthitta District of Kerala state. Being a part of the Periyar Tiger Reserve area in the Western Ghats mountain ranges, the temple suffocates for providing sufficient amenities for its pilgrims. For many years, a tussle between the TDB and the State Forest Department is going on regarding the issue of allotting more forest land to the shrine. Besides, there are several environmental issues relating to the pilgrimage.

Legacy of Sabarimala Temple

There is no generally agreed perception regarding the origin, history and administration of the temple in Hindu mythology or in any other documents (Sajeev, 2019: 11). The *Mala Araya* community, a section of tribal people claimed the right over the administration of the hill shrine. P. K. Sajeev, the General Secretary of *Mala Araya Maha Sabha* in an interview narrated the community's role in the hill shrine. He claimed that the Lord *Ayyappan* was born in the Mala Araya community to Kandan and Karuthamma, in a cave at Ponnambalamedu. The *Mala Arayas* looked after the temple till the 1800s. The customs of the Mala Araya community prevailed in Sabarimala; later, it was brahminised. The Thazhamon Madom family took charge of the temple only in 1942 when the King visited the temple and brought them for *puja*. Mala Araya community was evicted from Ponnambalamedu by the Forest Department and the TDB later.

According to Rajan Gurukkal, the reputed historian, the temple lay outside the *agamic* traditions; the Namboodiri *tantri* families of Vedic ritual tradition never cared much for it. No priest with the knowledge of *agamic* rules would dare to take responsibility for sustaining ritual purity in a forest temple. Only the Thazhamon, a family with no tradition of Vedic rites and *agamic* rituals would take up the job (Gurukkal, 2018). Till the 15th century CE, very few people visited the shrine during the annual festival in January to March including low-caste people living on the forest's fringes and some pilgrims from Tamil Nadu (Gurukkal, 2018).

However, the historical significance of the temple is evidenced by the writings of foreign authors like Xuanzang, Lt. Ward and Conner etc. Xuanzang calls it as *Churulimala* and Lt. Ward and Conner in their *Memoir of the Survey of Travancore and Cochin States* (1891), refers it to *Chourymulla Pagoda*. Historians and scholars argued that the Sabarimala temple was a Buddhist *vihara* before converting it into a Hindu temple. *Amarakosha* by Amarasimha mentions the term *Sastha* or *Dharmasastha* as one of the synonyms of Buddha. M. G. S. Narayanan, renowned historian, renounced this argument and according to him, there is no need to associate Sree Buddha with Lord *Ayyappa*. Buddha had renounced his kingdom and everything else for peace, while *Ayyappa* was a warrior (The Hindu, 2016: 44).

The history and mythology of Lord *Ayyappa* is closely connected with Pandalam royal palace and the King of Pandalam who is considered as his foster father constructed the temple on the wishes of *Ayyappa*. It is believed that the Pandalam kingdom was established around 903 AD extended over 1,000 square miles consisting of 18 holy hills including Sabarimala. In 1769, when Marthanda Varma established the kingdom of Travancore, Pandalam was not annexed but allowed to continue independent. After the invasion of Tipu in 1789, Pandalam King was asked to pay an amount to the Travancore Government towards the cost of the war. In order to pay the amount, the rulers of Pandalam hypothecated the income from Sabarimala temple towards this. In 1820 AD, the territories under Pandalam kingdom were assumed by Travancore as per the agreement; the administration of all the temples under Pandalam rulers got transferred to the Government of Travancore. After the integration of Travancore and Cochin, the administration of all these temples was handed over to the TDB.

As a custom, temple key and golden ornaments (Thanka Anki) are under the safe custody of Pandalam Palace. Pandalam palace enjoys ownership right by custom over the temple in spite of its administration is vested with the state sponsored Devaswom Boards. Pandalam Palace Committee stick on to their stand as the temple belongs to the devotees and the relation between the palace and the deity was that of a father-son relationship. The TDB is only the trustee of erstwhile Travancore temples. Their role was that of a guardian to ensure the protection of temple assets and continuance of the temple customs. Though the temple belonging to the palace had been brought under the TDB as per the Covenant, the palace is claiming its position as the original trustee (Personal Interview, 2019).

In the olden days, very few people visited the shrine and the temple was opened for a few days for worship. Ward and Conner in their *Geographical and Statistical Memoir of the Survey of Travancore and Cochin States* estimated that about 15000 pilgrims visited Sabarimala during the second half of the 19th century (Ward & Conner, 1893). Nagam Aiya, in his *Travancore State Manual* stated that during the beginning of the 20th century, about one lakhs pilgrims visited Sabarimala (1999: 598) and T. K. Velu Pillai in his *Travancore State Manual* accounts a phenomenal increase in the number of men, women and children who undertook the pilgrimage with ecstasy (1996: 621). Within a short span of period the temple attracted wide attention and lakhs of devotees visited the shrine from various parts. As a result of this increasing influx of pilgrims, the temple income has been steadily increased. The temple remains open only during the *mandala makaravilakku* festival (November to January) in a year, besides the first five days of every Malayalam month. In 1995-96, approximately 1 crore pilgrims visited the shrine and it was again increased to 2.5 crore during 2004-2005 (Radhakrishnan, 2005). Sabarimala temple is one of the income generators of the TDB and receipts from Sabarimala account for 30 to 40 percentage of the total income of the TDB. In the 1996-97 period, the total income of the temple was Rs 34.42 crores that enhanced to Rs 50 crores in 2001-02, Rs 67 crores in 2002, Rs 72 crores in 2004, Rs 243.69 crores in the 2016-17 period and Rs 342 crores in the year 2017-18.

Issue of Women Entry

The issue of entry of women in places of worship like Sabarimala, Shani Shingnapur, and Haji Ali is widely discussed at the national level that paved the way for a debate on *gender equality* Vs. *freedom of worship*. The restrictions on the entry of young women in Sabarimala as part of the age-old tradition attracted national attention when a group of young lawyers in New Delhi approached the Supreme Court in 2006 against it. The issue created divergent opinions; one section supported women entry, while the other who became the protagonists of temple rituals that prevented women of particular age group to enter in the temple. The left intellectuals predominantly argued that prior to 1991 women were freely allowed to enter the temple without considering their age. They pointed out the recollections of T. K. A. Nair, Principal Secretary to the former Prime Minister Manmohan Singh that he had his first rice-feeding ceremony on his mother's lap at Sabarimala in 1940. Similarly, the Queen of Travancore is also recorded as having visited the temple in 1939–40 when she was in her 40s (Manoj, 2018). Pointing out the above instances, they argued that restriction to a particular age group of women for worship is illegal and violation of Fundamental Rights. Reputed historian Rajan Gurukkal justified the women entry in Sabarimala temple on the ground that there are archival evidences of upper caste young women entering the temple till the eighties. Tribal families with women and children of all ages flocked to the temple until the sixties (Gurukkal, 2018). He also pointed out the contradiction that while upper caste households did observe menstrual pollution, for the tribal people, menstruation was auspicious and symbolic of fertility (Gurukkal, 2018).

Backward Hindu organisations like SNDP Yogam, KPMS and so on favoured the stand taken by the government in favour of women entry. Later SNDP Yogam shifted their earlier stand and expressed their allegiance with the believers. They anguished over the approach of *savarna* organisations for hijacking Sabarimala agitation without making a consensus among Hindu organisations. The disunity of the two leading Hindu organisations, the SNDP Yogam and NSS could be visible throughout the Sabarimala agitation.

The other sections of Hindu organisations and the right-wing political parties stand against women entry and pointed out that they should remain with the interests of the believers for protecting the age-old customs of the temple. Pandalam Royal Palace and organisations like the NSS, Yogakshema Sabha, RSS and its *parivar* organisations, Ayyappa Seva Sangham and political parties such as Congress, BJP, Kerala Congress and even Muslim League are against the governmental policy of favouring women entry and thereby the violation of the temple custom. They maintained that these customs were prevailed in the temple from time immemorial.

In the *Memoir of the Survey of the Travancore and Cochin States*, written by Lieutenants Ward and Conner and published in two parts in 1893 and 1901 proves that a traditional ban of some kind existed at Sabarimala. Renowned historian, M. G. S. Narayanan said that the temple had no importance until it was rebuilt in 1950 following a fire incident and till then hardly anybody went there. This new found popularity is said to have provoked the first formal restrictions (Manoj, 2018). Again in 1955 and '56, the Travancore Devaswom Board which controls the administration of Sabarimala, issued two notifications banning the entry of women in the age group of 10 and 55 from entering the temple, noting that this was contrary to "the fundamental principle underlying the *deity*. A similar notification was issued in 1972 also by the Board (Manoj, 2018).

In 1965, the Kerala Hindu Places of Public Worship (Authorisation of Entry) Act was enacted and Section 3 of the Act provides for places of public worship to be open to all sections and classes of Hindus. The Government of Kerala framed a rule accordingly; Kerala Hindu Places of Public Worship (Authorisation of Entry) Rules 1965, Section 3 of the rule stipulates certain conditions for temple worship. Thus, the ban on the entry of women of a certain age at Sabarimala temple has justified saying that the restriction was enforced under Rule 3 (b) of the Kerala Hindu Places of Public Worship (Authorisation of Entry) Rules, 1965.

In 1975, the Inspector General of Police in his report to the government stated that during the pilgrim season several women in the age group of 10-50 visited the shrine violating the temple traditions and customs. If this would continue the serenity of the pilgrimage might be ruined. Moreover, their entry might invite immoral activities of anti-social elements including thieves and the police might be unable to check this due to the influx of pilgrims. So, the coming of women in the age group may be restricted through advertising in media and those women who come violating the directions might be prevented at Pampa itself. The TDB accepted the IG's proposal and decided to send a letter to the government to implement the same with a slight modification that the upper age limits to be enhanced to 55 from 50 (TDB, 2004: 145).

The entry of women becomes a controversial question during the eighties. Two young women were prevented at Pampa by the volunteers of Ayyappa Seva Sangam, a devotees' organisation in 1982 on the ground that they are violating the traditional restriction (Rajagopal, 2018). The entry of women again hit the headlines in 1986 when an actress entered into the sannidhanam (temple premise) for the shooting of a Tamil movie *Nambinor Keduvathillai.* This was challenged in the Court by a devotee; Devaswom Board President and Members were the accused persons and subsequently the Court imposed a fine on the artist for violating temple custom.

Public Interest Litigation (PIL) of S. Mahendran

A landmark in the history of Sabarimala happened in 1991 when the KHC pronounced a remarkable verdict in the *Mahendran Vs. Travancore Devaswom Board* case by banning the entry of women of the age group 10-50 in the temple. The incident that led to the legal battle was the violation of the temple custom by a lady officer in the higher rank of Devaswom Board. Chandrika, the former Commissioner of TDB with members of her family including her daughter entered the shrine for the first *rice-feeding* ceremony of her grand-daughter in1990. Mahendran, a native of Changanacherry wrote a letter to the Chief Justice of the Kerala High Court pointing out the violation of custom and the Court considered it as a PIL and sent notice to the TDB authorities. The Court observed that the restriction imposed on women from worshipping at Sabarimala Shrine is in accordance with the usage prevalent from time immemorial. Such restrictions are not violative of Articles 15, 25 and 26 of the Constitution of India. The Court held that a religious denomination enjoys complete autonomy in deciding as to what rites and ceremonies are essential according to the tenets of the religion, under Article 26(b) of the Constitution (Mahendran, 1991). In the matter of temple entry, the prohibition is only in respect to women of a particular age group and not women as a class. Following this, a signboard that prevent women entry was displayed at the entrance of the Pamba Ganapathy temple and lady doctors, women police and Devaswom guards were posted to prevent the entry of women. B.Valsalakumri, the then Pathanamthitta District Collector visited the shrine by obtaining a Court order to see the civic amenities in 1994 sparked off another controversy in the state.

In another episode, while conducting a four-day *devaprasnam* (astrological observation) at Sabarimala in 2006, the astrologer Unnikrishna Panicker have predicted that the presence of a woman happened at the *sanctum sanctorum* of the temple. Shortly after, the famous film actress from the State of Karnataka, Jayamala revealed in public that she had entered the *sanctum sanctorum* of the temple by the surging crowd. Later it was found that the whole drama was a part of the conspiracy by the astrologer to earn fame. A criminal case was then filed against the party, the astrologer, his assistant and the actress for hurting the religious sentiments of the people by hatching out such a conspiracy. When the issue was blown as a thunder storm, probe was initiated by the Government of Kerala but after a short while, the case was dropped. Later in 2012, the KHC quashed the charges against the accused actress on the ground of insufficient evidence. The temple *tantri* (Chief Priest) performed a purification ceremony at the temple. When in 2011, another 35 year old lady, Saraswathi from Andhra Pradesh entered the temple complex and offered worship in violation of temple custom. She was spotted by Rapid Action Force personnel near Malikapuram temple premises and returned, but Temple *tantri* conducted purification ceremony as per the directions of the TDB (The Hindu, 2011, December 20).

PIL of Indian Young Lawyers Association

After a long fifteen years of the verdict of the KHC in the *Mahendran* case, a group of Delhi based young lawyers under the aegis of the *Indian Young Lawyers Association* approached the Supreme Court in 2006 seeking the entry of women of all age group to Sabarimala temple challenging the constitutional validity of Rule 3(b) of the Kerala Hindu Places of Public Worship (Authorisation of Entry) Rules 1965 and the notifications of the Travancore Devaswom Board. In the PIL, they argued that the Hindu women have a right to enter the temple as part of gender justice, their right to practice religion and the right to equality ensured by the Indian Constitution.

Table 4.1: Sabarimala women entry issue: chronicles of events

Sl. No.	Year	Events
1.	1820	Ward and Conner in their *Memoir of the Survey of Travancore and Cochin States* mention about the restrictions existed for the entry of women of a particular age group.
2.	1939	Reported visit of Maharaja of erstwhile Travancore along with the Maharani in Sabarimala temple.
3.	1940	T. K. A. Nair's first rice-feeding ceremony in 1940 at Sabarimala was on his mother's lap.
4.	1986	Kannada actress Jayamala's mysterious visit to the hill shrine and *darshan* at the *sanctum sanctorum*.

(Contd...)

5.	1986	Shooting of a Tamil film in which actress Jayashree and company danced near 18 holy steps- fined by the Court Rs 1,000 each.
6.	1990	The first rice-feeding ceremony of the grand-daughter of Chandrika, the former Devaswom Commissioner of TDB.
7.	1990	Mahendran sent a letter to the High Court citing violation of customs-The Court accepted it as PIL.
8.	1991	The High Court verdict banned the entry of young women at Sabarimala temple.
9.	1994	Pathanamthitta District Collector K.B. Valsalakumari visited the shrine.
10.	2006	The Indian Young Lawyers' Association approached the SC for lifting the ban on young women entry at Sabarimala.
11.	2018	The SC Verdict favouring the entry of women of all age groups in the temple with 4-1 majority; Justice Indu Malhotra dissented.
12.	2018	NSS and other organisations filed Review Petitions in the SC, was accepted to hear in an open court.
13.	2019	Two young women visited the shrine on 2nd January, *tantri* conducted a purification ceremony.
14.	2019	A contempt petition was filed in the SC against purification ceremony on 3rd January.
15.	2019	The SC accepted review petitions and the case is referred to a 7 Judge Bench.

The restriction is anti-Hindu in the sense that Hinduism never considers discrimination as a ritual or a ceremony and the religion accords to women a higher position compared to men. Moreover, the discrimination on the basis of biological factors of womanhood is not included under the purview of Article 26 of the Constitution. The petitioners contended that as a temple under the Travancore Devaswom Board which is a statutory body functioning with financial aid from the consolidated fund as per Article 290A of the Constitution and is governed as per the Travancore-Cochin Hindu Religious Institutions Act, 1950, such ill-practices could not be carried on. Again, temples in Kerala follow the same mode of worship and Sabarimala temple is one among them. Sabarimala Temple is not a separate religious denomination and does not have its separate administration. They questioned the myth of celibacy of the deity. The women devotees also go to Sabarimala seeking blessings of Lord Ayyappa and they are given the right by the Constitution. Thus, in their argument the petitioners stick on to Constitutional values such as gender equality, religious freedom and freedom of movement (*Indian Young Lawyers Association*, 2017).

The Counsel for the petitioner argued the restrictions as against Articles 14, 15 and 17 of the Constitution, that is, the custom is discriminatory, stigmatized and denial of the right to pray. The SC issued notice to the State Government, the TDB and temple *tantri* on 18th August 2006. When the case was brought before the SC, the State Government and the TDB responded paradoxically on the issue of women entry. The Travancore Devaswom Board filed an affidavit in the SC contending that the Board gave priority to temple traditions and customs and being the temple management, it has the right to frame rules for the shrine without the interference of the state. Ayyappa devotees constitute separate denomination with a definite identifiable character unlike the contention of the petitioners. It is also argued that the custom pertains to non-discriminatory as it was born from the belief that the deity is a *'naishtika brahmachari'* (eternal celibate) *(Indian Young Lawyers Association, 2017).*

The Government of Kerala led by the LDF filed an affidavit in 2007 favouring the contention raised by the petitioners for gender equality and right to freedom of worship which is ensured by the Constitution of India. The ideological difference between the LDF led government and the UDF nominees in the Board is clearly reflected in this conflicting view. Then the Board was disbanded by the State Government on the allegation of corruption through an amendment in the TCHRI Act 2007 which reduced the tenure of the Board into two years and included a woman member in the Board. This move may be observed as a calculated one to strengthen the demand raised by the petitioners. The stand taken by the government became very crucial for the subsequent Court proceedings. The succeeding UDF Government had taken away the provision for women reservation in the TDB through another amendment in the Devaswom Act in 2014.

Table 4.2: Parties involved in the Sabarimala women entry case (SC, 2006)

Parties	Sl. No	Name
Petitioner	1.	Indian Young Lawyers Association- Dr. Laxmi Shastiri, Prerna Kumari, Alka Sharma, Sudha Pal
Respondents	1.	State of Kerala
	2.	Travancore Devaswom Board
	3.	Chief *Tantri* of Sabarimala Temple
	4.	District Magistrate of Pathanamthitta
	5.	Nair Service Society
	6.	Akhil Bhartiya Ayyappa Seva Sangham
	7.	Ayyappa Seva Samithi
	8.	Ayyappa Pooja Samithi
	9.	Dharma Sastha Seva Samajam
	10.	Akhil Bharatiya Malayalee Sangh
	11.	Sabarimala Ayyappa Seva Samajam
	12.	Kerala Kshetra Samarakshana Samithi
	13.	Sabarimala Custom Protection Forum

Source: Supreme Court Observer, Retrieved from https://www.scobserver.in/court-case/sabrimala-temple-entry-case

In 2016, again the LDF Government came to power in Kerala, the Minister in charge of Devaswom, Kadakamppally Surendran and the then President of the TDB and former Congress MLA, Prayer Gopalakrishnan came into a tug of war on several issues connected with Sabarimala temple; the renaming of the temple, women entry issue etc. The move of the UDF appointed Board to rename Sree Dharma Sastha temple as Sree Ayyappa temple on 5th October, 2016 was blocked by the LDF government. Prayar Gopalakrishnan, in the women entry issue has called upon the Chief Minister and Devaswom Minister to initiate necessary steps to protect the age-old customs and tradition of the temple by which women in the age group of 10 to 50 years are not permitted to undertake the pilgrimage. He urged the government to take every possible step to oppose the move to destroy the temple. The Devaswom Board President said that he was ready to court arrest and go to jail for the sake of protecting the temple customs (The Hindu, 2016, May 27). Due to the conflicting interests of the Board and the Government, the Board was dissolved through an Ordinance in 2018, curtailing the tenure of the Board to two years and then installed a new Board of the Government's choice. Such a move of a democratic government to politicise temple administration had invited another controversy.

The new Devaswom Board came to power with A. Padmakumar, ex- MLA and the leader of the CPM as the new President. The newly formed Board cancelled the previous Board's decision to rename the temple. The NSS expressed displeasure over the decision to restore the official name of Sabarimala and demanded the State Government and the TDB to withdraw this move. NSS General Secretary, G. Sukumaran Nair sent a letter to the Chief Minister, Devaswom Minister and the President of the TDB in this regard (The New Indian Express, 2018, January 6).

In February 2016, the UDF Government filed an affidavit supporting the restrictions as part of temple's unique idol concept. The LDF Government came to power in the same year, filed another affidavit questioning the rituals, customs and observances pursued in the temple. By doing so, the government has taken a U-turn in the stand taken by its immediate predecessor. Earlier in March 2008, the Court referred the case to a three Judge Bench. But the case has been indefinitely postponed and came up for hearing after a long eight years in January 2016. Finally, in October 2017, the three Judge Bench consisting of Chief Justice Dipak Misra, Justice R. Banumathi and Justice Ashok Bhushan ordered to pass the case to a five-member Constitutional Bench. The three-Judge Bench considered the issues and raised the following points as questions for the purpose of reference to the Constitution Bench:

(i) Whether the exclusion of woman on the basis of biological factors amounts to discrimination and a violation of Articles 14, 15 and 17 and not protected by morality as expressed in Articles 25 and 26 of the Constitution?

(ii) Whether such exclusion is an essential religious practice under Article 25 and a religious institution can claim to have the right to manage its own affairs in the matters of religion?

(iii) Whether Ayyappa Temple managed by a statutory Board and financed denominational character out of the Consolidated Fund under Article 290-A of the Constitution of India to indulge in such practices violating constitutional principles or morality embedded in Articles 14, 15(3), 39(a) and 51-A (e)?

(iv) Whether Rule 3 of the Kerala Hindu Places of Public Worship (Authorisation of Entry) Rules permits 'religious denomination' to ban entry of women between the age of 10 to 50 years?

(v) Whether Rule 3(b) of the Kerala Hindu Places of Public Worship (Authorisation of Entry) Rules, 1965 is *ultra vires* the Kerala Hindu Places of Public Worship (Authorisation of Entry) Act, 1965 and, if treated to be *intra vires*, whether it will be violative of the provisions of Part III of the Constitution? *(Indian Young Lawyers Association, 2018).*

The Bombay High Court in its historic verdict in April, 2016 in the *Shani Shingnapur Temple case* held that it is the duty of the Government is to protect women's right of worship. Accordingly, a meeting of the Trustees of the temple decided to facilitate unrestricted entry to the *sanctum sanctorum* of the temple for all devotees, including men and women (The Hindu, 2016, April 8). This verdict may be considered as the first of its kind and became the forerunner of the Sabarimala women entry case.

The twelve years long legal battle for women entry created serious apprehension among the Hindu devotees all over the state. The TDB counsels K. Parasaran and K.K. Venugopal justified the ban on women's entry in tune with the tradition of the shrine and the religious questions posed in this writ can be determined by the temple *Tantri*. The apex court's observations are based on constitutional values that completely negate the arguments based on customs and rituals and in the stages of final hearing these were highlighted. The Court asserted that no temple can prevent women entry, managed by a statutory Board financed out of the consolidated fund by violating constitutional principles.

Chief Justice Dipak Misra stated that the Constitutional issues involved in this case are above spiritual considerations. The temple can claim constitutional protection on the ground of being a separate religious denomination; otherwise they cannot restrict the right to temple entry. The Court appointed two senior lawyers Raju Ramachandran and K. Ramamurthy as *amicus curiae* in the case to assist the Court. The *amicus curiae* expressed contradictory views and one of them, Ramamurthy favoured the restriction that is not violative of Articles 15, 25 and 26 of the Constitution; Articles 25 and 26 contain a guarantee for rituals and observations, ceremonies and modes of worship which are integral parts of religion. Religious practice based on religious faith adhered to and followed by millions of Hindus for over a millennium in consonance with natural rights of men and women is not violative of Fundamental Rights (*Indian Young Lawyers Association*, 2017). Raju Ramachandran, the other *amicus curiae* argued that entry to a public temple is a legal right and so the temple authorities have no power to curtail the right. The ban was discriminating women as a class and because of the biological factors their dignity could not be damaged. Finally, the Supreme Court referred to this case to a five-Judge Constitution Bench (*Indian Young Lawyers Association*, 2017).

This issue created a storm in state politics that divided opinions on *Right to pray Vs. Ready to wait* positioning. While activists seeking women entry have come out with social media campaigns like *happy to bleed,* a campaign against menstrual taboos that prevail in the society and *Right to Pray,* other Hindu women organisations have entered the battle ground with a counter campaign, *Ready to Wait.*

28th September, 2018 was a crucial day for the women entry issue on that day the SC of India issued a verdict in favour of the entry of women of all age group into the Sabarimala hill shrine. The five-Judge Constitution Bench headed by the Chief Justice Dipak Misra in a 4-1 majority judgement struck down Rule 3(b) of the Kerala Temple Entry Rules which denied the women between the age of 10 and 50 years the freedom of worship by barring them from entry into the temple. It is notable that the lone dissenting judgement in the case came from a woman judge, Justice Indu Malhotra. In her dissent note to the final decision she remarked that 'judiciary should not interfere in religious matters unless if there is any aggrieved person from that section of religion or if a tradition is a pernicious, oppressive, or social evil'. She also pointed out that what constitutes an essential religious practice is for the religious community to decide (*Indian Young Lawyers Association*, 2018).

In the SC judgment, Justice D. Y. Chandrachud stated that prohibiting women's entry was a form of untouchability.

Notions of "purity and pollution" which stigmatise individuals have no place in a constitutional order (The Indian Express, 2018, September 29). Fundamental Rights are only for individuals and not deities. The SC considered in this case not just gender discrimination, but also exclusion of women based on notions of caste supremacy and purity (Kannabiran, 2018). The SC in its verdict examined all aspects of temple tradition, religious beliefs, constitutional values, right to worship and nature of a religious denomination.

Table 4.3: Sabarimala temple verdict: A chronology of events

Sl.No.	Date and year	Events
1.	24th September, 1990	Mahendran's petition against violation of custom at Sabarimala in the KHC.
2.	5th April, 1991	The KHC verdict upholds the restriction on women of a particular age group in the temple.
3.	4th August, 2006	The Indian Young Lawyers Association approached the SC for seeking entry of women of all age group in Sabarimala temple.
4.	November, 2007	The LDF Government filed an affidavit in the SC supporting women entry.
	7th March, 2008	The Case was referred to a three-judge Bench.
5.	11th January, 2016	The SC questions the practice of banning of entry of women.
6.	6th February, 2016	The UDF Government submitted a fresh affidavit in the SC to safeguard the temple custom.
7.	11th April, 2016	The SC pronounced gender justice jeopardized by the ban.
8.	13th April, 2016	The SC said tradition could not justify the ban on the entry of women.
9.	7th November, 2016	The LDF government filed a fresh affidavit in the SC.
10.	13th October, 2017	The SC referred the case to the Constitution Bench.

(Contd...)

11.	27th October, 2017	Plea filed in the SC for the gender-equal bench to hear the case.
12.	17th July, 2018	Five-judge Constitution bench heard the case.
13.	19th July, 2018	The SC said women have a Fundamental Right to enter in the temple.
14.	24th July, 2018	The SC said that the case would be tested on "constitutional ethos".
15.	25th July, 2018	The NSS affirmed in the SC the celibate nature of the deity.
16.	26th July, 2018	The Supreme Court criticised the ban on the basis of physiological ground of menstruation.
17.	1st August, 2018	The SC reserved verdict.
18.	28th September, 2018	The SC, in 4:1 verdict, allowed entry of women in Sabarimala temple, on the ground that the ban amounts to the violation of the rights of Hindu women.
19.	22nd October, 2018	The SC decided to hear review petitions filed by more than 50 persons/ organisations.
20.	13th November, 2018	The SC decided to hear all review petitions on 22nd January, 2019.
21.	6th February, 2019	Heard review petitions and reserved for verdict; TDB favoured the SC verdict.
22.	14th November, 2019	The SC referred the case to a 7 Judge Bench

Table 4.4: Observations of Supreme Court on Sabarimala Verdict

Sl. No.	Juges	Observations
1.	Justice Dipak Misra (CJI)	The practice of age restrictions on women entry cannot be treated as an essential one. Ayyappa devotees do not constitute a separate religious denomination. Any rule based on biological characteristics cannot pass the uster of the constitutional test.
2.	Justice D.Y. Chandrachud	The Right to pray is equally applicable to both man and woman; Religion cannot deny women right to worship. To treat

(*Contd...*)

		women as children of lesser God is to blink at Constitutional morality. The custom as a form of "untouchability" cannot be allowed under the Constitution. A deity does not have constitutional rights.
3.	Justice Nariman	Menstruation is not impure; Fundamental Rights are essential for the transformation of society.
4.	Justice Indu Malhotra (Dissenting note)	Worshippers of Sabarimala temple constitute a separate religious denomination. The religious community is to decide religious practices and not the Court. The Court should not interfere unless if there is any aggrieved person from that section or religion; notions of rationality cannot be invoked in matters of religion.

Source: Young Lawyers Association Vs. State of Kerala (2018).

This judgement is not the only one of its kind from the judiciary; the apex court had earlier upheld the right of maintenance for Muslim women separated from their husbands, in the Shah Bano case in the mid-1980s. But a law was brought into negate it (Mohan, 2018). The Minister in-charge of Devaswom Kadakampally Surendran welcomed the verdict and described the Supreme Court verdict as historic. Human rights should not be denied in the name of faith as per the verdict (The Hindu, 2018, September 29).

Developments after Supreme Court Verdict on Women Entry

The verdict on women entry in Sabarimala has produced divergent views from various quarters; it was sufficient for creating polarisation in Kerala society. While the LDF government welcomed the verdict and proceeded for making necessary amenities for womenfolk in Sabarimala, the opposition parties the Congress and BJP like pro- Hindu political parties began to use the issue for their political mileage. Large scale resentment was experienced during the immediate post-verdict period. A section of the Hindu population became furious and proceeded to violent responses. RSS, VHP, ABASS, NSS, Yogakshemasabha, Pandalam Palace Managing Committee, *Akhila Kerala Tantri Samajam* exhorted their followers to react and the social atmosphere of the state became calamitous.

The SNDP Yogam, though expressed their displeasure with the Court verdict, did not go for protest as it considered the protest movements were hijacked by the NSS and other *savarna* organisations. But its political offshoot, BDJS, actively engaged in the protest with BJP. Kerala Pulayar Maha Sabha, an association of one of the Dalit community welcomed the Supreme Court verdict as it was the continuation of renaissance ethos; the Court had to interfere because the tradition cannot be changed through consensus (Deccan Chronicle, 2018, October 13,). Review petitions were filed before the Supreme Court to reconsider the verdict and the Court accepted them, though it was not a precedent. The Court in a significant move agreed to hear the case in open court.

The State Government and the TDB both became eager to implement the Court directive disregarding the feelings of devotees, alleged P. Rama Varma Raja, Chairman, Pandalam Palace Managing Committee. Organisations like NSS and Yogakshema Sabha and Pandalam Palace Managing Committee demanded the government and the TDB to file review petition immediately before the SC, but neither the TDB nor the government positively responded to the demand. They also pleaded the TDB to maintain *status quo* at the temple till the Supreme Court pronounce verdict on the review petition and to pressure the government to issue an Ordinance, if the apex court verdict on the review petition become unfavourable to maintain the tradition (Krishnakumar, 2018). But the Chief Minister ruled out the possibility of a review petition on the SC verdict banning women entry as illegal and unconstitutional.

Following the SC verdict, protest movements were organised by the believers across the state against the move to destroy temple traditions by the atheist led government. Large number of female devotees eagerly participated in the mass demonstrations (*namajapa yatras*) by chanting of *ayyappa manthras* and holding placards inscribing slogans like *Ready to Wait* (until menopause to visit the Sabarimala temple) and *save Sabarimala* (Krishnakumar, 2019). The massive participation of devotees including women in the *namajapa yatra* at Pandalam (the place where Lord Ayyappa was believed to be fostered) was a major impetus to the protest movements. *Sabarimala Karma Samithi* was formed to coordinate various protest movements by the *Sangh Parivar* organisations. The NSS was the first to come out against the Court verdict and directed its local *karayogams* to participate actively in its protest movements and prayer processions. The political parties such as the BJP and the Congress party declared their open support to the agitation led by the believers.

A day before the opening of the Sabarimala Temple after the verdict, the Union Home Ministry had issued a note to the Chief Secretaries as well as Director Generals of Police of Kerala, Karnataka and Tamil Nadu states to make adequate security arrangements at the Sabarimala Temple; all necessary precautionary measures to be taken to maintain law and order and appropriate security arrangements to prevent any untoward incident. The Centre had warned the Kerala government to take adequate security measures ahead of the opening of the Sabarimala Temple.

Attempts were made by several young ladies to offer prayer in the light of the SC verdict who was resisted by the Ayyappa devotees creating riot like situations in the temple premises and surrounding places of Nilackal and Pamba; the police had to use force many a time for removing protestors. On October 18, 2018, when a young journalist Suhasini Raj of the New York Times came escorted with heavy police security, a group of protestors blocked her and she was forced to return from the halfway point. In the next day Rehana Fathima, an activist was also blocked and forced to return owing to violent protests. Meanwhile, she was expelled from the Muslim community by Kerala Muslim Jama'at Council for hurting the Hindu religious sentiments (Times Now News, 2018). She was arrested by the police on the basis of a complaint by Radhakrishna Menon of the BJP for hurting religious sentiments through social media. She is a BSNL employee and following the arrest she was suspended from service. The mass entry of young women activists to the scene invited criticisms from different corners. The *Sangh Parivar* organisations suspected the move as part of the conspiracy of the ruling left forces to destroy the serenity of the holy shrine. Denying the allegation, the Minister for Devaswoms stated that the government has no intention to transform Sabarimala into a platform for activist intervention. Contrary to this statement, Kodiyeri Balakrishnan, State Secretary of CPI (M) stated that there was no ban on activists at Sabarimala (Krishnakumar, 2018).

With the protest movements became aggressive, Kerala police issued prohibitory orders at several key locations and declared Pamba and the *Sannidhanam* (immediate precincts of the temple) as special security zones. The police arrested over 3,345 people and registered 517 cases in connection with the violence happened during the protests. Many instances of violence and police *lathi* charges were reported at Nilakkal, Pamba and the precincts of Sabarimala. Following these unfortunate incidents, a state wide *hartal* was organised by the BJP which turned violent. The KHC on 29th October, 2018, issued directions to the State Government to file a report on police atrocities which took place during and after the violent protests at Sabarimala. A special mention was made in the 16th Lok Sabha by N. K. Premachandran, MP from Kerala about the calamitous situation after the verdict of the SC on women entry (Lok Sabha, 2018, December 28).

The police action towards Ayyappa devotees and protestors was criticised by the KHC in a case filed by a devotee from

Tamil Nadu seeking a direction from the Court that the Government and the Chief Minister had no authority to interfere in the affairs of the temple. The Court sought the details of prohibitory orders of the police in November 2018 and asked whether these officials were having any criminal antecedents and directed the government that experienced officials should be entrusted with the law and order. The Court also directed police not to obstruct chanting Ayyappa mantra at *Sannidhanam* (The New Indian Express, 2018, November 21). The Court directed the government not to interfere with the affairs of temple administration and its role is confined only to maintaining law and order. The Court warned the government not to cause any hardships to the pilgrims trekking to Sabarimala. The observation of the Court became a major setback to the government action at Sabarimala.

The KHC appointed a three-member panel on 27th November, 2018 to oversee the situation at Sabarimala temple after the Supreme Court verdict in the light of the series of violent incidents happened. P. R. Raman, a retired judge of the High Court, Justice Siri Jagan, Ombudsman for the Travancore and Cochin Devaswom Boards, A. Hemachandran, DGP and Chairman of the High-Power Committee, Sabarimala were the members of the panel. The Court also issued a warning to the protestors and observed that the temple was not a place for protests. The State Government followed stringent action against leaders of Hindu organisations like RSS and leaders of BJP at Sabarimala. K. P. Sasikala, President of the Hindu Aikya Vedi was taken into preventive custody on her way to Sabarimala on charges of making trouble at the temple. She was later produced before the Thiruvalla Magistrate and released on bail. Another leader K. Surendran, the BJP General Secretary was taken into custody by the police on 17th November, 2018 on his way to Sabarimala carrying the *irrumudikettu* (bundle containing offerings for the Lord) (The New Indian Express, 2018, November 18). The police registered as many as

15 criminal cases against him including conspiracy to commit culpable homicide. He got bail and released from jail after 22 days on 8th December 2018. The police blocked the escort vehicle of BJP leader and Union Minister Pon Radhakrishnan at Pamba while returning from Sabarimala.

Both the Congress and BJP exploited the situation politically by unleashing severe criticisms on the policies of the left government at Sabarimala. BJP structured a two-fold programme to protest against government policy of negligence at Sabarimala. First is a *rath yatra* (vehicle procession) from Kasargode to Pathanamthitta and the second, an indefinite hunger strike in front of the Government Secretariat. The first programme was a success in amassing public support, but the second failed to produce any tangible result. The indefinite hunger strike led by the party demanding the removal of restrictions in Sabarimala, withdrawal of all fake cases against its leader K. Surendran, taking action against officers who charged fake cases on the agitators etc., lasted indefinitely without any response from the part of the government. It was on 3rd December, 2018 that the indefinite *satyagraha* commenced. Top leaders of the party like A. N. Radhakrishnan, C. K. Padmanabhan, Sobha Surendran, Sivarajan, P. M. Velayudhan, V. T. Rema and P. K. Krishnadas were part of the agitation. An unfortunate incident happened amidst of the programme; a 50-year-old man committed suicide by setting fire in front of the *Satyagraha* venue by chanting *sarana mantra*. The BJP organised a statewide *hartal* against the incident and the conduct of series of *hartals* on the Sabarimala issue by the party evoked a bad image. The party had to withdraw the Satyagraha without any fruitful solution.

Meanwhile, Devaswom authorities expressed their dissatisfaction over the restrictions imposed by the police at *sannidhanam* by raising barricades. Devaswom Board Commissioner demanded the removal of barricades in front of Kanikka boxes as it badly affected the income of the temple.

According to the reports, a considerable decline happened in the number of pilgrims, consequent on the protest movements and police action. The Finance Minister of the state, T. M. Thomas Isaac observed that the Sabarimala issue adversely affected the state, state's finance and the rebuilding activities consequent on the worst natural disaster witnessed by the state in the last 100 years (Business Standard, 2018).

A Mumbai-based activist Trupti Desai of *Bhumata Brigade* could not even step out of Nedumbasserry airport on 16th November, 2018 due to the protest by the BJP and she returned with a vow to come again for Sabarimala *darshan*. Four transgenders who were earlier denied permission to visit the Sabarimala temple completed their *darshan* on 18th December, 2018, after securing permission (Outlook 2018, December, 18). Another team of 11 young women activists from Chennai-based NGO, *Manithi* tried to visit escorted by police on December 23, but blocked by the protestors. Two young women activists Bindu and Kanaka Durga were blocked by the protesters on 24th December, 2018.

Hindu organisations in the state under the aegis of the Sabarimala Karma Samithi (Sabarimala Action Council) organised *Ayyappa Jyothi (lighting the lamp)* from Kasaragod to Thiruvananthapuram on 26th December 2018 in protest of the breach of temple traditions. The programme could gain attention due to the participation of lakhs of women from all over the state. A women wall was erected as a symbol of renaissance ethos and values by the government and the LDF on 1st January 2019 which was also attended by lakhs of women. Both these programmes became successes in a sense due to the significance of the issue in the society, polity and culture of the state. Noted Hindu organisations the SNDP and the NSS stood in two extreme poles during the whole course of the issue. The SNDP Yogam supported the government sponsored women wall and the Yogam's General Secretary Vellappally Natesan was designated as the Chairman of the Government Committee constituted for the purpose. On the other hand, the NSS supported *Ayyappa Jyothi* due to its stand against violation of tradition.

Two women of menstruating age Bindu and Kanakadurga who tried to enter the temple earlier but failed, penetrated to the temple disguised as men, through the back entrance of the temple with police security on 2nd January 2019, the day after the state-sponsored women wall. Thus, they made history by becoming the first women to enter the temple after the Court verdict. The Chief Minister confirmed their entry and after the official confirmation of women entry, the temple *tantri*, Kandararu Rajeevaru closed the temple for an hour long 'purification ceremony', a traditional ritual performed in temples in the event of 'defilement' of the deity. The TDB sought explanation from the *tantri* for conducting purification ceremony as this was against the directive of the Supreme Court. In his explanations to the Board, he denied the allegations as baseless; but a contempt of Court was filed against him in the Supreme Court.

The legal proceedings against the *tantri* kicked up another controversy in state politics. NSS and the likeminded Hindu organisations favoured the *tantri's* action saying that in matters of temple rituals, the decision of the *tantri* is sacrosanct and he is the final authority on matters relating to temple rituals, rites, practices and ceremonies. As the 'spiritual engineer', his decisions in matters of temple ritual are unquestionable. Once the *tantri* is selected, he is treated as the representative of the deity.

The news of the entry of women produced disbelief and dismay among the believers and they became angered and a tensed situation was created all over the state. Law and order disrupted as the Hindu organisations became agitated that led to political clashes. The *Sangh Parivar* organisations conducted a state wide dawn-to-dusk *hartal* on 3rd January 2019 which evoked mixed response in the state. The Congress party observed the day as *black day*. SNDP Yogam expressed its dissatisfaction over the dramatic entry of women at Sabarimala and viewed the incident as an act of betrayal in the name of Kerala renaissance (Krishnakumar, 2019: 9). Political clashes between the BJP and CPM cadets at various parts of the state were reported which led to the death of an RSS worker at Pandalam.

Again, a controversy burst out when the State Government submitted a list of 51 women in menstrual age as entered in the temple during the annual pilgrimage after the SC verdict. The list included 24 women from Tamil Nadu, 21 from Andhra Pradesh, 3 from Goa and 1 each from Karnataka and Puducherry. But several discrepancies could be seen in the list as the media reported that three of them are men and the majority of them are women above the age of 50. Opposition parties alleged that the government is misleading the people and hurting the religious sentiments of the devotees. As per the official report, 7,564 women registered online for *Ayyappa darshan* and the government collected the list from this virtual queue system.

Ayyappa Bhakta Sangamam (Ayyappa Devotees' Gathering) was organised by the *Sabarimala Karma Samithi* on 20thJanuary, 2019 at Thiruvananthapuram in which thousands of people from five districts attended. The programme was inaugurated by Mata Amritanandamayi, a Hindu spiritual leader of Kerala who observed that the issues at Sabarimala were mishandled by those who do not know anything about the customs of temples; if the temples are destroyed, society will be the loser (The New Indian Express, 2019, January 21). The programme is regarded as the largest Hindu congregation ever in the history of Kerala.

The women entry issue has been raised several times in the Lok Sabha and State Legislative Assembly by the representatives of the Congress party. A private Bill was moved in the KLA in November 2018 by the Congress MLA, M. Vincent demanding a new legislation to protect the traditional rituals and customs of Sabarimala temple. But the speaker rejected the introduction of the Bill on the basis of the advice from the Law Department that it would be unconstitutional and against the Court verdict. Meanwhile, the UDF MP, N. K. Premachandran moved a private Bill, *The Sabarimala Sree Dharma Sastha Temple (Special Provisions) Bill, 2019 (bill No. 89)* in the 17th Lok Sabha on 21st June 2019. The bill was to provide for maintaining *status quo* on religious practices of the Sabarimala Temple, as existed on the 1st day of September, 2018 (prior to the SC verdict) and for matters connected therewith. Again Anto Antony, introduced the Sabarimala issue in the Lok Sabha under Rule 377 requesting to initiate legislative measures to overcome the SC verdict as the customs and traditions there have been observed by the devotees for a long time (Lok Sabha Proceedings, December 27, 2018).

The Devaswom Board entrusted the Devaswom Commissioner for filing a petition in the Court seeking more time to implement the SC judgment. When the review petitions came before the consideration of the SC, the TDB Counsel, Rakesh Dwivedi took a stand contradictory to the Board's decision supporting the implementation of the SC verdict. This created a tug of war between the Board President and the Commissioner. The Board sought explanation from the Commissioner for failing to abide by the Board's direction in the Supreme Court. The TDB Commissioner denied all these allegations. The CPM State Secretary intervened in the issue and summoned both the President and Commissioner to AKG Centre, the headquarter of CPI (M) at Thiruvananthapuram. The TDB President changed his stand after the intervention of the ruling party on the issue. The media reported that the President is proceeding to resign over the issue of side-lining him. The relation between the State Government and the President was at low ebb after he took a stance in favour of protecting the traditions in Sabarimala shrine. Deliberately or not the Board President abstained from Sabarimala, deputing a member K. P. Sankara Das and the Commissioner N. Vasu to oversee all arrangements. The government offered N. Vasu the Presidentship of the Board after the expiry of the term of Padmakumar.

The huge fall happened in the income from Sabarimala temple in 2018 due to the situation emerged after the SC verdict on women entry and the restrictions imposed by the police there which affected the functioning of each and every temple under the TDB. There happened a shortage of Rs 25.42 crores in the *kanikka* income and Rs 10.93 crore in the sale of *appam* and Rs 37.06 crores in the sale of *aravana* compared to the income of the previous year. Thus, during 2018-19, a total of Rs 100 crore deficits occurred in the income of Sabarimala. It is a fact that the depreciation in the income at Sabarimala would definitely be the result of the government policy of prompt implementation of the Court verdict and the subsequent police excesses and the unprecedented violent protests over the women entry issue. This shortage in income would affect the working of low-income temples and the disbursement of salary of the employees under the Board. To tackle the financial crisis, the Board sought financial help from the government. Meanwhile, the *sangh parivar* outfits began to unleash a propaganda that the government was siphoning off the money from the Sabarimala shrine. Allotting Rs 100 crore for the TDB in the 2019-20 state budget, the Finance Minister said that the government would not allow anybody to destabilize the TDB by dissuading devotees from offering money.

The Hindu organisations unleashed propaganda not to put any money at hundis in temples managed by the TDB as a mark of protest against the action of both the government and TDB evoked mixed response among the devotees.Whatever be the logic of the campaign, this move certainly affected the income of the temples considerably. The government and Devaswom Board openly criticised the campaign stating that the action will affect the subsistence of thousands of temple employees.

Politicisation of Sabarimala Issue

The Sabarimala women entry, police excesses, protests movements etc. reflected in the 17th Lok Sabha election campaign and voting behaviour. The Congress and the BJP used the issue of breach of custom at Sabarimala in their election campaigns, though the State Election Commissioner Tikkaram Meena issued directions not to use Sabarimala and Lord Ayyappa in the election campaign. The CPI (M) welcomed it but the BJP opposed. The BJP in its manifesto to the Lok Sabha election promised to secure constitutional protection on issues related to faith and belief. Prime Minister Narendra Modi while releasing the election manifesto stated that the Party would protect the subjects of faith, tradition and worship and rituals related to Sabarimala temple (The New Indian Express, 2019, April 9). In the election, BJP fielded K. Surendran, a popular leader of Sabarimala agitations in Pathanamthitta and Kummanam Rajasekharan, a leading Hindu leader in Thiruvananthapuram Lok Sabha constituencies with the hope of opening an account in the Lok Sabha, but when the result came, this hope became futile but their vote share increased considerably. A notable thing happened in the Lok Sabha poll is that the ruling party of the state, the LDF could win only a single seat. The party lost its strongholds like Attingal, Badagara, Kannur, Alathur, Palakkad and Kasargode constituencies. Later, in a post-poll evaluation report, the party central and state committees admitted that the entry of two women in Sabarimala temple did cause considerable impact among the voters to think against the Party.

It is a fact that BJP's electoral performance is considerably increased in Kerala after the issue of Sabarimala. Comparing the election statistics, it can be seen that in the Lok Sabha elections of 2014, the party got 19.4 lakh votes that has been increased to 21.2 lakh in 2016 Assembly elections and that again increased to 31.7 lakhs in 2019 Lok Sabha elections. The Party's vote share increased considerably due to the Hindu consolidation happened in the issue of women entry in Sabarimala. The Party got more than one lakh votes each in 14 constituencies. Still the people of Kerala hesitated to consider the BJP as a winning party, this feeling has been exploited by the Congress party well and they consolidated anti-left votes to its pocket. Political commentators rightly observed that "the BJP sowed but the Congress reaped". The Sabarimala issue helped the BJP to consolidate its vote bank, but they never reaped the benefits fully. The women entry issue in Sabarimala temple has attracted wide attention and the socio-political atmosphere of the state become the stage for arguments and counter arguments.

Table 4.5: Performance of the UDF, LDF and NDA in the Lok Sabha Election 2019

Sl. No.	Constituencies	UDF	LDF	NDA	WON
1	Kasaragod	474961	434523	1,76049	UDF
2	Kannur	529741	435182	68509	UDF
3	Vatakara	526755	442092	80128	UDF
4	Wayanad	706367	274597	78816	UDF
5	Kozhikode	493444	408219	1,61216	UDF
6	Malappuram	589873	329720	82332	UDF
7	Ponnani	521824	328551	1,10603	UDF
8	Palakkad	399274	387637	2,18556	UDF
9	Alathur	533815	374847	89837	UDF
10	Thrissur	415089	321456	2,93822	UDF
11	Chalakudy	473444	341170	1,54159	UDF
12	Ernakulam	491263	322110	1,37749	UDF
13	Idukki	498493	327440	78648	UDF
14	Kottayam	421046	314787	1,55135	UDF
15	Alappuzha	433790	443003	1,86278	LDF
16	Mavelikkara	437997	376497	1,32323	UDF
17	Pathanamthitta	380089	335476	2,95627	UDF
18	Kollam	497264	347492	1,02319	UDF
19	Attingal	380995	342748	2,48081	UDF
20	Thiruvananthapuram	416131	258556	3,16142	UDF
TOTAL VOTES		96,21,655	71,46,103	31,66,329	

The National Election Studies (NES) 2019 found that the Sabarimala issue was an important concern of the people of Kerala. The decision of the Supreme Court on Sabarimala temple was strongly opposed by more than six of every 10 respondents and somewhat opposed by another one of every 10. Among them, the opposition of women voters was much higher. The Supreme Court decision was opposed by more than two-thirds of the women respondents. Similarly, the handling of the Sabarimala temple issue by the LDF Government also received the same response from the people as more than half the respondents opposed it. This indicates a strong opposition to the Supreme Court verdict on Sabarimala as well as against the action taken by the LDF Government (Ibrahim, 2019).

Table 4.6: Opinion on the Verdict of Supreme Court on Sabarimala women entry

	Total	Male	Female
Fully support	13.7%	17.01%	10.01%
Somewhat support	12.4 %	16.1%	8.8%
Fully oppose	48.4%	41.7%	54.8%
Cannot say	8.2%	7.7%	8.6%
No response	4 %	2 .2%	5.5%

Source: CSDS data unit cited in K. M. Sajad Ibrahim. (2019), Decisive vote for UDF in Kerala, EPW, August 24, 2019, LIV (34).

After the Supreme Court verdict of September 28, 2018, major political parties tried to politicise the issue for reaping maximum political mileage and to boost up public opinion against the government decision to implement the verdict without consulting the stakeholders.

Review Petition on SC Verdict

More than 50 review petitions were filed against the SC verdict allowing women aged between 10 and 50 to enter in Sabarimala temple and for the protection of temple rituals and customs. The decisive petitions were filed by the chief priest of Sabarimala temple, NSS, All Kerala Brahmins' Association and former TDB Chief, Prayar Gopalakrishnan. Several women devotees also were among those who sought a review. The Court had agreed to hear all review petitions in an open court whether they should admit petitions, but had refused to provide stay for its earlier judgement. The five-judge Constitutional Bench of the Supreme Court was to hear the petition. The Kerala government, however, opposed the review petition and argued that exclusion of women from temple is not an essential practice of Hindu religion. They also argued that a ban on women because of menstruation is against the Constitution and essentially gender discrimination.

The argument put forward by the *Tantri* is that the temple allows the entry of all and there is no caste, gender and religious based exclusion. The fundamental right to worship also includes the right of the deity which is also formed part of the essential religious practice (Deccan Chronicle, 2019, November 14). Advocate K. Parasaran cited *Bijoe Emmanuel Vs. The State of Kerala*, where the Court established that religious beliefs held by persons cannot be tested on the grounds of rationality (Kantaru Rajeevaru, 2019). A. M. Singhvi and V. Giri, the counsels for Prayar Gopalakrishnan and *Tantri* argued on the non-applicability of Article 17 as it read as caste-based exclusion. Four women from Kerala, Reshma, Shanila, Bindu and Kanakadurga, supporters of women entry also have filed applications seeking to be heard as intervenors. It is an interesting fact that the TDB spent lakhs of rupees for its counsel for opposing the review petitions in the Court. This money is now other than the income from the temple including voluntary contributions of the devotees.

The SC on 14th November, 2019 referred the review petition to a seven- judge bench. Chief Justice Ranjan Gogoi, Justices A. M. Khanwilkar and Indu Malhotra observed that the restriction of women into religious places is not limited to Sabarimala alone, but the entry of women into mosques and the practice of female genital mutilation in the Dawoodi Bohra community are also to be re-examined. However, Justices R.F. Nariman, D.Y. Chandrachud gave dissenting verdicts in the case. However, the majority verdict did not say anything against the apex court's verdict on September 28, 2018 allowing women entry in the temple and pronounced no stay for the earlier judgement (The New Indian Express, 2019, November 14).The Court verdict evoked mixed response among Hindu organisations, the political leaders, jurists and the government. Soon after this, the Devaswom Minister firmly said that the State Government could not provide security to any woman visiting the shrine. Those who want police protection for entering in the temple should obtain a Court order for the purpose. Any activist will not be allowed to display their activism in Sabarimala. The CPM also took a wait and see approach in the issue (Times of India, 2019, November 16).

The fight for the entry of women in Sabarimala temple assumed larger dimensions. As per our Constitution, the restriction on women entry in Sabarimala is against the spirit of gender equality it ensures. Here the tussle is between religious tradition and beliefs on one side and rationalism, gender justice and constitutional rights on the other. Even many pro-Hindu organisations are arguing for equal treatment for women in the matter of worship. The RSS General Secretary Bhaiyyaji Joshi in his address to the National Council has said that unfair traditions have caused the ban of women in many temples; such unfair traditions should be disposed of with. Thus, in the beginning, there was no consensus even among the various Hindu organisations regarding the entry of women into the forest shrine. Temple entry movements by marginalised sections have historically been used as a symbol of protest against exclusion and as a challenge to the established power hierarchies in society. Banning entry to temples is especially discriminatory since it subverts the idea of everyone being equal to God and thus movements to enter the house of God assume a larger meaning. Years long legal battle on the issue created anxiety among the *Ayyappa* devotees.

The issue has two-fold dimensions; first is the human rights perspective and the other is religious perspective. Natural justice, gender justice and gender equality are the supporting pillars of human rights perspectives. Protection of temple tradition and customs are supporting arguments for the religious ground. Moreover, the entry of womenfolk in Sabarimala is not fully restricted and thousands of women devotees visit the shrine every year. Entry of women in a particular temple is not a means of gender equality or women empowerment. A consensus on the revision of temple customs in a time-bound manner among the stakeholders like Hindu leaders and saints is essential to solve the issue amicably. While taking the case of entry of women of a particular age group in Sabarimala temple the concern here is modernity regardless of traditional practices. The religious dimensions of the issue have been resisted by a group of people in the leftist stronghold society. But the Lok Sabha election results compelled the leftist to have a rethink on the issue.

5

Response on Temple Administration

Secularism envisages religious freedom to all citizens without the intervention of the state. It is strange that the political parties interfere in the internal matters of the religious institutions of particular communities in a secular state. Historical interpretation regarding the political interference over the administration of Hindu religious institutions in Kerala affirms that the erstwhile royal rule is instrumental for such a system and the successive democratic rule continues to overpower these institutions in disguise of their protection. Political parties, religious interest groups and caste organisations are actively involving in the issues concerned with the administration of temples in the state. This chapter makes an analysis of the views of political parties and Hindu organisations on various issues prevailing in the administration of Temples.

Role of Political Parties in Temple Administration

Political parties are an integral part of the democratisation of administration, be it the State Government or other local democratic bodies and they serve as intermediary structures between the society and the government (Asthana, 1988:1). Some of the political parties in state politics, who claim to be secular, are even involving in the administration of Devaswom Boards, the state machinery for regulating the Hindu religious institutions. But political control over these institutions through nominating party men to the Boards often creates controversies in state politics. Political nomination to various Devaswom governing bodies was criticised by the High Court several times.

In Kerala, all major political parties intervene in the administration of temples in one way or other. Both the LDF and UDF nominees rule Devaswom Boards, as the BJP is still not in the scene, so it opposes the political nomination and uses temple related issues for their political gains. Franklin. A. Presler in his monograph *Religion and Bureaucracy* points out that no government or political party has been able to resist incorporating the temple into its broader political strategy; whenever possible, temple resources, symbolic and material, have been used to build, stabilise or extended network of power and influence (Presler, 2008: 11). Major political parties in Kerala have their own outlook in temple related affairs and hold divergent views and perceptions on temple administration.

The Communist Party of India (Marxist) (CPI (M))

The Communist Party of India (Marxist), the leading political party in Kerala, has its influence among the backward communities of Hindu religion, particularly Ezhavas, SC and ST communities. It aims at a classless, casteless society and works for the removal of economic disparities exist in the society. Ideologically, the party represents atheism and considers religion as opium that creates havoc for class consciousness. But as part of power politics, they are also compelled to interfere in the affairs of the administration of temples. It dissociates with the spiritualism upheld by the temples, but associates with their administration in disguise of its materialistic perspective and do not initiate changes in their management. T. J. Nossitter observes that the party used the semi-governmental institutions and even religious institutions as an instrument of struggle in social and economic reconstitution, its members are overwhelmingly Hindus (1982: 367).

While examining the history of the Communist Party in the state since 1940, one can see that it is closely linked with the history of the Congress party (Fic, 1970: 8). In 1964, CPI (M) was formed under the leadership of A. K. Gopalan and E. M. S. Namboodiripad. Kerala Communism is distinctive in the sense that it is committed to the values like representative democracy and active socialism and was modified to the peculiar structure of Kerala society. CPI (M) has not much belief in the religious dogmas and is supposed to be an atheist having no faith in God and temple worship. Bukharin and Preobrazhensky in their work *The ABC of Communism* stated that religion and Communism are incompatible both theoretically and practically. In practice, Communism is mismatched with religious faith (1969: 247- 48). The Party sticks on to the principles of dialectical materialism which has been lenient towards the religious beliefs of supporters and fellow travellers. Party members are advised to shun such beliefs. Former Party Chief Prakash Karat said that the Party does not bar people with religious belief from joining, but they should not let their faith intrude into the affairs of the state. Clarifying the party's stand on religion, Karat in an article in the *People's Democracy*, the party mouthpiece, said that the Marxists are atheists and they believe in no religion, but Marxists understand the origin of religion and the role it plays in society (Karat, 2010). This is sufficient to indicate that the Marxists never underestimate the role of religion and the influence of religious institutions in society. The party leadership is affirmed that the party is not against any religion or religious beliefs but is against superstitious beliefs followed in the name of religion.

The CPM state conference held in 1990 moaned that there was an undesirable growing tendency among the party men to associate themselves with rituals and religious functions in places of worship (Govindankutty, 1990). Thus, in all sense the Party cadets were changed into believers in God and they are deviating from the basic principles of atheism. The Party in its rectification document of 2009 laid down that the party members have to eschew all social practices based on caste and religion which are alien to Communist norms. The Party exhorts its cadets not to organise religious ceremonies or personally conduct religious rituals (Karat, 2010). The CPI (M) in its Plenum held at Palakkad in 2013 had resolved to ban party members from being office-bearers of religious and caste outfits and from visiting places of worship for offering worship. This step was taken as part of the efforts to eradicate all tendencies that were considered inappropriate for a Marxist-Leninist organisation (The Pioneer, 2017, September 30).

Their ideological commitments compel the leaders of the Party to keep away deliberately from attending temple rituals. Chief Ministers, V. S. Achuthanandan in 2007, Pinarayi Vijayan in 2018 had avoided coming to the *sanctum sanctorum* of the Sree Ayyappa Temple, despite their official visit to Sabarimala for reviewing the preparations ahead of the pilgrimage season. G Sudhakaran, while holding the Devaswom portfolio during 2006-11 had visited temples, but did not partake in any rituals. Another notable event in this connection was Devaswom Minister Kadakampally Surendran's visit to Guruvayur temple in 2017 which triggered a controversy and created headache to the party leadership. The Minister visited the temple on *Ashtami Rohini* Day (birth day of Lord Krishna) and offered *pushpanjali* (offering) on behalf of his family members. Apart from making a donation, he reportedly offered prayers at the 'sacred steps' of the temple. He contributed money for *annadanam* as well (The Asian Age, 2017, October 30). The Party sought an explanation from the Minister in this regard and finally, the issue was amicably solved. The party members should follow the Constitution of the Party, but the followers of the Party have the right to follow their own path. Belief is personal and immeasurable one and it is difficult to identify a believer. The Party's stand is that temples should be run by Hindus and Hindu may be a person by birth or conversion, but not necessarily a person who had faith in God and temple worship (Govindankutty, 1990). The party believed that every Hindu, whether a believer in God or not should be given representation in the Devaswom governing bodies. Defining Hinduism in a particular manner is not possible.

Even in the midst of its atheist political ideology, the Party takes care to interfere in the administration of Hindu religious institutions of the state during its regime. By nominating party members to various Devaswom governing bodies and issuing ordinances and amendments in Devaswom Acts, the Party is trying to safeguard their political goals. The CPM-led government took a major step to appoint non-Brahmin priests including six Dalits in temples which is hailed as historic in the sense that it ensured social justice by giving a blow to the Brahmanical supremacy and putting an end to caste discrimination. This anti-caste democratic approach of the Party helped to some extent giving all Hindu believers their due share in priestly functions. It is impossible to differentiate the party men and exclude them from temple related affairs, so while constituting various committees like festival committees, they are naturally included. Kannur, being the stronghold of the Party, temple festivals are organised by the party men. Parassinikkadavu Muthuppan temple in Kannur has the temple governing body with members of the Party.The Party Branch Secretary in the temple village made an interesting remark that Muthappan is a rebel, a revolutionary and in that sense, he is a 'Communist God'. Around 90% of the temple committee members are party men (The New Indian Express, 2009, April 11). As a cadre political party, the CPM opposes temple-oriented activities of the RSS, a pro-Hindu cadre organisation in the state.

The Party holds the notion that the unassessed wealth belonging to the temples including the famous Sree Padmanabhaswamy Temple, Thiruvananthapuram is the wealth donated by the former kings who received it as tax or acquired in the course of annexing territory, should be treated as national wealth. The Party favours state controlled administrative set up for the Sree Padmanabhaswamy temple on the lines of the Guruvayur temple administration (The Hindu, 2011, September 20).

In the Sabarimala women entry issue, the CPM has expressed its own stand. The Party believes that it is unfair to keep the temple out of bounds for women of a particular age category and so it supports entry of women into Sabarimala temple for securing gender justice and Constitutional values. The CPM State Secretary Kodiyeri Balakrishnan in 2016 clarified that the Party stood for entry of women belonging to all age groups not only in Sabarimala but also in all temples in the state. In an article published in the party mouthpiece, *Deshabhimani*, he stated that the restriction at the hill shrine is an echo of an outdated class system which is keen to retain male dominance in the society and discriminate women from public space and places of worship. The government projected the implementation of the verdict of the Supreme Court regarding women entry as a part of continuing reformist values in the state.

The CPM-led LDF failed in 19 out of 20 Lok Sabha seats in Kerala during the Lok Sabha election of 2019 and secured only one seat. After the election, State Secretariat meeting of the Party in the first week of June 2019 evaluated that there had been depletion of votes from segments which traditionally stood with the Left. The State Government's decision to facilitate entry of women of all ages into Sabarimala temple in keeping with the Supreme Court order, had led to alienate a section of Hindu voters. So, the Party shifted its earlier stand and took a soft approach in the issue as the CPM State Secretariat remarked that the Party is with the believers.The Party observed that a section of party loyalists was "misled" by right-wing parties and groups in the Sabarimala issue. The stand taken by the Party to allow entry of women in Sabarimala definitely affected the poll prospects and the party suffered a major setback in the political history losing seats in its own strongholds.

Various Hindu leaders and organisations were highly critical of the CPM policy towards temple administration. The RSS started temple liberation movements against the Marxist interference in temple affairs that led to the formation of Hindu Front in state politics. In order to check the growing influence of Hindutwa organisations, the CPM also embarked on forming children's outfit *Balasangham on* the lines of *Balagokulam* of the RSS as a counter programme in the observance of *Sreekrishna Jayanthi* celebrations at Kannur. Social commentator B. R. P. Bhaskar tried to explain the CPM's dilemma in the following words, "Marxism decries religion but its followers know the importance of religion in our society and so cannot oppose it. This has led to a dichotomy and, at times, double standards in their approach" (The Telegraph India, 2012, November 11).

While upholding secular and renaissance values, the Party has always shown a keen interest in the administration of temples. The Party nominates leaders and activists who have close ties with the Party to various Devaswom governing bodies. The Party believes that political interference in temple administration is a part of democratisation of institutions in the state. The CPM has its own trade unions for Devaswom as well as temple employees in the state. Regarding the trade union activities among temple employees, the outlook of the Party is very clear as it believes an unavoidable thing to meet the problems of the employees. Even the living conditions of priests who offer rituals to God are pathetic as they struggle to meet their basic needs. Though the Party's policies regarding the management of Devaswoms invite criticisms from various corners due to its doctrinal insistence of atheism, the Party introduced several innovative steps in temple administration including handing over Devaswom recruitment to PSC (later replaced with Devaswom Recruitment Board), the formation of the MDB for Malabar temples etc. But it is a fact that the land reforms initiated by the Leftist government have obviously affected the survival of temples.

Indian National Congress (INC)

The Indian National Congress is a major national political party and being an umbrella organisation, it represents various sections of society including Hindu nationalists, Christians, Buddhists and other minority communities. Its ideology is deeply rooted in principles of Socialism, Liberalism and Gandhism (Gopakumar, 1984: 18). In all sense, the Congress Party is a secular platform that accommodates diverse interests under one roof. But the Party is vulnerable to pulls and pressures of religion and religious interest groups (Kurup, 2004: 149). The INC has a glorious past as the vanguard of anti-untouchability and temple entry movements in the state fighting against caste-based discriminations and protecting civil equality and social justice. T. K. Madhavan in the historic Kakinada session of the Congress in 1923 stated that temple entry was the birth right of all Hindus (Menon, 1994: 80). Anti-untouchability committees were formed in all villages due to the efforts of Madhavan under the auspices of the Congress Party and with the blessings of Mahatma Gandhi. During the conduct of the historic Vaikom and Guruvayur *Satyagrahas*, Congress volunteers actively participated.

The history of Devaswom Board for Travancore and Cochin temples is closely associated with the Congress Party. It was during the period of Congress rule in 1949 that Travancore Cochin Hindu Religious Institution Ordinance was promulgated and according to it the Travancore and Cochin Devaswom Boards were formed. The Congress leaders Mannathu Padmanabhan and R. Sankar led the first Devaswom Board (TDB), introduced several measures for Hindu unification through temple reforms. This created a headache to the Congress-led T. K. Narayana Pillai Ministry. Hindu leaders like Mannathu Padmanabhan and R. Sankar were fighting against the Congress policy of appeasing the Christian community and targeting Hindu religious institutions. As a result, both Mannam and Sankar were expelled from the Congress Party for the reason that they criticised the Christian interference on Hindu religious institutions (Sadasivan, 1997: 29). Finally, under the pressure of the Christian lobby in the Congress Party, the government introduced legislation to control Hindu religious institutions. There was an allegation against the Congress Party in 1984 for allotting one-hectare land for the building of a Christian church during the time of *Nilakkal agitation* under the pressure of the Kerala Congress Party (Jayaprasad, 1992: 194-96).

The Congress Party advocates autonomy of Devaswom Boards in the state. It is against the Marxist interference in temple administration due to their atheist policy. On the pretext of fighting against corruption, the Marxists intrude into the administrative machinery of Devaswoms and make them fettered. So, the Party believes that a consensus is needed to solve the issues prevailing in the administration of Devaswoms. It affirms that religious places are for the believers and the conversion of temples into a battleground of politics will not do any good for the temples or devotees. The ultimate result of the politicisation of temples will be the growth of Hindu communalism in the state. Ramesh Chennithala, the KPCC president in 2009 accused of the government for its interference in religious matters that would lead to a dangerous situation in a democracy (The Hindu, 2009, November 9). Prayar Gopalakrishnan, former MLA of the Indian National Congress and the former President of the TDB has expressed the opinion that the power of the state over Devaswom administration is limited; the government has the power only to nominate members to Devaswom Boards and not to dissolve them.

As stated earlier, the Congress is against the nomination of non-believers or atheists to the Devaswom Boards. As part of the political strategy to eliminate its rival leftists from temple administration, the Congress Governments in 1986 and 1994 made amendments for entrusting the administration of temples with the believers. In 1999, the LDF government through an amendment did away with the provision. Actually, the Congress Party is not against the political nomination in Devaswom governing bodies and many of its top-level leaders including former MLAs and MPs served as the chairmen and members of various Devaswom Boards. But the Party is against unnecessary governmental interference in the day-to-day administration of Devaswoms. The Party's trade union is very active in almost all the Devaswom Boards in Kerala, gained recognition in the referendum conducted in the TDB and CDB. Like the Communists, the Congress Party also concerned with the growing influence of the *Sangh Parivar* organisations over temples and devotees. The RSS and other Hindu organisations exploit temples for political advantages which indirectly led to the BJP's gains in elections.

With regard to Sabarimala women entry issue, the Congress Party's stand is clear; that the customs and traditions of the temple should be preserved and restriction imposed on the entry of women of a particular age group into Sabarimala temple should be sustained. In the Supreme Court, the Oommen Chandy Government submitted an affidavit clearly disfavouring the entry of women at Sabarimala against the stand taken by the previous LDF government. While the state Congress Party has taken a stand favouring the preservation of the customs and traditions of the Sabarimala temple, the national leadership of the Party differed in its attitude in the matter. The senior national leader of the Congress and former Union Minister, Jairam Ramesh and Shashi Tharoor, the Congress MP have favoured the entry of women in all temples saying that discrimination based on sex should be ended. Shashi Tharoor holds that the entry of women at Sabarimala has been opposed by raising the same kinds of arguments as had been raised against the entry of Dalits into temples in the thirties (News and Views, 2016). Meanwhile, the senior state Congress leader and a former

Member of TDB Ajay Tharayil through a facebook post sparked off another controversy regarding the entry of the non- Hindus in temples that those who believe in the temple and idol worship should be allowed in temples. In 2006, when a question arose on the appointment of 'non-Brahmin priests' in temples, then KPCC president Ramesh Chennithala's curious reply was to continue with the 'present system' of worship (The Hindu, 2006, January 4). This observation clearly indicates that the Party is stood for preserving temple rituals and customs rather than a reform.

Bharatiya Janata Party (BJP)

As a saffron political party, the BJP is a keen observer in temple-related affairs. In theory, the Party believes in the integral humanism propounded by Deen Dayal Upadhyaya and never represents the idea of 'Hindu Nation', but in practice, it represents the political viewpoint of the RSS (Jayaprasad, 1989: 301). The Party often uses temple and temple-related issues for consolidating its vote bank. It is highly committed to temple politics although in a different dimension.

The BJP emerged as the third force in Kerala politics by raising sensitive issues related with temple such as politicisation of its administration, nomination of non-believers in temple governing bodies, women entry issue in Sabarimala, encroachment on temple lands, attack on temples etc. It believes the temple as a symbol of Hindu unity and solidarity. Their support to Nilakkal agitation, temple liberation movements, temple de-politicisation movements, the policy taken towards Devaswom land encroachment, temple take over by the Malabar Devaswom Board etc. certainly made them popular among the Hindu community. They stood with the devotees in their protest against the takeover of Hanuman temple at Palakkad and Parthasarathy temple at Guruvayur by the MDB. They consistently demanded for the implementation of Sankaran Nair

Commission recommendations for the betterment of temple administration.

In the matter of political nomination to Devaswom Boards, the Party's stand can be seen in the observation of BJP's former President Kummanam Rajasekharan that temple administration should be depoliticised and members of Devaswom Committees should be believers in God and temple worship. Devaswom should be administered by representatives of devotees as in the case of several private temples in the state (Personal Interview, 2017). The BJP leader, O. Rajagopal remarked, if the temple administration is not distinct from politics it would spell disaster for secularism and communal amity (The Indian Express, 1991, June 9). The BJP accused both the Congress and Communist parties of their policies related to temples.

The Party's policy to nurture a temple oriented Hindu community in Kerala is actually with an eye at electoral dividends. In association with the RSS, the Party took the initiative to renovate temples, *kavus* and abandoned family temples. These activities helped it to make a hold in Kannur, once the communist citadel and the BJP vote share gradually increases in the region. The RSS leader Valsan Thillankeri observed that they groomed a temple-oriented community which then turns into a vote bank in favour of the BJP and this slowly reduces the influence of the CPM (The Indian Express, 2017, November 21). The Hindu Front (*Hindu Munnani*), a new outfit of RSS, entered in Kerala Politics in the eighties as a reaction against the minority appeasement policy of both the leftist and rightist political parties in Kerala. According to the Party, the present secularism is pseudo-secularism as it amounts to appeasement of minorities (Engineer, 1991, April 30). Their slogan 'Hindu votes for Hindus', made an impact on the electoral politics of Kerala. L. K. Advani, a senior BJP leader expressed that the BJP did not seek Hindu domination but only oppose the promotion of the interest of other communities at the expense of Hindus (The Hindu, 1986, March 15).

The Party stood against corruption in the Board administration. Many a times, it raised voice against illegal appointments to various Devaswom Boards. The former State President of the BJP, in 2015 urged the government to review all appointments made in the Devaswom Boards during the past 10 years (The Hindu, 2015, December 29). The Party also demanded to scrap off all Devaswom legislations enacted for politicising temple administration. The BJP former General Secretary K. G. Marar clarified that the administration of the places of worship of all the religions should be left solely to the believers (The Hindu, 1999, June 1). The party favoured the appointment of the non-Brahmin priests and the entry of non-Hindus in temples. In 1988, the Party opposed the Devaswom practice of preventing the *Harijan panchavadyaseva* (a type of devotional music) in the Guruvayur temple. The BJP leader K. G. Marar criticised such policies of the Board stating that no one should be denied the right to worship on the basis of caste considerations (The Indian Express, 1988, July 11). The BJP former President C.K. Padmanabhan also said that it is wrong to deny entry to anyone who is coming to the temple for worship (The Hindu, 2000, September 19).

The RSS and BJP share the same view that the sex and caste-based prejudices ruin the unity of Hindu society. In the issue of entry of women of a particular age group, the BJP stated that political parties should not interfere in the issue and it should be resolved through consensus among the stakeholders, customs and rituals "should change in accordance with time" (The Hindu, 2016, April 29). The BJP used temple related issues for their political advantages. The Party favours to start religious study centres and religious conventions in temples under the ambit of the Devaswom Boards to create awareness among various sections of the Hindu community and entice more people to the faith. Thus, the BJP and its parivar organisations try to increase their influence in Kerala through temple-oriented activities.

Communist Party of India (CPI)

The Preamble of the Constitution of the Communist Party of India states that the Party is a voluntary organisation of toiling people, intelligentsia and others devoted to the cause of Socialism and Communism. The Party's vision on religion is reflected in its Constitution that it espouses the right to faith of all sections of society subject to the condition that it should not permit preaching of hatred against any religion. The CPI was founded in the 1920s which was split into two factions, the CPI and CPI (M); the CPI being designated as rightist among the left group. The Party is one of the major leftist political parties in Kerala and through its cadre strength, aggressiveness and radical economic programme, appealed to a large number of people in Kerala belonging to all communities though the majority of its supporters are members of Ezhava community (Nair, 1994: 82).

According to the Communist notion, politicisation and democratisation are dialectically intertwined. As part of democratisation, the temples are to be administered by the nominees of political parties and in consonance with this policy, the Party also sends representatives to the temple governing bodies. They have representation in all the Devaswom governing bodies when the Left Front is in power. It is notable that none of the Party nominees hitherto faced allegations of corruption. But after the SC verdict on women entry, the CPI nominee in the TDB, K. P. Sankara Das had to face an allegation regarding the violation of Sabarimala temple custom by ascending 18 steps without carrying *irumudikettu*. Only the *tantris* and members of the erstwhile Pandalam royal family have the right to climb the steps without *irumudikettu* as per the prevailing custom.

Further in the Sabarimala issue, the Party supported the action of the government in implementing the SC verdict. The CPI National General Secretary Sudhakar Reddy accused of the right-wing political parties like the BJP and the Congress for indulging into dirty politics over the women entry issue to target the LDF government in Kerala by exploiting the religious sentiments of the people. He also pointed out the contradictions in the statements of the BJP- RSS leaders welcoming the judgement at the national level, but opposing it in the state. Both the BJP and the Congress were unnecessarily politicising the issue thereby exploiting the religious feelings of the people (First Post, 2018). The Government of Kerala revealed its stand in the Court that it has the constitutional obligation for ensuring gender justice thereby protecting the religious rights of the womenfolk. Though the Party supported the government policy in Sabarimala issue on the grounds of its constitutional duty, at the same time criticised the State Government failure in foreseeing the public response while implementing the Supreme Court verdict (The Hindu, 2019, June 13). The CPI has always supported for economic reservation to the forward castes in Devaswom recruitment. For a long, the Party is consistently demanding for that.

Revolutionary Socialist Party (RSP)

RSP is a leftist radical political party in Kerala dedicated to the cause of socialism through Marxist Leninist methods. At the national level, it emphasises the need for an armed revolution in a bourgeois set up. The ideological basis of the Party shows that they have little faith in the democratic method of ballot. It justifies its electoral participation as a way for mobilising the masses for revolution. Contradictory to their ideological posture, it nominates party leaders to various Devaswom governing bodies that manage the abodes of God in the state.

The RSP had its representation in the Devaswom Boards irrespective of the coalition it belonged to. For the first time in the history of the TDB, the Party nominee, Prakkulam Bhasi became its President in the sixties. Several other members of the Party became members of TDB including Chengarappalli

Damodaran Potti, Sankaran Nair, Prof. V. S. Madhavan Nair and Sicily. Once the party affiliated trade union became very powerful in the TDB; K. C. Vamadevan, Babu Divakaran, Damodaran Potti and several other leaders fought for the problems of temple employees in the state. Babu Divakaran belonged to the Party presented a private Bill in the Kerala Assembly, named as Kerala Private Devaswom Temple Employees Welfare Fund Bill, 1999 (KLA, 1999, December 17). A private Bill has also been moved by its MP, N. K. Premachandran in the Lok Sabha, seeking to conserve the customs and traditions of the Sabarimala temple.

Civil Society on Temple Administration

Civil Society is a political community, as Edmund Burke described as the 'little platoons' encompass institutions that are private in that they are independent of government and organised by individuals in pursuit of their own ends (Heywood, 2013: 17). The Oxford Concise Dictionary of Politics defined Civil Society as the set of intermediate associations which are neither the state nor the family includes voluntary associations (Mclean & McMillan, 2009: 81). It consists of a vast array of both formal and informal organisations, interest groups, cultural and religious organisations, civic and developmental associations, issue-oriented movements, the mass media, research and educational institutions and similar organisations. Thus, civil society refers to non-profitable voluntary associations and its sphere of activity lies in between the state and family and should include political parties and organisations as well. They are completely independent of the government and sometimes voice against governmental policies. Apart from the state-regulated temple administrative machinery, these civil society organisations play their active role in the realm of temple administration. Several civil society organisations based on caste and religion are functioning in the realm of temple administration in the state.

Caste-based Civil Society Organisations

The social composition of Kerala is significant as the study involves the administration of temples, the worshiping places of her majority community. Though Hinduism remains as the majority religion (54.73% as per 2011census), the minority communities are powerful in state politics due to the caste-wise stratification of the Hindu community. Religion-wise classification of population as per the 2011 census is explained in Figure 5.1.

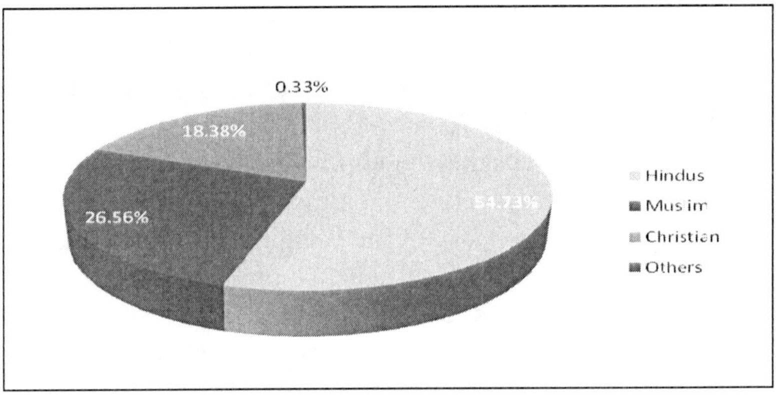

Fig. 5.1: Religion-wise classification of population.

Table 5.2: Caste-wise status of the Hindu population

Sl. No.	Community	Population* (%)
1	Nair	12.88
2	Other Forward Communities	1.77
3	Total Forward Communities	14.65
4	Ezhava	22.91
5	Other Backward Communities	8.48
6	Scheduled Castes	9.07
7	Scheduled Tribes	1.07
8	Total Backward Communities	31.39

*Studies based on the 2006 statistics of Kerala Sasthra Sahithya Parishad KP Aravindan. (2006), (Ed.). Kerala Padanam, Kerala Sasthra Sahithya Parishad, p. 33.

Among the total population, the backward communities constitute 31.39% of them the Ezhava community is the most powerful section constituting 22.91%. Nair community belonged to the forward section comprising of 12.88% of the total population. The composition of Kerala society on caste line is explained in the table (see table).

Sree Narayana Dharma Paripalana Yogam (SNDP Yogam)

In the socio-political scenario of the state, SNDP Yogam plays a decisive role in securing justice to the so-called *avarna* communities, particularly to the Ezhava people who constitute 22.91% of the total population and 40.79% of the total Hindu population (Aravindan, 2006: 34). SNDP Yogam, formed in 1903 primarily for managing the administration of Aruvippuram Siva Temple and propagating the ideas of the great saint Sree Narayana Guru. 'One Caste, One Religion and One God for man' is the message given by Guru to modern society. As a social reform movement, SNDP Yogam focused its activities on movements like temple entry, temperance movements and a movement for the proper representation of backward people in public services (Lawrence, 1988: 132). In the past, temple entry was restricted and the so-called untouchables were denied freedom of worship and so the Ezhava community decided not to co-operate with the temples where they had no accessibility (Khan, 2010: 58-59).

There were many reformers belonged to the Ezhava community who fought against the Brahmin monopoly in temple rituals. Sree Narayana Guru, Arattupuzha Velayudha Panicker, K. Ayyappan, C. Krishnan, Dr Palpu, Kumaran Asan, T. K. Madhavan were prominent among them. Arattupuzha Velayudha Panicker revolutionised temple worship by establishing a temple and installed a Siva deity in 1854 at Mangalathu village in the Karthikapalli Taluk in Central Travancore. The privileges and rights which were enjoyed by the upper classes for the right to worship in temples of Brahmanic tradition were brought down to the Ezhava class through his attempt (Arya, 2018). Dr Palpu founded the SNDP Yogam in 1903 which became the beacon for many future social reform movements. K. Ayyappan founded *Sahodara Sanghom* in 1917 for eliminating evils of caste and popularising *misrabhojanam* (interdining) among the Ezhavas and other inferior castes. C. Krishnan defied the orders of the Malabar Collector and walked along the approach roads to the Thali temple, Calicut on November 1, 1917 (Menon, 2008: 314-15). T. K. Madhavan and Kumaran Asan raised the issue of freedom of worship and movement through temple roads several times in the Assembly. Social exclusion, denial of freedom of movement and worship persuaded a sizable section of the Ezhavas to embrace Islam and Christianity.

Sree Narayana Guru's Concept of Temple Worship

Sree Narayana Guru, the philosopher-saint and architect of the *modern renaissance* in Kerala was born in 1856 in an Ezhava family at Chempazhanthi in Thiruvananthapuram. George Woodcock reminded that India as a whole may have produced its Gandhi, but Kerala is inclined to take more pride in their own great spiritual social leader, Gandhi's contemporary, the low caste sage Sree Narayana Guru with his tireless preaching of the doctrine 'one caste, one religion and one god' (1967: 36). Guru was a great visionary who propagated the idea of the essential goodness of man irrespective of religion, worked for a casteless society in which there is no exploitation of man by man. He discovered the essence of *advaita* philosophy and used it as an instrument for social liberation (Kumar, 2010: 149).

Guru pleaded for simplification of temple worship and insisted on radical reforms in temple rituals. Guru started his temple reform process by consecrating Aryan deities in many parts of the state with Sanskrit rituals for facilitating the freedom of worship to the *avarnas*. Through the *Aruvippuram* consecration in 1888, Guru revolutionised the concept of idol worship that had broken all chains created by the orthodox Brahmins in Kerala. Justice S. P. Iyer of Madras High Court remarked the Guru's temple building movement as a *parallel government* within Hinduism (Ayyappan, 1965: 135; King, 2015: 46). His temples were primarily built for the Ezhava community, but all classes were permitted to offer worship without distinction. Sree Narayana Guru's temples functioned almost parallel to that of the caste Hindus which denied entry to the Ezhavas (Menon, 1987: 205).

The consecration of Siva deity by Guru at Aruvippuram in 1888 contributed to the genesis of the social revolutionary movement in the state. Later, the temple management committee here was transformed into the SNDP Yogam in 1903. Guru's temple campaign was mainly intended to create awareness among the lower- class people regarding their freedom of worship. Guru deputed Ezhavas as officiating priests. He also wanted to convert the new temples as community centres and rallying points of Ezhava solidarity (Shaji, 2017: 90). Guru founded temples in South Travancore, North Travancore, Cochin, Malabar regions of Kerala and Mangalore in Karnataka state. Later he stopped consecration of idols in temples and discouraged the community for doing so as it amounts to colossal wastage of human resources by spending money on constructing temples (Kunjakkan, 2005: 38-39). The Ezhava community was inspired by the philosophical postulates of Guru and started a movement to fight for freedom of worship through temple entry.

SNDP Yogam and Temple Administration in Kerala

Sree Narayana Movements (SNM) in Kerala centred on temples was established by Guru. In the initial years, SNDP Yogam was a temple-oriented organisation constituted for the administration of Aruvippuram Temple consecrated by Sree Narayana Guru. Yogam manages several temples and a

Devaswom Secretary is in-charge of Devaswom affairs of Yogam. As a social reform organisation, SNDP Yogam always expressed its opposition against all forms of discrimination towards the Ezhava and other backward Hindu communities in the management of temples. SNDP Yogam leaders raised the issues of temple entry inside and outside the legislature and took an active part in the struggle for freedom of religion. R. Sankar, former General Secretary of the Yogam along with Mannathu Padmanabhan, the leader of Nair community, formed *Hindu Mahamandalam* in December 1950 to oppose the unnecessary governmental control over Hindu Religious institutions in the state.

SNDP Yogam's stand is notable for protecting the interests of the lower castes in the administration of Devaswoms in the state. It is the first Hindu organisation in the state that demanded backward classes' representation in all Devaswom Boards in Kerala. They took a firm stand on the appointment of a person from the backward community as the President of TDB; also, they pleaded to ensure reservation of backward communities in the administrative posts and posts of temple priests. SNDP Yogam General Secretary Vellappally Natesan expressed his concern regarding the inadequate representation of the backward communities in Devaswom Boards (The Indian Express, 1998, January 9). Almost 90% of the employees working in the TDB belong to forward communities; so, the recruitment to the Devaswom bodies should be entrusted with the state PSC to achieve social justice. The Director Board of the SNDP Yogam had urged the State Government in 2006 to give effect to 33% reservation for Other Backward Communities (OBCs) and scheduled castes in all appointments to the Travancore Devaswom Board and other Devaswoms in the state. (The Hindu, 2006, November 14). It was during the tenure of M. B. Sreekumar, the then Devaswom Secretary of SNDP Yogam as the TDB Member, successfully implemented reservation to the backward classes in the appointments to the TDB. The Yogam opposed the decision to implement economic reservation in Devaswom appointments by the LDF government in 2017. It felt that 90% of posts in Devaswoms are already occupied by the forward community members and so it is unconstitutional to give economic reservation to forward communities (Deccan Chronicle, 2017, November 18). Reservation to forward communities in Devaswom appointments on the basis of economic backwardness is against the spirit of the Constitution.

The Yogam also demands posting of non-Brahmin priests in Board temples. It defies the prevailing conservative actions of the Devaswom Boards in the state; be it the exclusion of non-Brahmin candidates from appointment as temple priests or conducting purification ceremony in the name of violating the orthodox customs of temples etc. Former General Secretary of SNDP Yogam K. Gopinathan in 1992 demanded the appointment of a non-Brahmin priest in the Sabarimala temple (Mathrubhumi, 1992, September 10). The Yogam gave moral support to the non-Brahmin priest appointed by the TDB in Chettikulangara temple of Mavelikkara Taluk, when a section of people protested over the appointment. The TDB fell into a dilemma and it planned to revert from its earlier decision of appointing non-Brahmin priest. Then the Yogam expressed its deep dissatisfaction and alleged that the TDB is still batting for upper-caste dominance violating Supreme Court verdicts (Deccan Chronicle, 2017, August 19). SNDP welcomed the later decision of the Devaswom Boards for appointing 63 non-Brahmin priests in various temples under its control. In its editorial, *Yoganadam*, the mouthpiece of the Yogam observed that if a Dalit could become the head of the nation then why could sans them to become the priests of temples (Natesan, 2000). The Yogam expressed dissatisfaction over the purification ceremony conducted after the marriage of the son of former Union Minister and leader of the Congress Party, Vayalar Ravi owing to the reason that his wife belongs to the Christian community. Subsequently, the Yogam convened an urgent

Council meeting at Guruvayur and passed a resolution stating that all believers are to be permitted to enter into temples and temple customs and rituals are to be modified according to the changing circumstances. It is the entry of non-believers and not non-Hindus to be prohibited from worshipping in temples (Yoganadam, 2000, October 1-15).

In the matter of introduction of a uniform law for the administration of Devaswoms throughout the state, the Yogam exhibited a negative stand. It strongly opposed the Devaswom Bill of 1997 which proposed a uniform law as that would hit the growth of Hindu temples financially and would deprive the autonomy of Devaswom Boards (The Indian Express, 1998, November 11). Interference of secular state over the administration of religious institutions of a particular community is wrong. Secularism is applicable to all religions. Political interference creates disunity among the Hindu community.

When Sabarimala women entry issue triggered controversy in the state, SNDP Yogam suspected it as part of a conspiracy to oust the LDF government and move to create a second liberation struggle in the state. The SNDP Yogam expressed a conflicting statement that women should not go to Sabarimala, but everyone should accept the Supreme Court verdict (The New Indian Express, 2018, October 10). Mohan Sankar, Executive Member of Sree Narayana Trusts observed that the government should take a compromising stand and consult with the stakeholders on the Sabarimala issue. The government has an obligation to protect the interests and respect the feelings of the devotees. BDJS, the political outfit of the SNDP Yogam supported the agitations organised by various Hindu organisations in the state against women entry. Vellappally Natesan, the General Secretary of the SNDP Yogam stated that the BJP is playing vote bank politics and is trying to destroy the Sabarimala temple (The Hindu, 2018, October 9). Addressing the media after the Yogam's Council meeting at

Cherthala, Natesan softened his stand on the Sabarimala controversy and said that Ezhava community could take part in the protests for protecting the traditions and customs of Sabarimala temple (Times of India, 2018, October 12).

When the government was determined in safeguarding the renaissance values of society by breaking the customs exists in Sabarimala, a Committee was constituted for this purpose under the Chairmanship of the Yogam General Secretary in December 2018 and the Committee decided to form a women wall from Kasaragod to Thiruvananthapuram on 1st January 2019. The decision of Yogam to cooperate with the government created controversies in state politics. The next day after the women's wall, two women activists entered into the Sabarimala temple. The incident persuaded the SNDP to rethink over the issue. Its General Secretary, Vellappally Natesan stated that the entry of women by stealth at Sabarimala was upsetting and distressing. His statement that Sabarimala temple is for the devotees and not for the activists clearly indicated his disappointment over the issue (Kerala Kaumudi, 2019, January 3).

The political interference and government control over the administration of Devaswom Boards are criticised by the Yogam and it urges for a decentralised and depoliticised administration for Devaswoms in the state. The SNDP Yogam demanded adequate representation for Ezhava community in the Devaswom administration (Yoganadam, 1999, July 1-15). The Yogam opposed the move of the government to wrest the control of the temples and mutts owned by the Sree Narayana community. In Travancore and Cochin, the religious institutions of the SNDP Yogam are not under the purview of Devaswom Acts. Vellappally Natesan in a statement remarked that the Yogam is ready to hand over all its temples to the Devaswom Boards, but others should also be ready to do the same so that equality would be ensured and discrimination based on castes would be eliminated (The Hindu, 2008, April

21). But the Devaswom Minister stated in the Legislative Assembly that the Government has not received any such proposal of transfer of temples to Devaswom Boards from the Yogam (KLA, 2008, June 26).

Nair Service Society (NSS)

Nair community is one among the prominent communities in Hindu religion which constitute 12.88% of the total population (Aravindan, 2006: 33). Once the community enjoyed power, rule and authority and belonged to the upper strata in the caste hierarchy and exercised a profound influence over temple management that has been considerably declined since the assumption of temples by Col. Munro in 1811.

Bharatha Kesari Mannathu Padmanabhan

The Nair Service Society (NSS) was established in 1914 with the aim of protecting the Nair community from out-dated religious observances and practices. It inaugurated a new era of social revolution in Kerala. The activities of NSS are still centering on the memories of its founder Mannathu Padmanabhan. As a humanist, social reformer, orator and a great leader, Mannathu Padmanabhan dedicated his life not only for his own community but also for the emancipation of the downtrodden classes. He opposed the worst features of Hinduism like caste-based pollution that denied the so-called 'untouchables' freedom of worship and sowed the seeds of social renaissance and civic equality in the Kerala society. Mannam opposed the Brahmanic hegemony in temple rituals. It was Mannam who had firstly challenged the wrong traditions and practices prevailed in temples. Even though the Brahmins are a microscopic minority in the Hindu religion, they controlled temple rituals and the Nairs blindly obliged as servants and supported alienating the *avarna* people from temple worship. He also questioned the rationality of cruelty practised in certain temples in the form of rituals like *garudanthookkam*, *padayani* etc.

Mannam had a clear vision on the role of temples in society. Temples are the possessions neither of the Brahmins nor Nairs, but of the Hindu community as a whole (Mannathu Padmanabhante Prasangangal, 2013: 24). He urged the government to use its effective authority and power to remove the pollution boards that denied the entry of *avarnas* in front of the leading temples in Travancore. It is to be remembered in this connection that about twenty years before the Temple Entry Proclamation, Mannathu Padmanabhan had thrown open his family shrine, Maranathu Kavu Devi Temple at Perunna, Changanacherry to all Hindus. He affirmed the role of temples in evoking the religious sentiments of the Hindu population and the mission of uniting the Hindu community. Through his vibrant speeches, he popularised the necessity of reforms in temples.

Mannathu Padmanabhan stood for a systematic administration for the temples in Travancore and his contribution in the realm is certainly significant. Mannam was critical over the interference of the state in the administration of Hindu temples. Though the temples were taken over by the government in the name of inefficient administration prevailed, no progress was seen achieved since then, he said. Anyway, the temples under the control of government are the common property solely for the use of the Hindu community (Mannathu Padmanabhante Prasangangal, 2013: 23). He stressed the need for liberating temples from the effective supervision of the government.

Mannam was highly critical of the double stand policy of the State Government in the matter of intervention in religious affairs. It is irrational that the government actively interferes in the internal affairs of a particular religious institution while others are left largely untouched. Either the government should take over all the religious institutions or relieve from engaging in the affairs of temple administration. If other communities have the capacity to manage their own religious institutions, the Hindus also can have that capacity. Moreover, it is unjust that the Hindus are denying civic equality. So he exhorted the Hindus for having united action without any caste distinctions for recapturing temples from governmental control (Mannathu Padmanabhante Prasangangal, 2013: 240-241). The role of Mannam and NSS in the historic temple entry movement is remarkable. The NSS passed a series of resolutions favouring temple entry of the *avarnas*. The *Savarna Jatha* led by Mannam in favour of *Vaikom Satyagraha* had its repercussions in the political and social atmosphere of that time.

Mannam as the President of the TDB

Both Mannam and Sankar visualised the revamping of Devaswom administration for the cultural regeneration of the Hindus (Kumaran, 1987: 351). As the President of the TDB, Mannam tried to introduce certain revolutionary reforms like starting of religious study centres (*mathapadasala*) attached to temples. He stressed the need for abolishing the existed system of Vedic study in *padasalas* exclusively for Brahmins and the feeding of Brahmins (in *oottupura* attached to temples) at the expense of the state and demanded to throw open the *mathapadasalas* that were working at the funds paid by the people to people from all castes (Kolenda, 2013: 184). Mannam and Sankar expressed their concern over the insufficiency of fund allotted by the government for Devaswom administration in lieu of the Devaswom land occupied and demanded enhancement of the statutory contribution to the Board.

During this period, the Board took a firm stand that temple administration should be entrusted with the Hindu people and ensure them opportunities for development through temple centred activities. The Board insisted on preserving the purity of temples and time-bound revision of temple customs and mode of worship. Temples should be made as centres of spiritual and cultural advancement for the Hindus and create unity among Hindus by eliminating the social evil of inequality (Sethunathan, 2015: 126). With the aim of consolidating all sections of Hindus irrespective of caste distinctions, Mannam and Sankar began to organise Hindu population. Both the leaders openly challenged the intervention of the government in the affairs of Devaswoms and felt it that the duty of the Devaswom Board is to organise Hindus through temples. The Congress leaders became aware of the threat posed by Mannam and Sankar and proceeded to move against the leaders. The Congress State Committee meeting held on 26th November, 1949 at VJT Hall, Thiruvananthapuram, decided to introduce legislation to control Devaswom administration in the state. Accordingly, through an amendment in 1950 in the existing Devaswom Act, the Devaswom Board was dissolved. Thus, through the calculated move of the Christian lobby in the Congress, Mannam and Sankar were expelled from the Board (Sethunathan, 2015: 120).

Mannam as the President of the TDB contributed much for the progress of the Hindu religion as well as the betterment of Hindu religious institutions. The promotion of religious education among all the Hindus, allotment of grants for religious publications, abolition of feast for Brahmins, measures to protect the sanctity of temples, procurement of land and construction of buildings for TDB headquarters at Nanthancode are among the major contributions of Mannam during the period (Anilkumar, 2016: 228). But under the political pressure, both Mannam and Sankar were expelled from the Board and the Congress Party. Soon after, Mannam and Sankar constituted the *Hindu Mahamandalam* in 1950 for spreading the message of Hindu unity. In the ensuing election for selecting members to the next Devaswom Board, the NSS nominee B. Paramu defeated the official candidate of the Congress Party, C.O. Madhavan which enshrines as a major event in the history of Devaswom administration in the state.

NSS on Temple Administration

The NSS, as a major social reform organisation in the state keenly observes the developments in the realm of Devaswom administration and expresses its opinion without any hesitation. The NSS has a clear and precise stand on various issues concerned with temple administration. Regarding the state interference and political control of Devaswom governing bodies in the state, the NSS is against such intervention by the government. Political nominations to the Devaswom committees are always resented by the NSS because in such a process, sometimes, even non-believers are being included. When in 1990 the Government planned to install non-believers in the Board, the NSS vehemently protested. It alleged that government interference in the day-to-day administration of temples is one of the reasons for the present state of affairs of Devaswom administration (The Hindu, 2008, July 27). The NSS strongly disagreed with the LDF government move in 1997 to consolidate Devaswom administration in the state without proper consultations. The delegates' meeting of the NSS in 1998 urged the government to retain the autonomy of Travancore Cochin Devaswom Boards. The NSS criticised the recommendations of Justice Chandrashekhara Menon regarding the formation of a separate administrative set up for Sabarimala temple (Malayala Manorama, 2000, June 9). The NSS also opposed the move of the LDF government to increase the number of members in Travancore and Cochin Devaswom Boards from 3 to 7. The NSS follows an equidistance policy towards *Sangh Parivar* organisations on the issue of de-politicisation of Devaswom administration.

The circumstances that led the NSS to wage Liberation Struggle against the first democratically elected Communist Government in Kerala were mainly the land legislations initiated by the E. M. S. Government. These land reforms had broken the financial stability of temples in Kerala, particularly in Malabar area. The NSS opposed the stringent provisions of the

Agrarian Reforms Bill and demanded exemption of the Devaswom lands from the purview of the Bill. Though several petitions were submitted to the government for excluding Devaswom property from the limit of the Bill, but were not accepted by the government. The Liberation Struggle commenced two days after the completion of the legislative process of the first Land Reform Bill. The NSS followed an adamant stand against the Land Reform Bill; its leader Mannathu Padmanabhan stated that since the NSS could not influence the ministry's policy, the ministry must go (Nossitter, 1982: 153). Thus, the government was thrown out of power due to the Liberation Struggle at the auspices of the NSS.

The stand taken by the NSS on the issues related to temple affairs is noteworthy. In the issue of appointing non-Brahmin priests, the NSS favoured the continuation of the hereditary monopoly of Brahmins in the priesthood jobs. In 2006, when TDB decided to appoint non-Brahmin priests in temples, the NSS openly resisted the move. Later, it changed its stand and started a tantric school at Thiruvalla in 2010 to give training to the Nair youth in the priesthood. The institution provides with a full-time, two-year course of study comprising 18 months of classes and a six-month internship at a temple. A debate on whether the worshippers would accept non-Brahmin priests has been triggered in 2013; when the NSS decided to appoint priests from the Nair community in temples managed by the organisation.

The NSS is adamant that temple customs and rituals should be properly protected. When the petition seeking women entry in Sabarimala temple was filed by the Young Lawyers' Association in the Supreme Court, NSS joined in the case as a party opposing the entry of women in the temple. The Supreme Court in its verdict positively viewed the entry of women in Sabarimala and the State Government led by the LDF promised all help to the women who wanted to enter into the temple. The NSS expressed its stand at this juncture that democratically elected government and the judiciary are bound to protect such age-old customs and traditions followed in a religious institution. The government could even explore the possibility of protecting such customs and traditions through appropriate legislation (The Hindu, 2016, January 13). The NSS urged the State Government to file a review petition and explore ways to bring an Ordinance to maintain the hill shrine's traditions. NSS General Secretary, G. Sukumaran Nair urged the government and the TDB to handle the issue more diligently (The New Indian Express, 2018, October 5). Finally, the NSS filed a review petition in the SC against Sabarimala verdict through senior Advocate K. Mohan Parasaran. NSS General Secretary stated that the government has been trying to promote atheism by destroying Sabarimala traditions.The NSS organised massive demonstrations by chanting *Ayyappa mantras* (prayer *yathras)* throughout the state in which thousands of devotees participated. According to the NSS, the government had amplified the problem which it could have resolved peacefully at the outset. The NSS criticized the decision of the TDB to seek an explanation from the *tantri* of Sabarimala temple for advising a "purification ritual" after the entry of two women. The NSS openly backed the lighting of lamps, *Ayyappa Jyothi*, organised by Hindu organisations on December 26, 2018 and exhorted all believers to take part in *Ayyappa Jyothi* irrespective of the political tilt of the organisers. It also criticised the wall of non-believers on January 1, 2019 by stating that the wall was the government's ploy to open Sabarimala to women when all else had failed (The Hindu, 2018, December 17). The NSS is in the forefront for the preservation of customs in Sabarimala and they are willing to spare energy as well as money for the legal battle. The role of NSS in this regard is memorable and laudable.

The decision of the TDB to introduce reservation for backward Hindus in Devaswom appointments and the government plan to hand over recruitments to KPSC irritated the NSS, as it would destabilise temple administration in the state. The PSC is a secular body and so it has no *locus standi* in this regard. In 2007, the NSS approached the Court against the government move. It pleaded for an independent Devaswom Recruitment Board as per the recommendations of Justice Paripoornan Commission. Later, the UDF government decided to constitute Devaswom Recruitment Board in 2013. When the LDF government assumed power in 2016, they decided to disband the Devaswom Recruitment Board which provoked the NSS and its annual conference in 2016 passed a resolution against the left government decision. Meanwhile, the government withdrew from this move and restructured the Recruitment Board by nominating their members. Reservation on economic criteria is what the NSS demands for long which is accepted by the left government and in 2017 the government decided to provide 10% reservation for economically backward sections of the forward Hindu communities in Devaswom Board employment. But the indefinite delay of implementing the decision irritated the NSS and this strained the relation between the two. The NSS demanded the State Government to enforce the decision sooner than later taking into account the realities (Service, 2018, January 15).

In a nutshell, the NSS is standing for complete autonomy of Devaswom Boards free from political interference and to promote a corruption-free and clean administration that make arrangements for the protection of temple traditions. It pleads for a unified Devaswom administration for all temples and temples should be entrusted with the believers. The NSS stands for the preservation of temple traditions and so it opposes issues like the entry of young women in Sabarimala and the entry of non-Hindus. The NSS believes that the progress of the organisation depends upon the progress of temples. The two temples near its head office at Perunnai, Maranathu Kavu Devi Temple and Thrikkannapuram temple are under the control of the NSS. Several other temples are also managed by the NSS Taluk Unions and Karayogams. As Nossitter points out, the

NSS once defended the interests of the community, later became a potent factor in Kerala politics (1982: 28). This statement signifies the role of NSS in the political scenario of the state.

Yogakshema Sabha

Yogakshema Sabha is a movement formed in 1908 for bringing about reforms among the Namboothiri community. It acts as a catalyst for the social renaissance in Kerala society. The Namboothiri community is firmly attached to temples and priesthood, being the traditional occupation of a Namboothiri and he had to lead a secluded cultural life. Through the intervention of Yogakshema Sabha new horizons are opened for the community. The land reforms introduced by Munro in 1811 certainly afflicted the Namboothiris and their dominance in temple administration. The slogan of the yogakshemasabha in those days was *to make Namboothiri as human beings* (Menon, 2008: 315). E. M. S. Namboodiripad and V. T. Bhattathiripad organised the young generation of the community against its orthodox and traditional leadership (Fic, 1970: 17). The radical activists in the Sabha condemned polygamy discarded their sacred thread and openly advocated for widow remarriage. Thus, through the formation of the Sabha, the Brahmin community became an organised force in the polity and society of Kerala.

Though the Brahmins adorned the upper strata in the caste hierarchy, the progressive Yogakshema Sabha took part even in the temple entry movements led by the downtrodden sections, amidst the opposition from orthodox Brahmins. Namboothiri Yogakshema Sabha in its meetings at Karalmanna in Palakkad and Haripad in Alappuzha passed resolutions against untouchability and demanded modernisation of traditions. Sabha organised a march from Sreekrishnapuram to Guruvayur temple in support of the Guruvayur Satyagraha. When a referendum had to be sought in favour of temple entry in connection with Guruvayur Satyagraha, V. T. Bhattathirippad, a reformer and leader of the Sabha took the initiative for securing the support of Namboothiri *savarna* people in this regard. In the past, the Namboothiri community faced manifold social disabilities on account of the outdated social and religious practices and traditions.

In their traditional priesthood occupation, the Namboothiris had to face grave issues such as low wages and poor service conditions. The Sabha intervened in these issues, demanded periodical revision of salary and other allowance to temple priests. Yogakshema Sabha urged the TDB to initiate immediate steps to revise the grade and pay-scales of priests now at par with the fourth class employees of the temples to the administrative officer/sub-group officer level. The Sabha took a daring stand on the issues connected with temple administration in the state. The nomination of non-believers in Devaswom administration, the intervention of government in temple customs and rituals etc., are the major concerns of the Sabha regarding temple administration. The Sabha constituted a five-member *Achara Parishad* (a committee of Hindu priests and religious scholars) in 2007 to study the need for changes in temple traditions. The Sabha took a firm stand against the entry of non-Hindus in Hindu shrines and the appointment of non-Brahmin priests in temples, according to it that will affect the sanctity of the temples (Times of India, 2017, October 20).

The Sabha is against politicisation of temple administration and nomination of non-believers in temple governing bodies. Trade union activities in temple premises affect the functioning of temples. Corruption allegations against temple staff become a major issue that affects the serenity of temples. In this regard, the Sabha demanded the State Government to take urgent steps to check official-level corruption in the administration of various temples attached to the Devaswom Boards. A sizable portion of the revenue collected at various temples had been allegedly diverted (The Hindu, 2011, October 14). The leakage of money through different channels creates financial stringency that affects the day-to-day affairs of temples.

The appointment of temple priests should be carried out on the basis of rules and restrictions prescribed in the age-old temple ritualistic rules. The service conditions of priests in private temples are another concern of the Sabha. It demands better service conditions, wage structure and a welfare fund for the betterment of priests in private temples. Yogakshema Sabha organised a meeting of various Brahmin communities in the state in 2007 for discussing the governmental move to bring legislation affecting the devotion and faith of Hindu believers. Amongst the demands of the Sabha, the one that the Minister-in-charge of Devaswoms should be a devotee of God is a noticeable one (Haindava Keralam, 2007, May 28). The Sabha questions the claims of government over Sree Padmanabhaswamy temple and its treasures. In the women entry issue at Sabarimala, the Sabha is against the government policy of violating temple traditions. The Sabha stood along with other Hindu organisations in opposing the government and the Board decisions to implement the Court verdict without proper consultations. The decision of the Board to seek an explanation from the temple *tantri* for advising purification ceremony after women entry in Sabarimala also irritated the Sabha.

Response of Dalit and Adivasi Organisations on Temple Administration

Out of the total population in Kerala, Dalits (9.8%) and Adivasis (1.14%) constitute around 11% (Mohan, 2011). Though the Constitution provides safeguards to these communities against various forms of exploitation and discrimination, still they are living as marginalised sections. Once the gates of temples were shut down before them and even after the temple entry proclamation they are often secluded and alienated from temple rites and rituals. The Dalit movements led by Ayyankali provided self-respect to these communities to resurge against oppression and caste domination. Unlike the Sree Narayana movement, Dalit movements did not attempt at challenging the caste orthodoxy through consecrating temples or establishing its own priesthood. Ayyankali tried to situate the Dalit community firmly within Hinduism and wreck its inhuman core from within (Prabhash, 2005). They largely worshipped the lower divinities and they were kept aloof from the temples of *savarna* communities. Consequent upon the large-scale conversion of these people to different faiths, the Hindu religion seemed weakened and reformers and leaders like Mahatma Gandhi intervened to redress the grievances of these sections. The Temple Entry Proclamation was made to restrict massive conversion; but as the *savarna* minds are not willing to accept this that prevented the re-entry of these people to the Hindu fold.

Today, Dalit representation is ensured in all the Devaswom governing committees and Temple Advisory Committees due to their organised efforts. A Malayalam daily reported in 2017 that among the total employees of the TDB, caste Hindus hold 96% of the jobs; out of the total 6,120 posts, the upper castes like Nairs and Namboothiris hold 5,870 numbers and the Ezhavas only 207 posts. The Dalit representation is terribly low at 20 posts or 0.32%. Similarly, according to the Right to Information records, 76% teachers in four aided colleges managed by the TDB belonged to the forward caste Hindus. Of the 186 teachers, 135 are Nairs and 6 are Namboothiris. The Left Front Government's decision to reserve jobs for the forward caste poor in Devaswom service has angered Kerala's Dalit, Adivasi and backward caste communities (Ameerudheen, 2017).

In 2018, the TDB took a historic decision to appoint five Dalits as priests to the temples under its control. Prayar Gopalakrishnan, the then president of TDB took personal initiative to take this historic decision in 2016.Thus, Kerala witnessed a revolutionary step that permitted the Dalits to perform priestly duties in Devaswom Board temples amidst the opposition of orthodox Hindus. The Cochin Devaswom Board also appointed priests from those belonging to the Scheduled Castes in 2018. The tribal people of Kerala also demanded on the same line to have the opportunity to take part in temple rituals. The *Mala Araya*, a tribal community who had certain rights in Sabarimala temple to perform lighting the lamp and to conduct *poojas* at Ponnambalamedu on the *Makaravilakku* (lighting of lamp in an auspicious day at Sabarimala temple on the first day of the Malayalam month, *Makaram*) day in January which was taken over by the TDB. *The Akhila Thiruvithamcore Mala Araya Maha Sabha* demanded the government to restore their right to conduct rituals connected with Sabarimala temple. They demanded to ensure a role for the community in the administration of Sabarimala temple and appoint a person from the tribe to the TDB as a member (The Hindu, 2011, March 8).

Religious Interest Groups

Religious interest groups had played a significant role in state politics even prior to the formation of the state. A number of Hindu organisations are functioning in the country for the promotion of Hindu culture and traditions. These organisations hold a common outlook concerned with the issues relating to temples and their administration. Resentment on such issues like the politicisation of temple administration, system of state control over Devaswom administration, nomination of non-believers in Devaswom governing bodies, lack of unified Devaswom administration have been expressed by them appropriately.

Akhila Bharatha Ayyappa Seva Sangham (ABASS)

Ayyappa Seva Sangham, a voluntary, non-political, non-profitable organisation was formed in 1945 with the task of spreading Ayyappa cult across the country. The mission of the organisation is to provide basic amenities to the pilgrims in

Sabarimala. Seva Sangham is an all India organisation having nearly 2570 branches and thousands of volunteer members and patrons. It manages about 260 temples in and outside Kerala, hospitals, clinics, etc.The activities of the Sanghom are centred on Sabarimala Ayyappa temple including free medical aid, healthcare, sanitation, provision of drinking water to the pilgrims. A Cardiology Centre is also functioning under the management of the Sanghom at Appachimedu at Sabarimala. The Sangham fosters co-ordination among various sections of the Hindus by organising classes and propagating essential principles of Hinduism (Srikant & Manoj, 2006:152). Serving as devotees' organisation, at times it acts as a pressure group for protecting the temple from the discriminatory attitude of the State as well as Central Governments and the TDB.

The Sangham is against large-scale development projects at Sabarimala for the reason that this may hurt the sentiments of the devotees, serene atmosphere of the temple and harmful to the flora and fauna there. It also opposes the moves to make the hill shrine a tourist centre (Indian Express, 1980, December 11). Exclusion of the temple from Periyar Tiger Reserve Zone, allotment of more forest land for the temple are their other major demands. The Sangham alleges lack of proper coordination among various government departments and the TDB as the major problem that Sabarimala temple faces. Ayyappa Seva Sangham demands the restoration of the right to light lamps at Ponnambalamedu by the *Mala Araya* tribal people in connection with the *Makaravilakku* festival (The Hindu, 2011, May 1).

Ayyappa Seva Sangham (ABASS), strongly opposed the verdict of the Court and the consequent government action for permitting the entry of women of all age group to the Sabarimala Ayyappa Temple contrary to the age-old traditions of the forest shrine. The Vice President of ABASS, D. Vijayakumar said that the judiciary is not supposed to interfere in matters relating to faith, custom and traditions prevailing in a place of worship and the Sangham would strongly oppose any move to hurt the sentiments of Ayyappa devotees (The Hindu, 2016, January 13).

The Sangham rendered its opinion regarding the issues of Devaswom administration. It accuses the Board of its non-obligatory functions that drain its economy to a considerable extent. Today most of the temples cannot perform the rituals as per the actual customs due to paucity of funds (GoK, 1974: 30). In the matter of political appointment also, the Sangham expresses its opinion; it is not fair to exercise governmental control over Hindu religious institutions and the members of Devaswom governing bodies should be believers in God and temple worship. It also demands the immediate implementation of the K. P. Sankaran Nair Commission Report to eliminate political interference on temple administration in the state (Indian Express, 1998, May 24). The Sangham expressed its protest against amendments in the Devaswom Act for political gains that aimed at sabotaging Hindu temples. It demanded the withdrawal of TCHRI Amendment Act, 1990 which redefined the term *Hindu* for political gains (The Indian Express, 1990, June 13). No account of Sabarimala pilgrimage will be completed without a mention of the yeoman service rendered by the volunteers of Seva Sangham (Vaidyanathan, 1996: 190). Applauded the services rendered by sanghom, the Kerala legislative committee on environment to study the environmental problems at Sabarimala and suggested that the TDB may effectively utilise it for providing basic amenities to the pilgrims (KLA, 1998: 59- 60).

Kshetra Samrakshana Samithi (Kerala Temple Protection Council- KTPC)

Kshetra Samrakshana Samithi is one among the sister organisations of RSS, working for the upliftment and protection of Hindu temples and their customs. This organisation has its genesis on the miserable conditions of temples in the Malabar region. A temple renovation movement in Malabar initiated by Kerala Gandhi, K. Kelappan paved the way for the formation of an organisation totally devoted to temple welfare. Thus, in 1966, Malabar temple protection Samithi was constituted, later the organisation got moral support from various Hindu *parivar* organisations. Under the initiative of Madhavji in 1977, Kerala Kshetra Samrakshana Samithi (KKSS) was registered. Madhavji wrote a book entitled *Kshethra Chaithanya Rahasyam* in which he formulated a scheme for temple worship. The aim of the Samithi is to consolidate the Hindu society through the temples and making the temple as a centre of communal worship irrespective of caste distinctions. This was for the first time that a common body was formed to protect the interest of the temple devotees and to oppose the political dominance in the administration of the temples in Kerala (Jayaprasad, 1989: 302).

The KTPC is solely engaging in temple-oriented activities. The Samithi arranges *mathapadasala* to give religious teachings to the younger generation. The Council undertook the renovation of many dilapidated temples in the State. A series of struggles in the state including temple liberation struggle, parallel Devaswom Board agitation etc. have been conducted under the aegis of the Council. The Council exhorted Hindus to be united in the wake of numerous instances of temple molestation and stressed the need for organising temple protection forces (Nair, 1994: 303). It condemned the attack on temples and participated in the agitation led by various Hindu organisations against the destruction of idols of Palukachi Mala temple at Kottiyoor in Kannur district.

One of the missions of the Samithi is to liberate temples from the clutches of politics. It urges the government to entrust the temple administration with the devotees along with other Hindu organisations, the KTPC organised agitation in 1988 for the liberation of temples from political control saying that a secular state had no right to interfere in the management of temples as it does not intervene in the affairs of Church and Mosque (Nair, 1994: 132). As a protest against the nomination of non-believers in Devaswom Boards and anti-Hindu provisions in the controversial Devaswom Bill, parallel Devaswom Board agitation was started in 1990.

Samithi opposes the system of nominating politicians to Devaswom Boards and demands that the revenue of the temples should be utilised for the benefit of the Hindus. Temple should be administered by believers. The Samithi urged the Devaswom governing bodies to establish a Hindu international university for imparting knowledge about Hindu culture and values in the model of Tirupati University in the name of Sree Padmanabhaswamy with the help of valuable treasures found in the temple. The Samithi demanded a uniform administration for Hindu temples in the state on the lines suggested by Sankaran Nair Commission Report. A corruption free Devaswom administration for temples in the state and measures for preventing alienation of temple land are also included among the demands of the Samithi.

In its annual conference in 2008, the Samithi passed a resolution urging to throw open the doors of Hindu temples to those from other religions, provided they affirm their faith in Hindu rituals and traditions. The resolution stated that temples should allow entry to all who respect temple practices, customs and rituals (Myriad, 2016: 10-11). The Samithi favours the implementation of a master plan for the development of Sabarimala without any delay for providing more amenities to the pilgrims. There are hundreds of temples under the control of the Samithi and it has branches in almost all the temples in the state including those under the control of Devaswom Boards. The Samithi proposed an alternative scheme for the administration of Malabar temples; the day-to-day administration of the temples is to be entrusted with a committee selected from the devotees. An apex committee should be formed with prominent astrologers, Hindu scholars, tantric experts, representatives of Hindu organisations and religious activists as advisory members (The Indian Express, 1995, December 3).

When the Sabarimala women entry issue came up, the Samithi protested against the meddling of the secular government with the age-old practices and customs. It warned the government that violating such practices like the ban of young women to enter the temple may create anxiety to the believers. The Samithi favours the setting up of a High-Power Committee with statutory power for the smooth conduct of the Sabarimala pilgrimage so as to provide basic facilities for the pilgrims (The Hindu, 1999, March 28). As a prominent temple-oriented organisation, the Samithi's contributions are valuable. It gives prime importance to renovate the temples and to preserve their spiritual values by promoting religious discourses and *bhajans.* The Samithi prefers a devotee centred administrative set up for temples instead of politically controlled Devaswom Boards.

Sree Ramadasa Mission

Without mentioning the role played by Sree *Rama Dasa Mission* and its spiritual head Swamy Satyananda Saraswathy, the study on temple centred Hindu reform movement in contemporary society is meaningless. Swamy Satyananda Saraswathy, the disciple of Neelakanda Gurupadar, was the founder of Hindu unity forum, an umbrella organisation for protecting the Hindu interest in the state. He propagated the message of Hindu dharma in India and abroad (Nair, 1994:303).

Swamy Satyananda Saraswathy was the spiritual leader and a frontline campaigner of several Hindu rights movements in Kerala. As a great saint Swamy sowed the seeds of temple oriented movements in twentieth-century Kerala. Swamy Satyananda Saraswathy played a key role in the temple related movements in the state. He was the president of the Nilackal Action Committee and played a key role in Guruvayoor Temple Liberation Struggle and agitations against Devaswom Bill. Swami was an ardent critic of politicisation of temple administration and trade unionism in temples that tarnish the rites, rituals and serenity of temple atmosphere. In order to protect the pristine purity of Hindu religion and to re-infuse among the people respect for the ancient heritage Swamy Satyananda Saraswathy contributed much. (Souvenir 1995:7) According to Swamy, temple culture revolves around *mantras,* idol and culture. The entry of non-believers will produce anti-waves which will erode the Chaitanya (Menon, 1990 June 3). Satyananda Saraswathy was the architect of temple liberation agitations and the chairman of seven members high power committee of various Hindu leaders for temple liberation movement, the first organised mass movement for liberating temples from political control (The Hindu, 1988, May 8). Swami led an agitation in front of Guruvayur temple in 1988 demanded the dissolution of Guruvayur devaswom managing committee by eliminating non-believers and reconstitution of the devaswom committee on the basis of KP Sankaran Nair Commission Report (Kerala Kaumudi, 1988, July 2). A temple liberation march was organised in 1988 under his leadership from Sree Padmanabha Swami temple to Raj Bhavan and submitted a mass petition to the Governor demanding hand over of temple administration and temple properties to the Hindu devotees. Under the initiative of Satyananda Saraswathy, a Masterplan was prepared for the holy Sabarimala Ayyappa temple, which proposed a scheme for temple complex which would enable nearly 25 lakh pilgrims to offer at prayers at a time. The *Harivarasanam* project scheme has been drawn with special emphasis on ecological and environmental balance (Indian Express, 1995, December 3). In the year 2000, a meeting of Hindu saints and organisations was convened by the Sree Ramadasa mission for freeing temple administration from the clutches of political parties and to end corruption and maladministration (New Indian Express, 2000 July 3). With the death of the spiritual leader Swamy Satyananda Saraswathi in 2006, an era of Hindu renaissance in Kerala has been ended.

Rashtriya Swayamsevak Sangh (RSS)

RSS, the most powerful Hindu nationalist group in India was founded in 1925 at Nagpur by Keshav Baliram Hedgewar. Being a Hindu nationalist organisation, the ideology of RSS is deeply rooted in Hindu culture and tradition. In Kerala, the RSS *shakhas* (branches) are functioning mainly in temple premises. It organised several agitations primarily for protecting Hindu interests through temple related issues. The RSS opposes the interference of the government in the internal administration of temples and politicisation of temple administration. The RSS started a campaign in the state from 1982 onwards emphasising the issues like the plight of temple administration, inadequacy of Devaswom grants, attacks on temples etc. (Jayaprasdad, 1989: 176-77). But the RSS often succeeded in exploiting temple politicisation issues for consolidating the caste ridden Hindu community. *Thali* temple issue, *Nilakkal* issue and the women entry issue in Sabarimala have been utilised by the RSS for Hindu consolidation. It has a *parivar* organisation in the state, namely Kshetra Samrakshana Samithi dedicated solely for temple related affairs. Besides the Samithi, the RSS has other offshoots like Sabarimala Ayyappa Seva Samajam, Hindu Aiykyavedi, Vishva Hindu Parishad etc., for temple welfare activities. The RSS manages several private temples in the state and some of them are functioning exceptionally well. In a resolution passed by the RSS in 1988 stated that for the healthy growth of a secular state, religious freedom with no political interference is a basic necessity (The Hindu, 1988, May 8).Coming to the issues related with the administration of temples, the RSS is vigilant in raising matters in public forums thereby exploiting Hindu sentiments for creating the polarisation. The RSS is on an undeclared war with the government in power whether it is the LDF or the UDF relating to the management of temples. Their hostility towards the LDF is due to their atheism; to the UDF, corruption. The nomination of non-believers in temple governing bodies, encroachment of temple lands, neglect of

Devaswom Boards towards Hindu temples etc. are opposed by the RSS. Under the auspices of the RSS, a Hindu Front was formed in 1980 that led to the communalisation of state politics. Their slogan was 'Hindu vote for Hindus' in politics. This Hindu Front is the forerunner of BJP in the state. In 1982, *Vishal Hindu Sammelan* was organised under their initiative which became a landmark in the Hindu consolidation movements in Kerala. The major theme for discussion in this meeting was the plight of the temples controlled by the State Government through Devaswom Boards. The *Sammelan* demanded the liberation of temple administration from the clutches of the government. Consequent on the memorandum submitted to the Governor by the *Vishal Hindu Sammelan* on December 7, 1982, the government appointed K. P. Sankaran Nair Commission to study all the issues in temple administration.

The RSS undertook several temples related movements in the state. *Thali* temple agitation, *Palukachi Mala* temple agitation, *Nilakkal* agitation and *save Sabarimala* agitation are important among them. *Thali* temple agitation, the first organised agitation of RSS on temple related issue happened in 1968, got active support from various Hindu organisations. The second incident in this regard was the *Palukachi Mala* agitation of 1978 to protest the destruction of idols in the Palukachi Mala temple at Kottiyoor in Thalassery Taluk in Kannur District. The RSS sponsored agitation got full support from major Hindu organisations like the NSS and SNDP. They organised a long protest march with the destroyed idols from Thalassery to Cape Comorin and destroyed idols were thrown to the sea. A new idol was installed in the temple on 30, March 1979 (Jayaprasad, 1992: 192).

In 1983, Kerala witnessed a Hindu- Christian confrontation over *Nilakkal* issue; the issue relating to the construction of a Church in Nilakkal near Sabarimala temple. The government allegedly comes under the pressure from the Church and Kerala

Congress decided to grant government land for the construction of a Church close to Sabarimala temple in the high ranges (Gopakumar, 1986: 78). Finally, as a settlement the Christian leaders agreed to construct a Church far away from the Nilakkal temple. Through this agitation, the RSS could create a feeling of consciousness among the Hindu community on temple related issues. The RSS volunteers blocked the then Kerala Chief Minister, K. Karunakaran at Guruvayur temple on 15th June, 1983. The Nilakkal issue created a unique consciousness among the Hindus that paved the way for the formation of a Hindu Front in state politics. In the Sabarimala woman entry issue, the credibility of the RSS has been questioned by many on the ground that the stand it taken initially was favouring the entry of women of all age groups in the temple. RSS General Secretary Bhaiyyaji Joshi said in a television interview that while women are being allowed in the majority of temples in the country, there was no need for taking a different stand in the Sabarimala issue. He admitted that the custom is wrong and it should be abandoned (Mathrubhumi, 2016, July 25). P. Parameswaran and R. Hari, the intellectual leaders of the RSS stated that if women are demanding temple entry, they should be allowed to visit the temple. After the verdict of the Supreme Court, the RSS changed its earlier stand and began to oppose women entry understanding the religious pulse of the majority Hindu public. Subsequently, the RSS organised Ayyappa devotees to form *Sabarimala Karma Samithi* for coordinating the protest movements. It organised a series of programmes like *Ayyappa Jyothi* on December 26, 2018 and *Ayyappa bhakta sanghamom* (a meeting of Ayyappa devotees) at Thiruvananthapuram in 2019 to express the solidarity to 'save Sabarimala' campaign.

Thanthra Vidyapeedham

RSS revolutionised the traditional concept of the priesthood by setting up a Thanthra Vidyapeedham in 1972 at Guruvayur (later shifted to Aluva) for training youths in temple priesthood including Dalits and other non-Brahmin communities. A unique educational institution for Thanthrashasthra by the name "Thanthra Vidyapeedham" formally launched with the blessings of Kaanchi Kaama Koti Peettham Sankaraachaarya Jayendra Saraswathi, on June 23, 1972. Its vision to appoint non-Brahmins as priests in temples helped to reinforce the internal unity of the Hindu society. At present, RSS cadets are active in Temple Advisory Committees, governing bodies of private temples, festival committees, renovation committees etc.

Vishva Hindu Parishad (VHP)

Vishva Hindu Parishad (VHP) is a leading Hindu platform in India having branches abroad for propagating the message of Hinduism throughout the universe. It is widely recognised as the ideological initiator of a 'Hindu Unity' Movement. Swami Chinmayananda, a Hindu saint from Kerala put forward the idea of a world Hindu conference in 1963 which has been materialised in 1964 through the formation of the VHP (Jaffrelot, 1996: 194). Spearheading the ideology of Hindu nationalism, the VHP is playing a crucial role in the Hindu awakening programmes in the state. The VHP started a movement responsible for consolidating the unorganised religious sects to a sort of centralised structure (Jaffrelot, 2007: 19). It formulated a programme which includes the establishment of autonomous Boards to Hindu temple management. The VHP stood for autonomy of Hindu religious institutions and so it wants to scrap of all legislations regarding the control of temples. Thus, it launched temple liberation movements from 1988. According to the VHP, a secular state has no right to control temples, particularly when it did not control church and mosque (Nair, 1994: 132).

In Kerala, the VHP started its activities in 1966. It became the spearhead of Hindu militancy at the beginning of the 1980s. The aims of the VHP are to consolidate and strengthen the Hindu society, to protect and spread Hindu values, both ethical and spiritual and to make them relevant in contemporary society and to establish and strengthen the links among the Hindus living in different countries. There are 22 temples and mutts under the direct management of the VHP in Kerala (Jayaprasad, 1992: 219-220). The VHP is absolutely against the interference of political parties in temple administration. In 1999, the organisation along with Temple Protection Council approached the High Court against the government move to fill the vacancies of political nominees in Guruvayur Devaswom Committee (The Indian Express, 1999, July 11). The VHP opposed the move of Guruvayur Devaswom to deposit its income to the state treasury as it violates the Devaswom Acts. This shows that the organisation is vigilant in observing even the financial transactions of Devaswoms.

The VHP in 2007 presented a draft proposal for the formation of the Malabar Devaswom Board to Governor, Chief Minister and Devaswom Minister. In the proposal it demanded the inclusion of elected members of Temple Advisory Committees and a representative of the employee in the Board. It criticised the move of the LDF government to enhance the strength of members to the TDB and CDB. They asked if the government failed to control a three-member Board, it would not be able to control a Board with more members. It would only lead to misuse of the Devaswom funds (The Hindu, 2007, November 29). In the Sabarimala women entry issue, the VHP stood with the devotees and raised the allegation that the government's stand was a part of a conspiracy to hurt the sentiments of devotees and destroy the importance of the hill shrine. The VHP's stand in the matter is that women entry in the shrine should be subjected to the decision of temple *tantri* on the basis of astrological observation and the judiciary has no say in such matters.

There are widespread criticisms against the activities of the VHP as they try to communalise the social system using temple and related issues. Former Chief Minister A. K. Antony termed it as a religious fundamentalist group in the Assembly (KLA, 2002, July 23). Though it claims a Hindu organisation, only a microscopic minority of Hindus extend support to their activities. Ram Puniyani, a critic of Sangh Parivar Organisations viewed that the VHP has emerged as the major retrograde force has politicised the saints, communalised the social space and also created new institutions around its socio-political agenda (Puniyani, 2009: 39).

Hindu Aikya Vedi (HAV)

The Hindu Aikya Vedi (HAV) is a *parivar* organisation of the RSS formed in 1992 to protect the interests of the Hindus. It follows the CAP model (Coordination, Agitation and Propaganda) action plan in their activities. It intervenes in matters concerned with Hindu religious institutions, like their administration, role of government and Devaswom Boards in it, financial maladministration, corruption, politicisation etc. It also engages in the protection of traditions, customs and interferes when these are violated. When Sabarimala women entry issue came into limelight, the organisation boldly reacted against the Court verdict and the immediate governmental initiative to implement the verdict.

The HAV has expressed an unambiguous stand on various issues concerned with Hindu interests, particularly in temple-related affairs. They constantly demand the revamping of temple administration by giving representation to believers. According to it, a secular government should not get involved in the affairs of the places of worship of any community. Devaswom administration should be on the basis of a uniform Devaswom law and demanded an Ordinance for this. Its former General Secretary Kummanam Rajasekharan views that the nomination to the temple administrative bodies should not be on political grounds rather believers should be entrusted with the task of temple administration.

HAV demanded for setting up of an independent Devaswom Board comprising of devotees free from political patronage. A state wide temple protection march was organised demanding depoliticisation of temple administration and to ensure adequate representation of devotees in it. Government, by controlling temple administration is denying justice to the Hindus. It raised the allegation of plundering the temple wealth by the government in disguise of political control. It is ironical that the government while advocating decentralisation, in the case of temples it tries to centralise power through Devaswom Boards. A memorandum was submitted to the government in 2001 and 2007 demanding depoliticised Devaswom bodies. They opposed the proposal to hand over Devaswom recruitment to PSC on the ground that a secular institution had no right to interfere in the activities of religious entities. The HAV demanded that a new Devaswom Recruitment Board comprising of experts from the Hindu community be constituted for Devaswom recruitment.

After the formation of the Malabar Devaswom Board, more and more temples were being taken over which irritated the HAV. According to the organisation, it is paradoxical that while temples in Malabar are taken over by the MDB on the grounds of lack of governmental control for rectifying corruption, at the same time the government dissolved the TDB citing corruption and mismanagement (The New Indian Express 2017, November 15). The utilisation of income from temples for government purposes during natural calamities etc., is resented by the Hindu organisations. During the flood in 2018, various Devaswom Boards issued directions to the temples and its employees to contribute to the Chief Minister's Relief Fund. The Commissioner of Malabar Devaswom Board had directed the temples under its supervision to collect Rs 5 lakh each from 22 temples, Rs 2.5 lakhs from two temples each, and Rs 1 lakh each from the remaining 33 temples towards flood fund. The High Court of Kerala quashed the Commissioner's directions when it was challenged in the Court. The HAV is against the directions of the Boards for compulsory donation to the Chief Minister's Relief Fund as the temples are not a government department and so compulsory donation is arbitrary. The HAV demanded the state government to take steps to ensure corruption-free administration for temples, otherwise the fate of temples will be disastrous.

The HAV gives special attention to provide basic amenities for the pilgrims in Sabarimala. It submitted the *harivarasanam* project to the State Government for Sabarimala development that was accepted by the government in 1995. As a *parivar* organisation, the HAV extends all support to other Hindu organisations' agitations to preserve the traditions of Sabarimala. The HAV is not against the appointment of non-Brahmin priests in temples. According to the organisation, it is not the caste but proper knowledge in temple rituals should be the condition to become priests in temples. The organisation favoured the entry of non-Hindus in temples provided that they should have faith in the Hindu religion and obey the customs of the temple. For the efforts to preserve temple rituals, the HAV receives extensive support from various Hindu outfits including NSS, SNDP Yogam, Yogakshema Sabha and a section of Pulayar Maha Sabha.

For some time, a debate is ongoing regarding the administration of temples by the government sponsored Devaswom governing bodies and the flaws in their policies and attitudes towards temples. As part of democratisation of temple administration, political participation is inevitable. The political parties are interested in engaging into the affairs of temples particularly due to their influence on the Hindu public, the majority population. Even if politics is inevitable in a democratic polity, its involvement in the affairs of religious institutions may hamper its serenity. Trade unionism, nepotism etc., are the worst features of politicisation in the administration of temples. The responses of the Civil Society and Hindu organisations are against political interference and governmental control. With the controversial women entry issue the debate regarding politics of temple administration become live and could get national as well as international attention.

6

Alternative Models of Administration

Temples are the manifestations of spiritual aspirations of the Hindu community. Worship in temples was mostly a private affair in the early period, but later when temples emerged as centres that fostering art, architecture and learning and thus became effective devices of social transformation. The ethos of social renaissance happened in Kerala through temple related movements. Inequity in the social stratification necessitated reformation; temples became the venues of social renaissance. Consequent on the temple entry movements, Temple Entry Proclamations were issued firstly in the princely state of Travancore, later in Cochin and temple entry Act in the Malabar region. Contributions of reformers are to be remembered here. The universal temple entry not only boosted the process of social change which ensured freedom of worship to the downtrodden sections, but helped the sustainability of temple economy thereby the state exchequer then. With the prospering of temple revenue, the financial administration should also be properly regulated through accounting and auditing of funds. When the monarchy was transformed into democracy, all the temples that were under the control of the King were transferred to the government. When the monarchy was completely abolished, temple administration became the strongholds of political bosses. The first democratically elected government in Kerala led by E. M. S. Namboodiripad followed an equidistance policy towards religious institutions in the state. But successive governments intervened in the autonomy of Devaswom Boards by making amendments in the principal Devaswom Acts.

The inception of governmental control over temple administration in the princely state of Travancore had been taken place with the assumption of temples and their treasures by Dewan Col. Munro in 1811 through an executive order. The Revenue Department became the sole custodian of temple administration. The first regulation on temple administration was passed in 1903, the Hindu Religious Endowment Regulation which empowered the government to intervene in the affairs of temples whenever necessary. Eventually, the separation of Devaswom from the Revenue Department became a necessity. The temples in the state were placed under a separate administrative mechanism under a Devaswom Commissioner in 1922; the expenditure to be met from the general revenue of the state.

The ethos of social renaissance happened in Kerala through temple related movements. Inequity in the social stratification necessitated reformation; temples became the venues of social renaissance. Consequent on the temple entry movements, Temple Entry Proclamations were issued firstly in the princely state of Travancore, later in Cochin and temple entry Act in the Malabar region. Contributions of reformers are to be remembered here. The universal temple entry not only boosted the process of social change which ensured freedom of worship to the downtrodden sections, but helped the sustainability of temple economy thereby the state exchequer then. With the prospering of temple revenue, the financial administration should also be properly regulated through accounting and auditing of funds. With the integration of Travancore Cochin states in 1949, through a tripartite agreement in the Covenant, Devaswom Boards were created for the management of temple fund and administration; the temples along with their properties were transferred to the Devaswom Boards by the rulers. An annuity was instituted as compensation to TDB and Sree Padmanabhaswamy temple as per the Covenant which was later on constitutionally protected as per Article 290A. Travancore - Cochin Hindu Religious Institutions Act, 1950 was enacted for temple governance in respective princely states. Rulers of both the states retained the power of nominating one member each to the Devaswom Boards till the abolition of Privy Purse in 1971.

The linguistic reorganisation of states and the formation of the Kerala State remain as another phase in the study of the politics of temple administration in Kerala. The reorganisation resulted in the transfer of 490 temples of erstwhile south Travancore territory to the Madras state. The temples in Malabar remain under the Madras laws till today with certain modifications, though separate MDB came in to existence in 2008. When the monarchy was transformed into democracy, all the temples that were under the control of the King were transferred to the government. When the monarchy was completely abolished, temple administration became the strongholds of political bosses. The first democratically elected government in Kerala led by E. M. S. Namboodiripad followed an equidistance policy towards religious institutions in the state. But successive governments intervened in the autonomy of Devaswom Boards by making amendments in the principal Devaswom Acts.

The study mainly focused on the administration of temples under the state management, vested with autonomous bodies called Devaswom Boards or Devaswom Managing Committees. The administration of private temples is excluded due to the lack of organised pattern in their administration. Devaswom governing bodies in the state are constituted as per the provisions of various Devaswom Acts. For administrative convenience, the temples are grouped on regional basis such as Travancore, Cochin and Malabar. Travancore Devaswom Board is the custodian of temples in Travancore except the reputed Sree Padmanabhaswamy Temple which is under the control of Travancore royal family. Temples in the erstwhile Cochin state is administered mainly by the CDB, while Koodalmanickam temple at Irinjalakkuda in the same state is managed by Koodalmanickam Devaswom Managing Committee. The temples in Malabar region have a separate and distinctive administrative system managed by the respective trustees and the MDB has only a supervisory role there. The administration of Guruvayur Sree Krishna temple is carried out by the Guruvayur Devaswom Managing Committee. Thus, at present the temples in Kerala are administered by three Devaswom Boards and two Devaswom Managing Committees as per the four Devaswom Acts. The study enquired how the diverse laws of Devaswoms affect the administration of temples particularly the low-income temples in Malabar where the absence of common pooling of fund, like that of the Travancore and Cochin Devaswoms, poses difficulties in supporting the low-income temples. One of the objectives of the study was to enquire how relevant is to the temples in the state, a unified administrative system binding the temples of the whole state.

Temple as an Integrating Force

The role of the temples once in the society was powerful and acted as a disintegrating force which segmentalised the Hindu society on caste lines. The upper strata of the society, especially the Brahmins enjoyed all privileges as managers of temples, promulgated caste pollution rules, and thus monopolised all the spheres of state administration as well as temple administration. The lower strata in the caste hierarchy were kept aloof from the vicinity of God and considered as even 'unapproachable' and had to observe *theendal* or distance-pollution rules. They worshipped God remaining beyond the outer walls of the temples. Thus, these sections had to bear severe social exclusion and so these agitated sections began to disown Hinduism and Hindu Gods.

These affairs began to change as a result of social renaissance and the relentless efforts of reformers. The formation of social reform organisations like SNDP Yogam, Sadhu Jana Paripalana Sanghom, Yogakshema Sabha and the NSS in the beginning of 20th century paved the way for Hindu unity in the state. The contributions of these organisations to social renaissance are through the temple related activities. The movements for social justice and civic equality were organised at Vaikom, Sucindram, Ambalappuzha, Koodalmanickam and Guruvayur temples proved that temples were forces of Hindu integration. With the Temple Entry Proclamations, the pollution rules began to be flexible and in the modern era, all sections of Hindus are given access to worship inside the temples without any discrimination.

Kerala witnessed Hindu consolidation movements at various phases of her history in connection with temple affairs. *Hindu Mahamandalam*, the first Hindu consolidation movement was formed in 1950 by Mannathu Padmanabhan and R. Sankar, the leaders of two powerful communities- Nairs and Ezhavas, against the discriminatory attitude of the government towards Hindu temples. Another instance of Hindu consolidation occurred during Nilakkal temple agitation. A Hindu front (*Hindu Munnani*) was formally inaugurated in the 1980s in connection with temple related issues. Brahmin monopoly in the field of priesthood also began to be ceased; non-Brahmin priests are being appointed in temples today. In *Adithayan Vs. The Travancore Devaswom Board* case, 2002, the SC observed that the persons duly qualified cannot be prohibited on the ground that such person is not a Brahmin by birth or pedigree. Dalits are nominated in Devaswom governing bodies and other administrative posts. Today, temples became centres of common worship integrating all Hindus beyond the boundaries of caste. Appointment of non-Brahmin priests in temples and introduction of reservation for backward Hindus are the policy options of the government that helped to eliminate caste-based segregations which resulted in Hindu integration. Hindu organisations often use issues in temples to consolidate their power. The Sabarimala women entry issue added stimulus for the integration of Hindu community. The Hindu unity felt during the women entry issue in Sabarimala is an instance of Hindu consolidation based on temple related movements in the state.

Findings of the Study

Political parties either left or right wings never want to spare any opportunity in involving in the affairs of temples to promote their political mileage and temple related issues often determine the dynamics of Kerala politics. Temples are highly influential in the social order as their influence on the society is enormous. In Kerala, there is no village without a temple and the daily life of every Hindu irrespective of status, gender and caste distinctions is closely associated with temples. Temple related issues always left their imprints in state politics from even prior to the formation of the Kerala state. The creation of the TDB in 1949 and the formation of the *Hindu Mahamandalam* became turning points in the history of communal polarisation in state politics. Later, several temple related issues like Kottiyoor temple issue, impacts of land reforms legislations, Thali temple agitation, Nilakkal issue, issues related with the management of Sree Padmanabhaswamy temple, appointment of non-Brahmin priests, Sabarimala women entry issue etc., determined the contemporary political discourses. The formation of the Hindu Front in 1980s became the predecessor of Hindutva politics in the state.

Even in Devaswom Boards and Temple Advisory Committees, political nominations can be seen. Devaswoms afford employment opportunities to large number of people in temples, educational institutions and other establishments under their control. Thousands of students get chances of education in Devaswom Board institutions. So these factors persuade the political parties to have an eye on the administration of Devaswom Boards. Both leftist and rightist political parties interfere in temple administration to promote their political mileage. Women entry issue in Sabarimala is politically exploited by both the Congress and BJP in the 2019 Lok Sabha election. As a Hindutva political outfit, the BJP consolidated its vote bank politics, but they never reap the benefits fully. Another allegation emerged during the Sabarimala issue was regarding the politicisation of the issue.In the Lok Sabha election 2019, the INC and the BJP used Sabarimala as a major issue in their campaigning against the policies of the ruling party and both of them reaped its benefits also.

It is a matter of great concern that a secular state which has to follow equi-distance policy in religious affairs, actively interfere in the internal and spiritual affairs of the religious institutions of particular community. This can be viewed as a breach of right to freedom of religion. A feeling is there among the devotees that they are deprived of the right to administer their own religious institutions as they are alienated from temple administration. The Temple Advisory Committees constituted in temples that ensured devotees representation, but excessive political interference in these committees created controversies. Elections to the TAC in many temples are conducted with the help of police security and tense situations prevail in temple premises.

The absence of a unified system of law for the Devaswom administration is another pertinent issue. The demand for codification of Devaswom laws is strong for a long period from the part of politicians, administrators, various Commissions, judicial verdicts and devotees. It is a fact that the existing Devaswom laws are out-dated. Devaswom Boards in the state follow unscientific and diversified classification of temples.

Temples in different regions in the state are followed common rituals, customs with slight changes, but they are categorised in a different manner. Temples are categorised on the basis of income or expenditure rather than their importance or historical significance. Majority of the temples under various Devaswoms in the state are not self-supportive and so they have to depend on self-reliant temples for their survival.

Corruption is widespread in Devaswom administration in the state. Mismanagement and misappropriation of funds, theft of valuables, favouritism are the different forms of corruption. Large scale leakage of money in diverse ways affected the temple economy considerably. Economic crisis is often happened in Devaswom administration due to the creation of unnecessary posts in temples, financial indiscipline, large scale temple land alienation and corruption. Entertaining of non-remunerative schemes, paucity of government grants etc. are other major causes of financial problems faced by the temple administration. Annuity to temples by the government is inadequate to meet their expenditure. The Board spends huge amounts for meeting establishment charges every year which is steadily rising due to the hike in pay and allowances of employees.

The present system of administration prevailing in Malabar is defective as the MDB has no effective control over the affairs of temples under their supervision. Lack of common pooling of fund in Malabar temples is one of the major challenges to the low-income temples and their employees. There is no uniformity in salary and other service conditions of temple employees in the state and the service conditions of employees of low-income temples in Malabar are very pitiable. The gravity of encroachment of temple land, particularly in Malabar is very alarming. Both the temple authorities and the revenue officials are responsible for such a massive intrusion to the Devaswom land. This laxity has led the impoverishment of Hindu religious institutions in Malabar which is actually deplorable.

There are several grave issues prevailed in the management of Sabarimala temple. The TDB, the supervising authority treated the temple only as a milch cow. It failed to provide basic amenities to the devotees like toilet facilities, drinking water facilities, facilities for proper accommodation etc. Environmental degradation due to the heavy influx of pilgrims created great concern. The Sabarimala women entry issue and the consequent violation of tradition have been greatly resented by not only the devotees but the general public as well. The issue has been politicised by major political parties in Kerala for their political mileage. The policy taken by the LDF government in the issue has been badly affected its political prospects that reflected in the 2019 Lok Sabha elections. After the Supreme Court's decision to hand over the review petitions to a 7 Judge Bench, the government and the Devaswom Board changed their earlier attitude regarding women entry that provided some sort of relief to the believers.

Temple employees in the state, except employees in Malabar are scared of the Board authorities due to their political influence and power to take disciplinary action. Even priests in temples are afraid of them rather than the deity they worship. Devaswom Board employees who participated in the survey for identifying the issues they face, revealed their dissatisfaction on the performance of the Board mainly due to politicisation and corruption prevailing in temple administration.

The study has two-fold dimension; the first being the politics of temple administration and the other, politics in temple administration. Both are correlated concepts as the first is the analysis of policy options in temple governance and the other is issues connected with the internal administration of temples i.e., pertaining to the affairs in the sacred areas. Though the study touches both the aspects, more emphasis has been given to policy options and their drawbacks in the implementation. The study analysed the various issues that meted out by the temples in Kerala in the administrative sphere. The pertinent question addressed here is whether a secular state's interference in the internal affairs of a particular community's religious institutions is justifiable. Other significant issues like the degeneration of Devaswom Boards, created for the administration of Hindu temples to the status of political institutions, corruption, mismanagement, misutilisation of funds and trade unionism among the temple employees etc. paved the way for losing the credibility of the Devaswom Boards.

Suggestions of the Study

The study found out that the prevailing administrative systems for the temples in Kerala need radical reforms and restructuring. For ensuring administrative efficiency, transparency in financial administration and recruitment process, a total revamping of the prevailing administrative mechanism is needed. Temple economy needs urgent attention. Remunerative Schemes like effective utilisation of drained and unused Devaswom lands, measures to regain encroached temple lands and their protection are urgent steps for boosting up temple economy.

Modification and unification of temple legislations, temple rituals, customs and conventions are imperative for the effective carrying out of administration of temples. Outdated Devaswom laws should be modified. It is to be remembered that the existing Devaswom laws in the state were formulated prior to the formation of Kerala state. Periodical revision and unification of Devaswom laws are essential for the smooth conduct of the administration of temples. Unification of Devaswom law is a herculean task owing to the heterogeneous administrative set up prevailing for the temples; of course, historical reasons are there behind the diversified administration for the temples in the state. Like the administrative set up existing for the religious institutions in other South Indian states, Kerala Government also should take appropriate action to coordinate and unify Devaswom laws existing in the erstwhile three regions;

Travancore, Cochin and Malabar that will help to solve the grave administrative issues prevailing.

Two types of administrative systems are proposed through the study. One is a separate administrative system for popular and famous temples in Kerala, in the Guruvayur Devaswom model of administration and the other is an integrated administrative system for all temples in the state like that of other south Indian states of Tamil Nadu and Andhra Pradesh. Complete delinking of temple affairs from the effective control of the state is not possible in the present system of administration. More representation should be given to local devotees in the day-to-day administration of temples. Administration of temples should be handed over to Local Advisory Committees and in this model; the state has only a supervisory role. A Hindu Religious Department became essential to coordinate activities of temple administration in the state. There should be an apex Monitoring Committee as the High-Level Committee recommended; a President and four Members of the Committee shall be nominated by the Governor of the State. The Minister-in-charge of Devaswom becomes the Chairman of the Committee. The essential qualification to become members of the Committee should be belief in God and temple worship and they should be absolutely free from politics. Term of members should be fixed as three or four years. Representation should be given to devotees, temple *tantri,* women and SC and ST communities.

A good corruption free mechanism is essential for temple administration in the state. Devaswom Ombudsman mechanism should be strengthened. The Kerala High Court from 2007 appointed retired Judges as Ombudsmen to supervise the functioning of the Devaswom Boards and to enquire about the serious allegations of maladministration against the Board members, other officers and temple employees. Empowerment and strengthening of Ombudsman's services for all Devaswoms in the state is essential to combat with corruption in temple administration. A state level Audit Department is essential for proper auditing in the Devaswoms. A foolproof accounting and auditing are essential and officers from Accountant General Office should be entrusted with the power of auditing in Devaswoms in the state. Auditors should be appointed on deputation basis from the Accountant General's Office. A state level Vigilance Cell is also recommended.

The introduction of a Devaswom Recruitment Board for selecting officials to Devaswoms is of course an innovative step. This can be viewed as a first step towards the unification of temple administration in the state. At present the Recruitment Board has only limited power over appointments as it has no power to make appointments in educational institutions under various Devaswom Boards. There are serious allegations of corruption in the appointment of teachers to schools and colleges under various Devaswom Committees. Members and Chairman of the Board should be persons of honesty and integrity than politically supported ones for ensuring impartiality in appointments. Those who are facing Vigilance enquiry or allegations of corruption should not be appointed as Board Members.

A State Institute for Temple Administration should be set up as in the case of Andhra Pradesh for conducting orientation and refresher courses for temple employees in the state. Training in temple rites and rituals to interested youths to enable them to perform priestly duties in temples should also be started. The state sponsored institutes will enable the non-caste Hindus to study priestly duties. Temple Advisory Committees are to be strengthened in all temples under Devaswom Boards. Advisory committees for leading temples like Guruvayur, Koodalmanickam, Sabarimala etc., should be constituted by the government incorporating representatives of Hindu organisations. Political considerations should be avoided while constituting Temple Advisory Committees. Reputed persons with integrity residing in temple premises should also be incorporated. Temple premises should not be allowed to use for political propaganda or any type of arms training. Controversial issues like the entry of women of a particular age group in Sabarimala temple, entry of non-Hindus in temples etc., are to be settled in consultation with the stakeholders. Caste should not be a criterion for selecting high priests in temples.

The Reports of various Commissions on Devaswom administration that are kept in the cold storage and the government never paid attention for implementing these recommendations. Kuttikrishna Menon and Sankaran Nair Commission reports are of much value in this regard and the government should make a rethinking in implementing the vital recommendations of these Commissions for the interests of the temples. Also, the government should take into confidence the Hindu organisations while introducing reforms in the sphere of temple administration. In order to eradicate corruption and misappropriation of funds from the Devaswom administration, the Board should first take an uncompromising stand. Repeated occurrence of corruption indicates that the current mechanism of auditing is highly flawed and porous. Measures should be taken for strict auditing of the receipts and expenditures of temples on a regular basis. It is better to avoid pilfering than appointing Commissions or declaring Vigilance enquiry after each incident of corruption. Commissions and enquiries will only cost the Board more than what is lost. Departmental actions against the corrupt officials will not yield the desired result either as they may come back with renewed vigour, thanks to their strong political connections. Rules should be suitably amended to ensure that the guilty are shown the door. All these measures can avoid corruption in the Devaswoms to a great extent. The government can also do something to reduce corruption in the Devaswoms. Government should ensure that only people with proven integrity are nominated as members of Devaswom

Boards. Only a clean and transparent Board can speak against corruption and proceed against the delinquent.

Freedom of religion and worship are the most significant rights guaranteed by the Constitution of India to its citizens. Discrimination of human beings on the ground of religion or belief is an affront to human dignity. The administrative control over temples by a secular government is totally unethical and unjust and it would violate the freedom of religion guaranteed in the Constitution of India. For the growth of a healthy secular state, religious freedom should be given to its citizens without political interference. Politicisation leads to corruption and other related issues. It is a grave injustice to the Hindu society if a secular government makes temples grounds for political gains and pressure game politics, leaving free the religious institutions of other religious groups. Such discrimination creates a strong sense of group solidarity among the Hindu community which sowed the seed of Hindu communalism in the state.

APPENDICES

Appendix - I

The Covenant

Entered into by rules of Travancore and Cochin for the formation of the United States of Travancore and Cochin

(Article 8)-Relevant Part of the Covenant deals with Devaswom affairs

(Article 8)

(a) The obligation of the Covenanting State of Travancore to contribute from its general revenues a sum of Rs 50 lakhs every year to the *Devaswom Fund* as provided for in the *Devaswom* (Amendment) Proclamation, 1123 ME. and a sum of Rs One lakh every year to *Sree Pandaravaga* referred to in Provision (A) to sub-section (1) of Section 23 of the Travancore Interim Constitution Act 1123 ME., shall for the appointed day, be an obligation of the United State and the said amounts shall be payable there from and the *Raj Pramukh* shall cause the said amounts to be paid every year to the Travancore Devaswom Board and the Executive Officer referred to in sub-clause (b) of this Article respectively.

(b) The administration of Sree Padmanabhaswamy Temple, the *Sree Pandaravaga* properties and all other properties and funds of the said temple now vested in trust in the Ruler of the Covenanting State of Travancore and the sum of Rs One lakh transferred from year to year under the provisions of clause (a) of this article, and the sum of five lakhs of rupees contributed from year to year towards the expenditure in the Sree Padmanabhaswamy temple under sub-clause (c) of this article, shall, with effect from the first day August 1949, be conducted, subject to the control and supervision of the Ruler of Travancore, by an Executive Officer appointed by him. There shall be a Committee known by the name of the Sree

Padmanabhaswamy Temple Committee composed of three Hindu Members to be nominated by the Ruler of Travancore to advise him in the discharge of his functions. Suits by or against the Sree Padmana bhaswamy Temple or in respect of its properties shall be instituted in the name of the said Executive Officer.

(c) The administration of the incorporated and unincorporated Devaswoms and of Hindu Religious Institutions and Endowments, and all their properties and fund as well as the fund constituted under the Devaswom Proclamation 1097 ME., and the surplus fund constituted under the Devaswom (Amendment) Proclamation, 1122 M.E., which are under the management of the Ruler of the Covenanting State of Travancore and the sum of Rs 50 lakhs transferred from year to year under clause a shall with effect from the first day of August 1949, vest in a Board known by the name of the Travancore Devaswom Board. An annual contribution of five lakhs of rupees shall be made by the Travancore Devaswom Board from aforesaid sum of Rs 50 lakhs towards the expenditure in the Sree Padmanabhaswamy Temple.

(d) The administration of the incorporated and unincorporated Devaswoms and Hindu Religious Institutions, which are under the management of the Ruler of the Covenanting State of Cochin under Section 50G of the Government of Cochin Act XX of 1113 ME., or under the provisions of the Cochin Hindu Religious Institutions Act, I of 1081 ME., and all their properties and funds and of the estates under the management of the Devaswom Department of the covenanting State of Cochin shall with effect from the first day of August 1949 vest in a Board known by the name of the Cochin Devaswom Board:

Provided that the regulation and control of all rituals and ceremonies in the Temple of Sree Poornathrayeesa at Trippunithura and in the Pazayannore Bhagavathy Temple at Pazayannore shall continue to be exercised as hitherto by the Ruler of Cochin.

(e) The Board referred to in sub-clause (c) of this Article shall consist of Three Hindu Members, one of whom shall be nominated by the Ruler of the Covenanting State of Travancore, one by the Hindus among the Council of Ministers and one elected by the Hindu Members of the Legislative Assembly of the United State.

(f) The Board referred to in sub-clause (d) of this article shall consist of three Hindu Members, one of whom shall be nominated by the Ruler of the covenanting State of Cochin, one by the Hindus among the Council of Ministers, and one elected by the Hindu Members of the Legislative Assembly of the United State.

(g) Each of the aforesaid Board shall be a separate body corporate having perpetual succession and a common seal with powers to hold and acquire properties and shall by its name sue and be sued.

(h) Subject to the provisions of this Article, the constitution, powers and duties of the Board aforesaid shall be such as may be determined hereafter by law enacted by competent authority.

Source: Travancore Devaswom Manual. (2011), Vol. II, pp.179-186.

Appendix - II

Jurisdiction areas of Devaswom governing bodies in Kerala

Sl. No	Act	Board	District/Area
1.	Madras Hindu Religious & Charitable Endowment Act (Act XIX) of 1951-Amended in 2008	Malabar Devaswom Board	Kasargod, Kannur, Wayanad, Kozhikkod Malappuram Districts and Palakkad (excluding some portion of Chittur Taluk) Chavakkad Taluk of Thrissur and portion of Cochin Taluk of Ernakulam District
2.	Travancore–Cochin Hindu Religious Institution Act 1950 (Act XV of 1950)	Travancore Devaswom Board/Cochin Devaswom Board	Portion of Chittur taluk (which formed part of erstwhile Cochin state) Ernakulam district (excluding the portion of Cochin taluk) and Idukki, Kottayam, Alappuzha, Pathanamthitta, Kollam and Thiruvananthapuram districts
3.	Guruvayur Devaswom Act 1978 (Act XIV of 1978)	Guruvayur Devaswom Managing Committee	Guruvayur Sree Krishna Temple and Minor Temples
4.	Koodal Manickam Devaswom Act 1971	Koodalmanickam Devaswom Management Committee	Koodalmanickam Temple, Irinjalakkuda and its subordinate temples

Appendix - III

Lists of various commissions on Temple Administration (1950-2018)

Sl. No.	Name of Commission	Chairman of the Commission	Year	Subject of Enquiry	Appointing Authority
1.	Sabarimala Temple Arson Enquiry Commission 1950	K. Kesava Menon	1957	Sabarimala temple fire case	State Government
2.	Hindu Religious Endowment Commission	C. P. Ramaswamy Aiyyer	1962	Study on religious endowments	Central Government
3.	High Level Committee for unification of Laws relating to Hindu Religious Institutions	Kuttikrishna Menon	1964	Devaswom reforms/unification of Devaswom laws	State Government
4.	Devaswom Employees Salary Revision Committee	Kainikkara Padmanabha Pillai	1966	Salary revision of TDB	State Government
5.	Guruvayur temple fire Enquiry Commission	Ganghadharan Thampy	1971	Guruvayur temple fire incident	State Government
6.	Report on the financial position and other allied matters of CDB	Bhaskaran Nair	1974	Financial position of CDB	State Government
7.	Report on the financial position and other allied matters of TDB	C. R. Krishna Moorthy	1973	Financial position of TDB	State Government
8.	Kerala Devaswom Administrative Reform Commission	K. P. Sankaran Nair	1984	Devaswom Reforms	State Government
9.	Report on the Travancore and Cochin Devaswom Boards	V. Ramachandran	1991	Study on Sabarimala TDB and CDB	High Court of Kerala
10.	Justice Chandra Shekhara Menon Commission	Justice Chandra Shekhara Menon	2000	Sabarimala Stampede	State Government
11.	Krishnan Unni Commission	Krishnan Unni	2003	Irregularities in Guruvayur Devaswom	High Court
12.	Justice M. R. Hariharan Nair Commission on Pullumedu tragedy	Justice M. R. Hariharan Nair	2011	Sabarimala Pullumedu tragedy	State Government
13.	High Power Commission	Justice Paripoornan	2007	Irregularities in TDB	High Court
14.	K. Jayakumar Committee	K. Jayakumar	2016	Pay and service conditions of Malabar Devaswom employees	State Government
15.	The Law Reforms Committee	Adv. Gopalakrishnan	2017	Malabar Devaswom Board	State Government

Appendix - IV

List of Devaswom /Amendments enacted in the KLA Since 1957

Sl. No.	Bill/Amendments	Year
1.	The Koodalmanickam Devaswom Proclamation (Amendment) Bill, 1957 (Act 3 of 1957)	1957
2.	The Travancore–Cochin Hindu Religious Institutions (Amendment) Bill, 1958 (Act 36 of 1958)	1958
3.	The Madras Hindu Religious and Charitable Endowments (Amendment) Bill, 1963 (Act 41 of 1963).	1963
4.	The Madras Hindu Religious and Charitable Endowments (Amendment) Bill, 1967 (Act 13 of 1967)	1967
5.	The Madras Hindu Religious and Charitable Endowments (Amendment) Bill, 1968 (Act 12 of 1968)	1968
6.	The Guruvayur Devaswom Bill (Act 6 of 1971)	1971
7.	The Koodalmanickam Devaswom Bill(Act 7 of 1971)	1971
8.	Guruvayur Devaswom (Amendment) Bill 1972 (Act 28 of 1972	1972
9.	The Travancore Cochin Hindu Religious Institutions (Amendment) Bill, 1974 (Act 20 of 1974)	1974
10.	The Travancore Cochin Hindu Religious Institutions (Amendment) Bill, 1974 (Act 21 of 1976)	1976
11.	The Koodalmanickam Devaswom (Amendment) Bill, 1976 (Act 22 of 1976)	1976
12.	The Guruvayur Devaswom Bill, 1978 (Act 14 of 1978)	1978
13.	The Madras Hindu Religious and Charitable Endowments (Third Amendment) Bill, 1980 (Act 11 of 1981)	1981
14.	The Travancore Cochin Hindu Religious Institutions (Amendment) Bill, 1988 (Act 14 of 1990)	1990
15.	The Travancore - Cochin Hindu Religious Institutions (Amendment) Bill, 1989 (Act 15 of 1990)	1990
16.	The Travancore - Cochin Hindu Religious Institutions (Third Amendment) Bill, 1990(Act 20 of 1990)	1990

(Contd...)

16.	The Travancore - Cochin Hindu Religious Institutions (Third Amendment) Bill, 1990 (Act 20 of 1990)	1990
17.	The Travancore - Cochin Hindu Religious Institutions (Fourth Amendment) Bill, 1990 (Act 3 of 1991)	1991
18.	The Travancore-Cochin Hindu Religious Institutions (Amendment) Bill, 1994 (Act 3 of 1994)	1994
19.	The Travancore-Cochin Hindu Religious Institutions (Amendment) Bill, 1995 (Act 10 of 1995)	1995
20.	The Guruvayur Devaswom (Amendment) Bill, 1998 (Act 7 of 1998)	1998
21.	The Guruvayur Devaswom (Amendment) Bill, 1999	1999
22.	The Travancore–Cochin Hindu Religious Institutions (Amendment) Bill,1999 (Act 9 of 1999)	1999
23.	The Guruvayur Devaswom (Amendment) Bill, 2001	2001
24.	The Koodalmanickam Devaswom Bill, 2002	2002
25.	The Travancore–Cochin Hindu Religious Institutions (Amendment) Bill, 2007	2007
26.	The Travancore-Cochin Hindu Religious Institutions (Amendment) Act 2 of 2014	2014
27.	The Madras Hindu Religious and Charitable Endowments (Amendment) Act 2 of 2014	2014
28.	Kerala Devaswom Recruitment Board Act 16, 2015	2015
29.	The Kerala Devaswom Recruitment Board (Amendment) Act, 2016 (Act 22 of 2016)	2016
30.	Madras Hindu Religious and Charitable Endowments (Amendment) Act 12, 2018	2018
31.	Travancore-Cochin Hindu Religious Institutions (Amendment) Act, 2018	2018

Source: Retrieved from www.niyamabha.org

Bibliography

I. Primary Sources

A. Official Publications

Acts and Ordinances of Kerala, 1991. (1992), Thiruvananthapuram: The Law Department, Government of Kerala.

Census of India, 1891. (1894), Travancore, Report, Vol. 1.

Census of India,1931. (1932), Vol. XXVIII, Travancore, Part I, Report, by Kunjan Pillai, N, Trivandrum.

Census of India, 1941. (1942), Vol. XXV, *Travancore*, Part I, by A. Narayana Tampi, Trivandrum.

Census of India, 2011, Kerala District *Census Handbook, Thrissur*, (Series 33, Part XII), Directorate of Census Operations, Kerala.

Kerala Budget Speech, 2019-20 by Thomas Isaac, (2019), Retrieved from http://niyamasabha.org.

Kerala Gazette, Extra Ordinary. (1971). March 11, XVI, (154), Retrieved from http://statelibrary.kerala.gov.in/gazette/index.php.

Kerala Gazette, Extra Ordinary. (1976). August 24, 1976, XXI, (497), Retrieved from http://statelibrary.kerala.gov.in/gazette/index.php.

The Regulations and Proclamations of Travancore, Vol. V. (1929). Government of Travancore.

B. Commission Reports

Justice Chandrasekhara Menon Commission of Inquiry on Stampede Tragedy at Sabarimala, (2000). Final Report, Vol. I- IV, Unpublished Report, High Court of Kerala.

Kerala Devaswom Administrative Reform Commission Report (K. P. Sankaran Nair Commission Report), (1984), Ernakulam: Government Press.

Law Reform Committee Report (K. Gopalakrishnan Committee Report on Malabar Devaswom Board). (2017),Unpublished Report, Government of Kerala.

Report of the Temple Entry Enquiry Committee. (1934), Government of Travancore.

Report of the Travancore and Cochin Integration Committee. (1949), Thiruvananthapuram: Government Press.

Report of the Hindu Religious Endowments Commission. (1962), Government of India.

Report of the High- Level Committee for the Unification of Laws relating to Hindu Religious Institutions and Endowments (Kuttikrishna Menon Committee Report). (1964), Unpublished Report, Government of Kerala.

Report of the Devaswom Employees Salary Revision Committee (Kainikkara Padmanabha Pillai Committee). (1966).Unpublished Report, Thiruvananthapuram: Government of Kerala.

Report on the Financial Position and other Allied Matters of Travancore Devaswom Board (C. R. Krishnamurthy Commission Report). (1974). Unpublished Report, Government of Kerala.

*Report on the Travancore and Cochin Devaswom Boards (*High Power Commission Report). (1990). Unpublished Report, High Court of Kerala.

Report of the Enquiry Commissioner-Complaints, Regarding Guruvayur Devaswom (Krishnan Unni Commission Report). (1993). Unpublished Report, High Court of Kerala.

Report, *Issues of Environmental Pollution in Sabarimala*, (1998), 10th KLA Committee on Environment, (1996-98), 13th Report, Thiruvananthapuram: Legislative Assembly Secretariat.

Report on Environmental Impact Assessment of Diversion of Forest Land at Sabarimala. (2000). Unpublished Report, Peechi : Kerala Forest Research Institute (KFRI).

Report on the Pilgrimage to Sabarimala- Human Problems and Ecology. (2005). New Delhi: Lok Sabha Secretariat, Retrieved from http:// 164.100.47.193/ lsscommittee/Public%20Accounts/14_Public% 20Accounts_18.

Report of the High-Power Commission to Enquire into the Affairs of the Travancore Devaswom Board (Justice Paripoornan Commission Report). (2006). Part I, Unpublished Report, High Court of Kerala.

C. Administration Reports/Budgets

Administration Report of the Malabar Devaswom Board, 2017-18, Kozhikode: MDB.

Administration Report of the Travancore Devaswom Board for 1966-67. (1968), Thiruvananthapuram: Travancore Devaswom Board.

Administration Report of the Travancore Devaswom Board for 1967-68. (1969), Thiruvananthapuram: Travancore Devaswom Board.

Guruvayur Devaswom Administration Report, 1976, (1977), Guruvayur Devaswom Managing Committee.

Kerala State Administration Report, 1967-68, (1968), Thiruvananthapuram: The Government Press.

Kerala State Administration Report, 1969-70, (1970), Thiruvananthapuram: The Government Press.

Kerala State Administration Report, 1970-71. (1971), Thiruvananthapuram: The Government Press.

Kerala State Administration Report, 1971-72. (1972), Thiruvananthapuram: The Government Press.

Report on the Administration of Cochin for the Years 1909- 1910. (1911), Government of Cochin.

Report on the Administration of Cochin for the years, 1912-13, (1913), Government of Cochin.

Report on the Administration of Travancore for the Years, 1921-1922, (1923), Government of Travancore.

Report on the Administration of Travancore for the Years, 1926-1927, (1928), Government of Travancore.

Report on the Administration of Travancore for the Years, 1927-28, (1929), Thiruvananthapuram: Government Press.

Report on the Administration of the Devaswom Department for the years 1934-35, (1935), Government of Travancore.

Report on the Administration of the Devaswom Department for the years 1935- 36, (1936), Government of Travancore.

Report on the Administration of the Devaswom Department for the years 1936-37, (1937), Government of Travancore.

Report on the Administration of Travancore for the Years, 1936-37, (1938), Government of Travancore.

Report on the Administration of Cochin for the years, 1937-38, (1939), Ernakulam: Cochin Government Press.

Report on the Administration of Travancore for the Years, 1944-45, (1946), Government of Travancore.

Report on the Administration of Travancore for the Years, 1946-47, (1948), Government of Travancore.

Report on the Administration of Travancore and Cochin for the Years, 1948-49. (1950).

Report on the Administration of Travancore for the Years, 1952-1953. (1954), Thiruvananthapuram: Government Press.

Travancore Devaswom Board Budget for the year 1996-97. (1997), Thiruvananthapuram: Travancore Devaswom Board.

D. Manuals

The Cochin Devaswom Board Manual. (2014), Thrissur: Cochin Devaswom Board.

The Travancore Devaswom Manual, Vol. I. (2004), Thiruvananthapuram: Travancore Devaswom Board.

The Travancore Devaswom Manual, Vol. II. (2011), Thiruvananthapuram: Travancore Devaswom Board.

The Travancore Land Revenue Manual, Vol. IV. (1916), Thiruvananthapuram.

E. Legislative Proceedings

Abstract Proceedings of the Travancore Legislative Council. 3rd Session, 1903, December 5, Retrieved from *http://klaproceedings.niyamasabha.org*.

Abstract Proceedings of the Travancore Legislative Council. First Session, 1921, June 2, Retrieved from *http://klaproceedings.niyamasabha.org*.

Abstract Proceedings of the Travancore Legislative Council. 5th Session, 1924, 20th September, Retrieved from *http://klaproceedings.niyamasabha.org*.

Abstract Proceedings of the Travancore Legislative Council. First Session, 1925, February 6, Retrieved from *http://klaproceedings.niyamasabha.org*

Lok Sabha Proceedings. (2018), December 27, Retrieved from *http://loksabhaph*.nic.in.

Lok Sabha Proceedings. (2018), December 28, Retrieved from http://loksabhaph.nic.in/Debates.

Proceedings of the Kerala Legislative Assembly. (1958), 1957, December 20, Official Report, III (8), Thiruvananthapuram: Government Press.

Proceedings of the Kerala Legislative Assembly. (1960), 1959, March 13, Official Report, VII (17), Thiruvananthapuram: Government Press.

Proceedings of the Kerala Legislative Assembly. (1962), 1962, March 14, Official Report, IV (10), Thiruvananthapuram: Government Press.

Proceedings of the Kerala Legislative Assembly. (1976), 1976, February 25, Official Report, XL (9), Thiruvananthapuram: Government Press.

Proceedings of the Kerala Legislative Assembly. (1979), 1977, August 5, Official Report, XLIV (24), Thiruvananthapuram: Government Press.

Proceedings of the Kerala Legislative Assembly. (1978), March 3, Retrieved from http://klaproceedings.niyamasabha.org.

Proceedings of the Kerala Legislative Assembly. (1983), Fourth Session, 1980, December 11, Official Report, LII (2), Ernakulam: Government Press. LXIV (D), (14), Government of Kerala.

Proceedings of the Kerala Legislative Assembly. (1986), November 27, Official Report, LXVIII (28), Government of Kerala.

Proceedings of the Kerala Legislative Assembly. (1987), July 31, Official Report, LXXI (30), Government of Kerala.

Proceedings of the Kerala Legislative Assembly. (1990), March 20, Official Report, LXXIX (2), Government of Kerala.

Proceedings of the Kerala Legislative Assembly. (1990), June 20, Official Report, LXXX (13), Government of Kerala.

Proceedings of the Kerala Legislative Assembly. (1997), December 22, Official Report, 103 (11), Secretariat of Kerala Legislature, Government of Kerala.

Proceedings of the Kerala Legislative Assembly. (1999), April 13, Official Report, 107 (13), Secretariat of Kerala Legislature, Government of Kerala.

Proceedings of the Kerala Legislative Assembly. (1999), July 21, Official Report, 108 (23), Secretariat of Kerala Legislature, Government of Kerala.

Proceedings of the Kerala Legislative Assembly. (1999). December 17, Official Report, 109 (5), Secretariat of Kerala Legislature, Government of Kerala.

Proceedings of the Kerala Legislative Assembly. (2001), March 7, Official Report, 113 (12), Secretariat of Kerala Legislature, Government of Kerala.

Proceedings of the Kerala Legislative Assembly. (2002), July 23, Official Report, CXVII (26), Government of Kerala.

Proceedings of the Kerala Legislative Assembly. (2004). July 21, Official Report, CXXI (18) Secretariat of Kerala Legislature, Government of Kerala. CXXI (23) Secretariat of Kerala Legislature, Government of Kerala.

Proceedings of the Kerala Legislative Assembly. (2006), October 16, Official Report, CXXX (16) Secretariat of Kerala Legislature, Government of Kerala.

Proceedings of the Kerala Legislative Assembly. 2007, July 4, Official Report, 133(8), Thiruvananthapuram: Secretariat of Kerala Legislature.

Proceedings of the Kerala Legislative Assembly. (2008), June 26, Official Report, CXXXVI (4), Government of Kerala.

Proceedings of the Kerala Legislative Assembly. (2009), September 16, Official Report, Government of Kerala.

Proceedings of the Kerala Legislative Assembly. (2010), July 28, Official Report, 143 (23), Government of Kerala.

Proceedings of the Kerala Legislative Assembly. (2011), June 29, Official Report, 146 (6), Thiruvananthapuram: Secretariat of Kerala Legislature.

Proceedings of the Kerala Legislative Assembly. (2014), July 10, Official Report, 156 (22), Secretariat of Kerala Legislature, Government of Kerala.

Proceedings of the Travancore-Cochin Legislative Assembly. (1950), 1949 November 29, Thiruvananthapuram: Government Press.

Proceedings of the Travancore-Cochin Legislative Assembly. First Session, 1950, April 5, Official Report, 1 (24).

Proceedings of the Travancore-Cochin Legislative Assembly. First Session, 1950, April 12, Official Report, 1 (26).

Proceedings of the Travancore-Cochin Legislative Assembly. Second Session, 1950, November 2, Official Report, 1I (12).

Proceedings of the Travancore-Cochin Legislative Assembly. First Session, 1955, January 29, Official Report, XII (3).

Proceedings of the Travancore Sree Moolam Popular Assembly. 1907, January 9, Retrieved from http://klaproceedings.niyamasabha.org.

Proceedings of the Travancore Sree Moolam Popular Assembly. 1916, March 1, Retrieved from http://klaproceedings.niyamasabha.org.

Proceedings of the Travancore Sree Moolam Popular Assembly. 1920, March 3, Retrieved from http://klaproceedings.niyamasabha.org.

Proceedings of the Travancore Sree Moolam Popular Assembly. 1921, March 10, Retrieved from http://klaproceedings.niyamasabha.org

Proceedings of the Travancore Sree Moolam Popular Assembly. 1921, March 11, Retrieved from http://klaproceedings.niyamasabha.org.

Proceedings of the Travancore Sree Moolam Popular Assembly. 1921, June 2, Retrieved from http://klaproceedings.niyamasabha.org.

Proceedings of the Travancore Sree Moolam Popular Assembly. 1922. March 12, Retrieved from http://klaproceedings.niyamasabha.org.

Proceedings of the Travancore Sree Moolam Popular Assembly. 1925, February 6, Retrieved from http://klaproceedings.niyamasabha.org.

Proceedings of the Travancore Sree Moolam Popular Assembly. 1932, March 10, Retrieved from http://klaproceedings.niyamasabha.org.

Proceedings of the United State of Travancore-Cochin Legislative Assembly. 1949, November 29, Official Report, III (1).

Proceedings of the United State of Travancore-Cochin Legislative Assembly. 1950, January 21, Retrieved from http://klaproceedings.niyamasabha.org.

F. Cases Referred

C. K. Rajan Vs. State of Kerala and others (1994). AIR 1994, Ker 179, High Court of Kerala, Retrieved from https://indiankanoon.org/doc/663416/.

Devaraja Shenoy Vs. State of Madras, (1957), Retrieved from https://indiankanoon.org/doc/916111.

Gopalakrishnan Nair Vs. State of Kerala (2005), Retrieved from https://indiankanoon.org/doc/1639944/

Indian Young Lawyers Association Vs. The State of Kerala (2018) WP(C). No.373 of 2006, Supreme Court, Retrieved from https://indiankanoon. org/doc/163639357/

Kantaru Rajeevaru Vs. Indian Young Lawyers Association, (2019), Supreme Court of India, Retrieved from https://indiankanoon.org/doc/120364030/.

Mahendran Vs. The Secretary, Travancore Devaswom Board, Kerala High Court, on 5 April 1991 [AIR 1993 Ker 42].

M. Muraleedharan Nair Vs. State of Kerala and others (1991). Kerala High Court AIR. 1991, Ker. 25, Retrieved from https://indiankanoon.org/doc/847844

N. Adithayan Vs. The Travancore Devaswom Board, (1996). AIR 1996 Ker 169, High Court, Retrieved from https://indiankanoon.org/doc/1865241/.

N. Adithayan Vs. The Travancore Devaswom Board, (2002), AIR 2002, SC 3538, Supreme Court, Retrieved from https://indiankanoon.org/doc/1705114/.

Re: Temples in the Erstwhile Malabar Vs. Unknown (1994) on 21 July, 1994, High Court of Kerala, AIR. 1995, Ker. 172, Retrieved from https://indiankanoon.org/doc/381419/.

Subramanian Swamy Vs. State of Tamil Nadu & Others (2013), Supreme Court of India, Retrieved from https://indiankanoon.org/doc/130581093/.

T. G. Mohandas Vs. State of Kerala (2018), High Court of Kerala, WP(C).No. 33301 of 2015, Retrieved from https://indiankanoon.org/doc/134485723/.

Tharamel Krishnan Vs. Guruvayur Devaswom Managing Committee (1978), High Court of Kerala, AIR. 1978, Ker. 68. Retrieved from https://indiankanoon.org/doc/48525/.

The Commissioner, Hindu Religious Endowments, Madras Vs. Sree Lakshmindra Tirtha Swamiar of Sri Shirur Mutt, Supreme Court of India, on 16 April 1954 1954 AIR 282, 1954 SCR 1005, Retrieved from https://indiankanoon.org/doc/1430396/.

G. Devaswom Acts

- Guruvayur Devaswom (Amendment) Act, 1978.
- Guruvayur Devaswom (Amendment) Act, (Act 20) of 2001.
- Kerala Devaswom Recruitment Board Act, 2015.
- Koodalmanickam Devaswom Act,1971.
- Koodalmanickam Devaswom Act, 2005, (Act 2 of 2007).
- Madras Hindu Religious Charitable Endowment Act, 1951.

- Madras Hindu Religious Charitable Endowment (Amendment) Act, 2008.
- Madras Hindu Religious Charitable Endowment (Amendment) Act, 2014.
- Travancore- Cochin Hindu Religious Institution Act, 1950.
- Travancore- Cochin Hindu Religious Institution (Amendment) Act, 1974.
- Travancore- Cochin Hindu Religious Institution (Amendment) Act, 2007.
- Travancore- Cochin Hindu Religious Institution (Amendment) Act, 2014.
- Travancore-Cochin Hindu Religious Institution (Amendment) Act, 2018.

II. Secondary Sources

A. Books

Aiyangar, S. Krishnaswami. (1931). *Evolution of Hindu Administrative Institutions in South India*, Chennai: University of Madras Publication.

Aiya, V. Nagam. (1999). *The Travancore State Manual.* (Vols. I– III), Thiruvananthapuram: Kerala Gazetteers Department (Original work published 1906).

Aiyer, S. Parameswara, Ulloor. (1998). *Progress of Travancore under H. H. Sree Moolam Thirunal*, Thiruvananthapuram: Department of Cultural Publications, Government of Kerala.

Aiyyer, S. Ramanath. (1903). *A Brief Sketch of Travancore: The Model State of India, the Country, its People and its Progress under the Maharajah*, Thiruvananthapuram: Modern Star Press.

Aravindan, K. P. (2006), (Ed.). *Kerala Padanam, Keralam Engane Jeevikkunnu? Keralam Engane Chinthikkunnu?.* (M), Kozhikode: Kerala Sasthra Sahithya Parishad.

Asthana, Puspa. (1988). *Party System in India: Development or Decay*, New Delhi: Criterion Publications.

Ayyappan, A. (1965). *Social Revolution in a Kerala Village, A Study in Culture Change*, New York: Asia Publishing House.

Ayyar, P. V. Jagadisa. (1993). *South Indian Shrines*, New Delhi: Asian Educational Services.

Balakrishnan, V. & Leeladevi, R. (1982). *Mannathu Padmanabhan and the Revival of Nairs,* New Delhi: Vikas Publishing House.

Beteille, Andre. (2013). "Caste and Political Group formation in Tamil Nadu", In Kaviraj, Sudipta. (Ed.). *Politics in India*, New Delhi: Oxford.

Bukharin, Nikolai& Preobrazhensky, Evegenii. (1969). *The ABC of Communism*, Penguin Books, Retrieved from https:// www.marxists.org/ archive/ bukharin/works/1920/abc/11.htm.

Chander, N. Jose. (1981). *The Legislative Process in Kerala*, Thiruvananthapuram: Kerala Academy of Political Science.

Clothey, W. Fred. (2006). *Religion in India: A Historical Introduction*, London: Routledge.

Desai, Mahadeva. (1937). *Epic of Travancore*, Ahmadabad: Navajivan Karyalaya.

Dhanagre, D. N. (2005). "Civil Society State and Democracy: Contextualizing a Discourse", In Jayaram, N. (Ed.). *On Civil Society: Issues and Perspectives*, New Delhi: Sage Publications.

Edwards, Michael. (2011). "Introduction: Civil Society and the Geometry of Human Relations", In Edwards, Michael. (Ed.), *The Oxford Handbook of Civil Society*, New York: Oxford University Press.

Fic, M. Victor. (1970). *Kerala: Yenan of India Rise of Communist Power,* 1937-*1969*, Bombay: Nachiketa Publications.

Gaur, Mahendra. (Ed.). (2006). *Indian Affairs Annual 2006: Parliament* Vol. 4, New Delhi: Kalpaz publications.

Gopakumar, G. (1984). *The Congress party and State Politics*, New Delhi: Deep and Deep Publishers.

.........(1986). *Regional Political Parties and State Politics*, New Delhi: Deep and Deep Publishers.

Gouri Lakshmi Bayi, Aswathi Thirunal. (2018). *Sree Padmanabhaswamy Temple*, (4th Edn.) Mumbai: Bharatiya Vidya Bhavan.

.........(1998). *Thulasi Garland*, Mumbai: Bharatiya Vidya Bhavan.

Heywood, Andrew. (2013). *Key Concepts in Politics*. New York: Palgrave Macmillan.

Innes, C. A. (1951). *Madras District Gazetteers, Malabar, Vol. I*, Madras: Government Press.

Jaffrelot, Christopher. (1996). *The Hindu Nationalist Movement and Indian Politics*, Columbia University Press.

.........(2007). *Hindu Nationalism: A Reader*, Princeton University Press.

Jayaprasad, K. (1991). RSS and Hindu Nationalism: Inroads in a Leftist Stronghold, New Delhi: Deep and Deep Publishers.

Jayaram, N. (2005). "Civil Society: An Introduction to the Discourse", In Jayaram, N. (Ed.), *On Civil Society: Issues and Perspectives*, New Delhi: Sage Publications.

Jayashanker, S. (1997). *Temples of Kerala*, Thiruvananthapuram: Directorate of Census Operations, Kerala.

.... (2002). *Temples of Wayanad District*, Thiruvananthapuram: Directorate of Census Operations, Kerala.

.... (2006). *Temples of Thrissur District,* Thiruvananthapuram: Directorate of Census Operations, Kerala.

Jeffrey, Robin. (1978). "Travancore: Status Class and Growth of Radical Politics 1860-1940". In Jeffrey, Robin. (Ed.), *People, Princes and Paramount Power: Society and Politics in the Indian Princely States,* New Delhi: Oxford University Press.

Jodhka, S. Surinder. (2012). "Caste and Politics", In Jayal, Gopal. Niraja & Mehta, Bhanu, Pratap. (Eds.), *The Oxford Companion to Politics in India*, Oxford University Press.

Justice Reddy, O. Chinnappa. (2006). *Religion, Caste and the Threat to Secularism*, Thiruvananthapuram: Department of Publications, University of Kerala.

Khan, M. M. (2010). "Negotiating the Hindu state and Nationalism Travails in the Making of a Community". In Raman, K. Ravi. (Ed.), *Development, Democracy and the State: Critiquing the Kerala Model of Development*, New York: Routledge.

King, Mary Elizabeth. (2015). *Gandhian Non-violent Struggle and Untouchability in South India*, New Delhi: India Oxford University Press.

Kothari, Rajani. (2004). "Introduction: Caste in Indian Politics". In Kothari, Rajni. (Ed.), *Caste in Indian Politics*, Hyderabad: Orient Longman.

Kothari, Rajani. (2013). "Caste and Political Group Formation in Tamil Nadu", In Kaviraj, Sudipta (Ed.). *Politics in India*, Oxford University Press.

Kumar, P. Suresh. (1994). *Political Evolution in Kerala Travancore 1859-1938*, New Delhi: Pheonx Publishing House.

Kumaran, M. K. (1985). *R Sankar*. (M), Thiruvananthapuram: Department of Cultural Publications.

Kunjakkan, K, A. (2005). *Sree Narayana Guru: An Apostle of Humanism*, Thiruvananthapuram.

Kunjan Pillai, P. N, Elamkulam. (1970). *Studies in Kerala History*, Kottayam: National Book Stall.

Kurup, G, Radhakrishna. (2004). *Politics of Congress Factionalism in Kerala Since 1982*, New Delhi: Kalpaz Publications.

Kurup, K. K. N. (2014). *Guruvayur Kshetram Puravruthavum Charithravum*. (M), Kozhikkode: Mathrubhumi Books.

Kusuman, K. K. (2000). "Vaikom Satyagraha; the Lead of T. K. Madhavan". In Alaisar, J. et.al. (Eds.). *Aspects of South Indian History*, Nagercoil: Rajesh Publications.

Logan, William. (1887). *Malabar Manual*. Vol. I, Madras: Government Press. Lopez, Lawrence. (1988). A *Social History of Modern Kerala*, Thirvnanthapuram.

Mateer, S. Samuel. (1871). *The Land of Charity: A Descriptive Account of Travancore and its People, with Special Reference to Missionary Labour*, London: J. Snow and Co.

Mathew, George. (1989). *Communal Roads to a Secular Kerala*, New Delhi: Concept Publishing House.

Menon, A. Sreedhara. (1985). A *Survey of Kerala History*, Kottayam: National Book Stall.

.........(1987). *Kerala History and its Makers*, Kottayam: DC Books.

.........(2008). *The Legacy of Kerala*, Kottayam : DC Books.

Menon, C. Achutha, (1995). The *Cochin State Manual* (Original work published 1911), Thiruvananthapuram: Kerala Gazetteers Department.

Menon, K. P. Padmanabha. (1945). *History of Kerala,* Vol. IV, Cochin: Asian Educational Services.

Menon, M, Dileep. (1994). *Caste, Nationalism and Communism in South India – Malabar 1900-1948*, New Delhi: Foundation Books.

Menon, P. K. K, (1972). *The History of Freedom Movement in Kerala*. Vol. II, Trivandrum: Kerala Regional Records Survey Committee.

Menon, P. Shungoonny. (1878). *History of Travancore from the Earliest Times*, Madras: Higginbotham and Co.

Menon, V. P. (1955). *The Story of the Integration of the Indian States.* London: Longmans Green and Co.

Muller, F. Max (1867). *Chips from a German workshop*, Vol.1, London: Longmans Green and Co, Retrieved from https://ia801601.us.archive.org/8/items/I n.ernet.dli.2015.17446 8/2015. 174468.Chips-From- A-German-Workshop.pd.

Nair, A. Balakrishnan. (1994). *The Government and Politics of Kerala*, Thiruvananthapuram: Indira Publications.

Nair, K. Ramachandran. (2006). *The History of Trade Union Movement in Kerala*, Thiruvananthapuram: The Kerala Institute of Labour and Employment.

Nair, S. Vijayaraghavan. (1998). *Vadakkunathan Temple Complex: Trichur*, Mumbai: Manan Prakashan.

Nambiar, A. C. K. (2005). *Population, Development and the Environment: The Dynamic Interface*, New Delhi: Serials Publications.

Narayanan, M. G. S. (1972). *Cultural Symbiosis in Kerala*, Thiruvananthapuram: Kerala Historical Society.

Nehru, Jawaharlal. (1994). *The Discovery of India*, New Delhi: Oxford University Press.

Nossitter, T.J. (1982). *Communism in Kerala: A Study in Political Adaptation*, Bombay: Oxford University Press.

NSS. (2013). *Mannathu Padmanabhante Prasangangal* (M), Perunna: Nair Service Society.

Ouwerkerk, Louis. (2004). *No Elephants for the Maharajas: Social and Political Change in the Princely State of Travancore (1921-1947),* New Delhi: Manohar Publications.

Padhy, Krushna Singh. (1986). *Corruption in politics: A Case study*, New Delhi: BR Publishing Corporation.

Padmanabhan, Mannathu (1998), *Reminiscences of My Life*. (Trans. by P. C. Menon), Changanacherry: Nair Service Society.

Panicker, K. N. (2016). *Essays on the History and Society of Kerala*, Thiruvanathapuram: KCHR.

Perumal, Nilkan. (1937). *A Hindu Reformation*, Madras, R J Ram and Company.

Pillai, Sreekanteswaram, Padmanabha, (1989). *Sabdatharavali* (Malayalam Lexicon).

Pillai, T. K, Velu, (1996). The Travancore State Manual, Vols. I- IV (Original work published in 1940), Thiruvananthapuram.

Pillay, K. K. (2002). *The Sucindram Temple. (2nd ed.)*, Madras: Kala Kshetra Publications.

Prakash, R. (2006). *V. K. Varadhachari's Hindu Religious and Charitable Endowments* (revised). Lucknow: Eastern Book Company.

Pressler, A. Franklin, (2008 edn.). *Religion under Bureaucracy Policy and Administration for Hindu Temples in South India*, Cambridge University Press.

Raines, John. (2002). *Marx on Religion*, Philadelphia: Temple University Press.

Raja, P. K. S. (1953). *Medieval Kerala*, Madras: Annamalai University.

Ramachandran (Ed.), *Issues in Indian Public Administration*, New Delhi: IBH & Oxford.

Ramesan, R. P. (2006). *Travancore Cochin Hindu Religious Institutions Act & Rules*, Ernakulum: Law Books Centre.

.... (2014). *Madras Hindu Religious and Charitable Endowments Act, 1951 & Rules*, Ernakulum: Law Book Centre.

Rao, C. Anna. (1995). *Administration of Temples*, Tirupathi: Thirumala Tirupathy Devasthanam.

Rao, U, Mahabala. (1986). "Management issues in the field of Labour in Kerala", In Padma Ramachandran (Ed.). *Issues in Indian Public Administration*, New Delhi: IBH & Oxford.

Raveendran, T. K. (1972). *Asan and Social Revolution in Kerala*, Thiruvananthapuram: Kerala Historical Society.

Rudolph, I. Lloyd. (1984). *Cultural Policy in India*, Delhi: Chanakya Publications.

Sadasivan, S. N. (1977). *Party and Democracy in India*, New Delhi: Tata Mc Graw- Hill Publishers.

.........(2000). *A Social History of India*, New Delhi: A. P. H. Publishing Corporation.

.... (2005). *Political and Administrative Integration of Princely States*, New Delhi: Mittal Publications.

Sajeev, P. K. (2019). *Sabarimala Ayyappan Malaaraya Daivam (M)*, Kottayam: DC Books.

Sarkar, H. (1978). *An Architectural Survey of Temples of Kerala*, New Delhi: Archaeological Survey of India.

Selvam, S. (2003). *Religion, State and Social Policy: Changing Social Organisation of Hindu Temples*, New Delhi: Kanishka Publishers.

Seth, Pepita. (2009). *Heaven on Earth: The Universe of Kerala's Guruvayur Temple*, New Delhi: Niyogi Books.

Sethunathan, P. (2015). *NSS Shatakam* (M), Perunna: Nair Service Society.

Shaji, A. (2017). *Politicisation of Caste Relations in a Princely State: Communal Politics in Modern Travancore (1891-1947)*, Gurgaon: Zorba Books.

Shukla, Nilesh Madhusudan. (2013). *Hindu Temple Management*, New Delhi: Global Vision Publishing House.

Sinha, P. R. N, Bala Sinha, Indu. et.al. (2017). *Industrial Relations, Trade Unions and Labour Legislation* (2nd ed.), Delhi: Pearson.

Smith, David. (2002). "Hinduism", In Woodhead, Linda. et. al., (ed.). *Religions in the Modern World*, New York: Routledge.

Smith, D. E. (1963). *India as a Secular State*, Princeton N J, Princeton University Press.

Smith, D. E. (2012). "India as a Secular State", In Bhargava, Rajeev. (Ed.) (2012 re- print), *Secularism and its Critics*, New Delhi: Oxford University Press.

Smith, H. George. (1989). *Atheism: The Case against God*, USA: Prometheus.

Somarajan, C. N. (1986). *Role of Gandhi in Vaikom Satyagraha*, Kundara: Raj Publications.

Sree Ramakrishna Math, *Vivekananda's Work on Hinduism*, Madras.

Srikant & Manoj, C.V. (2006). *Sabarimala, its Timeless Message*, Kanhagad: Integral Books.

Tharoor, Shashi. (2018). *Why I am a Hindu*, New Delhi: Aleph Books.

Vaidyanathan, K. R. (1996). *Pilgrimage to Sabari*, Bombay: Bhartiya Vidya Bhavan.

.... (1998). *Sri Krishna: The Lord of Guruvayur*, Mumbai: Bhartiya Vidya Bhavan.

Vasanthan, S. K. (2006). *Nadanna Vazhikal Kerala Samskara Charithram* (M), Thrissur: Malayala Padana Gaveshana Kendram.

Veluthat, Kesavan. (2009). *The Early Medieval in South India*, Oxford University Press.

Walzer, M. (1998). "The Idea of Civil Society: A Path to Social Reconstruction", In E J Dionne. (ed.). *Community Works: The Revival of Civil Society in America*, Washington, DC: Brooking Institution Press.

Ward & Conner. (1893). *Memoir of the Survey of Travancore and Cochin States*, Vol. 4.

Webb, Sidney and Beatrice Webb. (1950). *The History of Trade Unionism*, London: Longmans Green and Co.

Woodcock, George. (1967). *Kerala: A Portrait of the Malabar Coast*, London: Faber and Faber.

Woodhead, Linda. (2002). "Studying Religion and Modernity", In Woodhead, Linda. et.al. (ed.). *Religions in the Modern World*, New York: Rutledge.

Yesudas, R. N. (1977). *Colonel John Munro in Travancore*, Thiruvananthapuram: Kerala Historical Society.

B. Articles

Aathira, Konikkara. (2018). "History is being Deliberately Neglected: Sabarimala and the Brahminisation of an Adivasi Deity", *The Caravan Magazine*, 2018, October 28. Retrieved from https:// caravanmagazine. in/religion/pk-sajeev-sabarimala-mala-araya-brahminisation-adivasi-deity.

Aiyer, S. Parameswara, Ulloor. (1931). "Col. Munro", Kerala Society Papers, II. (7). In Thankappan. K. K. (ed.). *Kerala Society Papers*, Vol. I & II. Thiruvananthapuram: Kerala Gazetteers Department, (1997).

Ameerudheen, T. A. (2017). "Why Communist Parties in Kerala are Insistent on Job Reservation for Upper-Caste Poor", *Scroll.in*, December 01, Retrieved from https://scroll.in/article/859286/why-communist-parties-in-kerala-are- insistent-on-job-reservation-for-upper-caste-poor.

Arya, P. (2018). "Arattupuzha Velayudha Panicker: A Pioneer Social Reformer of Ezhava Community in Kerala", *International Research Journal of Management, Science & Technology, 9* (9) retrieved from https://www.academia.edu/38006588/Arattupuzha_Velayudha_ Panicker_ A_Pioneer_Social_Reformer_of_Ezhava_Community_ in_Kerala_ARYA_ P.

Dauhashanti & Paanchajanyaa, (2017, March 29). "Irinjalakkuda Temple: Ending of Traditional Practices and Welfare Schemes by Secular State", Retrieved from https://www.hindupost.in/ irinjalakkuda-temple-ending-traditional- practices-welfare-schemes-secular-state/.

Deol, H. S. (1989). "Employer- Employee Relations- Critique of the Participatory Concept", *Administrative Change*, *XVII* (1), 1989, July-December.

Govindankutty. (1990). "Politics of Temple Control", *The Indian Express*. July 19.

Gurukkal, Rajan. (2015). "Don't Convert Sabarimala into a City, Appeals", *Kerala Editor*, December 14, Retrieved from https:// keralaeditor.com/ dont-make-sabarimala-a-city-gurukkal/.

Gurukkal, Rajan. (2018, December 23). "Sabarimala: The past and present", *The New Indian Express*, Retrieved from https:// indianexpress.com/article/ opinion/columns/sabarimala-temple-lord-ayyappa-protests-5505598/.

Ibrahim, K. M. Sajad. (2019). "Decisive vote for UDF in Kerala", *Economic and Political Weekly*, IV (34). August 24.

Jaysawal, Neelmani. (2013). "Role of Civil Society and its Impact on Social Capital", *IOSR Journal of Humanities and Social Science*, 11 (1) 98-106, May – June. Retrieved from www.iosrjournals.org.

Jithesh, P. M. (2018). "Appropriation of Ayyappa Cult: The History and Hinduisation of Sabarimala Temple," *The Wire*, October 12, Retrieved from https://thewire.in/history/appropriation-of-ayyappa-cult-the-history- and-hinduisation-of-sabarimala-temple.

Kannabiran, Kalpana. (2018). "Denying Women Entry to the Sabarimala Temple Amounts to Untouchability," *The Wire*, July 19, Retrieved from https://thewire.in/law/sabarimala-temple-women-entry-supreme-court.

Karat, Prakash. (2010). "CPI (M), Rectification and Religion", *People's Democracy*, XXXIV (03). January 17, 2010, Retrieved from https:/ /archives. peoplesdemocracy.in/2010/0117_pd/01172010_2.html.

Kiruthika, D. "Constitutional Validity of the Hindu Religious and Charitable Endowment Act", http://www.legalservicesindia.com/ article/1687/ Constitutional-Validity-of-the-Hindu-Religious-and-Charitable- Endowment- Act.html.

Konikkara, Aathira. (2018). "History is being Deliberately Neglected: Sabarimala and the Brahminisation of an Adivasi Deity," *The Caravan Magazine*, October 28, Retrieved from https:// caravanmagazine.in/religion/pk-sajeev- sabarimala-mala-araya-brahminisation-adivasi-deity.

Krishnakumar, R. (2018). "Battleground Sabarimala", *Frontline*. 2018, November 09.

Krishnakumar, R, (2019). "Politics at Play", *Frontline*, 2019, February 01.

Manoj, Rohan. (2018). "Sabarimala: Restrictions on Women a Recent Phenomenon", *Outlook Magazine*, October 11, Retrieved from https://www.outlookindia.com/magazine/story/the-courts-went-tantri/300769pdf.

Mathur, A. B. (1990). "The State of Public Administration in India Today- Some Observations," *Administrative Change*, June- July 1991, XVIII (1, 2). 30. Jaipur: The Centre for Administrative Change.

Menon, T. K. Krishna. (June, 1980). "Malabar Temples", *Bulletin of the Rama Varma Research Institute*, V (ii), Thrissur: Kerala Sahitya Academy.

Mohanan, B. (1998). "Controlling Corruption at the Grass Roots," *ISDA Journal* 8 (2, 3, 4), April-December.

Mohan, R. (2018). "Sabari Saga: Beyond what is Obvious", December 23, *Sunday Chronicle*, Deccan Chronicle.

Mohan, Sanal. (2011). "Land struggles in contemporary Kerala", *The Hindu Business Line*, 2011, December 19, Retrieved from https://www.thehindubusinessline.com.

Myriad, K. Santhosh. (2016). "Hues of Earth, Guruvayur Sree Krishna Temple- Tryst with the Sublime", Chennai: *The Hindu* Group Publication.

Natesan, Vellappally. (2000). "Rashtrathekkalum Valutho Kshetram" (M), *Yoganadam*, 26 (5), November, 1-15.

Nayyar, Sanjeev. (2019). "How Hindu Temples Came under Government Control", April, 10 https://www.esamskriti.com/e/National-Affairs/Ideas- ad-Policy/How-Hindu-temples-came-under-Government-control-1.aspx.

Pillai, Sreedhar. (1988, May 15). "Marxists in Kerala take over Guruvayur Sree Krishna Temple Administration", *India Today*, Retrieved from https://www.indiatoday.in/magazine/indiascope/story/19880515-marxists- in-kerela-take-over-guruvayoor-sree-krishna-temple-administration- 797262-1988-05-15.

Prabhash, J. (2005). "Social Change and Mobility through Protest: Dalit Movements in the Erstwhile Princely State of Travancore, Kerala", *Journal of Vikalp Alternatives*, August 2005. Retrieved from docplayer.net/51915031-August-contextualising-dalit-movement-in-south- india-selfh.

Puri, Geeta. (2008). "Hindutva Movement and Politics: The Case of Vishwa Hindu Parishad", In Prem Bhas Memorial Lecture, delivered by Geeta Puri at Gandhi Peace Foundation, New Delhi, February 9, 2008, Retrieved from http://www.sacw.net/DC/CommunalismCollection/ArticlesArchive/GeetaP uriAug08.html.

Radhakrishnan, M. G. (2005). "Reserved for God", *India Today*, November 7, Retrieved from indiatoday.intoday.in/story/periyar-tiger-reserve-land- transfered-to-sabarimala-temple-ecosystem-under-threat/1/192796.html.

Raja, Raja Varma (1932). "Travancore Dynastic Records", *Kerala Society Papers*, II. (8), 1931- 32.

Rajagopal, P. K. (2018). "Religious Freedom and Gender justice: Women Entry Issues in Sabarimala Temple", *Research Guru*, 11 (4), March, Retrieved from http://www.researchguru.net/volume/Volume%2011/Issue%204/RG23.pdf.

Ramakumar, R & Nair, K. N. (2009). "State, Politics and Civil Society: A Note on the Experience of Kerala", Retrieved from https://www.scribd.com/doc/55710427/ramakumar-nair-kerala-civil-society.

Ramesh, T. R. (2016). "Supreme Court Judgment in Chidambaram Temple Case: What Next?", *Vijayavani.com*, May 16, Retrieved from http://vijayvaani.com/Article Display.aspx?aid=3892.

Remani, K. K. (2015). "New Dimension of Social Change: Reflections on Mahatma Ayyankali's Dalit Mobilisation in Cochin State", *International Journal of Humanities and Social Science Invention*, 4 (1). January, 1, http://ww.ijhssi.org/papers/v4(1)/Version-2/E0412033036.pdf.

Roopesh, O. B. (2018). "Sabarimala Protest Politics of Standardising Religious Pluralism", *Economic & Political Weekly*, Vol. LIII, No. 49, December15, Retrieved from https://www.epw.in/journal/2018/49 commentary/ sabarimala- protest.html.

Sharma, Cheenu. (2016). "Gender Equality: Access to the Places of Worship", *The World Journal on Juristic Polity*, November, Retrieved from www.jurip.org.

Swamy, Subramanian. (2014). "Freeing temples from State Control", *The Hindu*, January 20, Retrieved from https://www.thehindu.com/opinion/ lead/freeing-temples-from-state-control/article5594132.ece.

Tarabout, Gilles. (2018). "Ruling on Rituals: Courts of Law and Religious Practices in Contemporary Hinduism", *SAMAJ*, Retrieved from https://journals.openedition.org/samaj/4451.

Thampi, Leela. (1996). "Protection of Temples, the Need of the Hour", *Sree Rama Navami Hindu Mahasammelan Souvenir*, 1994-95.

Vamadevan, K. C. (1974). "Travancore Devaswom Employees Union: Innale Innu"(M), *Travancore Devaswom Employees Union Souvenir*, Thiruvananthapuram.

C. Ph. D Theses

Anilkumar, S. (2016). *Nair Service Society: Socio- Political Change in Kerala* (Unpublished Doctoral Dissertation), Thiruvananthapuram: University of Kerala.

Bhai, A. Thulasi. (1986). *History of the Agitation for Temple Entry in Kerala* (Unpublished Doctoral Dissertation), Thiruvananthapuram: University of Kerala.

Jayaprasad, K. (1989). *Impact of Hindu Nationalism on Kerala Society and Politics: A Study of RSS* (Doctoral Dissertation), Thiruvananthapuram: University of Kerala.

Kumar, E. (2010). *People's participation and evolution of legislature in Travancore (1888-1948): A Historical Study* (Unpublished Doctoral Dissertation). Thiruvananthapuram: University of Kerala.

Kumar, P. Suresh. (2002). *History of Social Legislation in Travancore State* (Doctoral Dissertation), Mahatma Gandhi University, Retrieved from https://shodhganga.inflibnet.ac.in/handle/10603/6480.

Madhusoodhanan, C. K. (2010). *Study on the Nature of the Relationship between the State and the Management of Hindu Temples in Kerala* (Unpublished Doctoral Dissertation), Social Sciences, Tata Institute of Social Sciences, http://shodhganga.inflibnet.ac.inhttp:/ / hdl.handle.net/10603/2708.

Menon, A. Gopalakrishnan (1983). *History of Sree Padmanabhaswamy Temple till 1758* (Unpublished Doctoral Dissertation). Thiruvananthapuram: University of Kerala.

Mohanan, Vijaya, T. K. (1997). *History of Devaswom Administration in Travancore, 1811-1936* (Unpublished Doctoral Dissertation). Thiruvananthapuram: University of Kerala.

Nair, D. N, Krishnan. (1999). *History of Temple Administration in Travancore with special reference to Kanyakumari District 1922-1960*

(Unpublished Doctoral Dissertation). M.S. University, Retrieved from Shodhgangainflibnet,http://hdl.handle.net/10603/61441.

Sivathambika. (1991). *The Untouchables and their Struggle for Temple Entry in Kerala since 1920* (Unpublished Doctoral Dissertation). M G University, Retrieved from www.mgutheses.in.

Zacaria, T. V. (2012). *Interface Between Environmental and Trade Union Movements in Kerala* (Unpublished Doctoral Dissertation), Political Science, University of Mysore, Retrieved from http://hdl.handle.net/10603/37068.

D. Newspapers

- Deccan Chronicle Daily.
- Janmabhumi Daily.
- Kerala Kaumudy Daily.
- Malayala Manorama Daily.
- Mathrubhumi Daily.
- The Hindu Daily.
- The Indian Express Daily.
- The New Indian Express Daily.
- The Times of India Daily.

E. Periodicals

- Bhakthapriya (Guruvayur Devaswom).
- Outlook.
- Sannidhanam (TDB).
- Service (Nair Service Society).
- Yoganadam (SNDP Yogam).

F. Websites

- http://archive.indianexpress.com
- http://www.asianage.com
- https://www.business-standard.com
- https://www.cochindevaswomboard.org
- https://www.deccanherald.com
- https://economictimes.indiatimes.com
- https://english.mathrubhumi .com

- www.guruvayurdevaswom.org
- https://indiankanoon.org.
- http://kdrb.kerala.gov.in.
- http://klaproceedings.niyamasabha.org.
- http://www.koodalmanickam.com
- www.malabardevaswom.kerala.gov.in
- http://www.newsandviews.org.in
- http://www.newindianexpress.com
- https://www.telegraphindia.com.
- http://www.thehindu.com
- https://timesofindia.indiatimes.com
- https://tnhrce.gov.in
- http://travancoredevaswomboard.org

Index

D

Q

R

T

U

V